EMINENT DOMAIN

Books by John Keats

YOU MIGHT AS WELL LIVE

SEE EUROPE NEXT TIME YOU GO THERE

THE NEW ROMANS

HOWARD HUGHES

THE SHEEPSKIN PSYCHOSIS

THEY FOUGHT ALONE

THE INSOLENT CHARIOTS

SCHOOLS WITHOUT SCHOLARS

THE CRACK IN THE PICTURE WINDOW

EMINENT DOMAIN

The Louisiana Purchase
and the
Making of America

by JOHN KEATS

CHARTERHOUSE / NEW YORK

Foreword

IT seems to me that most readings in American history fail to fit the story of America into its proper European context, which is that of Europeans adventuring in a New World. Much less often do they suggest that the United States owes its existence to a series of European accidents, events, and princely caprices over which the Americans had no control and on which they had little, if any, influence.

I believe it important for us to understand our origins, not only because the story is interesting in itself, but also because the story will render more explicable our attitudes, prejudices, and relationships with the French- and British-descended Canadians, and Indian- and Spanish-descended Mexicans with whom we share our continent.

This book seeks to provide the context and to show that American history was simply a transatlantic extension of European history up to Napoleon's time. It shows who the Europeans were who came to the New World, why they came, how and why they behaved as they did upon their arrival, and how and why it was that the Latin nations failed in contention with the British for mastery of the continent. The book ends with the purchase of Louisiana, for it is my belief that this curious and wholly unlooked-for transaction marked the beginning of the end of Europe's determination of American events. For more than a century following the purchase, the Americans were, as Talleyrand suggested they should be, busy making the most of their bargain, gaining their place in the world. In retrospect, it seems quite remarkable that the Europeans let them do it.

To say these things is not to denigrate American accomplishments. It is simply to reflect on facts. For America, up to 1803, almost all the facts of life were European ones. It is a point of view not often taught in American schools, although I think it should be. I think to understand a man, it is always helpful to know who his parents were and what his childhood was. And so, I think, with nations. Our nation's parents were Europeans, and this book represents my vision of who those parents were and how and why we were enabled to survive our most precarious infancy.

J. K.
Philadelphia and
Rockport, Ontario
September 1972

Contents

[vii]

Contents

PART ONE

Louisiana
and the
New Jerusalem

I

A Thought
While Bathing

Тне three men who met by candlelight were revolutionaries. Like their masters, Napoleon Bonaparte and Thomas Jefferson, they had lived all their adult lives amid plots and treasons, at
the very center of deadly cabals. They had survived wars and
reigns of terror. They were mutually suspicious of one another
for excellent reasons, and they met in secret in April in Paris in
the gathering shadows of still another war.

Two of them were Americans: Robert Livingston, a deaf old
man who was ambassador to France; and James Monroe, a personal friend and political colleague of President Jefferson, who
had been sent by him to attend this extraordinary meeting as a
special envoy with plenipotentiary powers. Livingston detested
Monroe and resented his presence.

The third man was the Marquis de Barbé-Marbois, treasurer
of France. He was a diplomat who had served the Bourbons, then
the Directory, and was now the servant of the First Consul. He
had been chosen not so much for his political artistry as for the
reason he had lived in Revolutionary America and had married a

[3]

Philadelphian. It was thus presumed that the Americans would regard him as a friend. Otherwise, he danced to the strings Napoleon pulled. The Americans, however, believed they saw, just behind Barbé-Marbois, the enigmatic, sardonic, and venal figure of Talleyrand, the apostate bishop who was Napoleon's first minister. In this, they were much mistaken.

The ostensible purpose of the meeting was to compose American claims on France arising from a war the two nations had recently waged against one another at sea and, more important, to determine whether France could grant, guarantee, or sell to the United States navigational rights along the Mississippi River and/or a trading port on the Gulf of Mexico. But behind this ostensible purpose, which was real enough so far as the Americans were concerned, were the ambitions of Napoleon and the anxieties of Jefferson.

Napoleon intended to make war on Britain. He cared nothing for the United States, whose friendship or enmity was unimportant to him, but he was entirely willing to use the little republic, in any way he could, to claw at the British. A splendid, simple, beautifully ironic idea had shortly before occurred to Napoleon while he was bathing. When he told Barbé-Marbois what it was, the marquis looked stunned, and Napoleon laughed.

For his part, Jefferson found nothing laughable in the secret negotiations under way in Paris. His political career was in jeopardy, and so was the precarious unity, if not the very existence, of his infant nation. In 1803 the United States was politically fragile, virtually without an army or a navy, without a friend in the world, and its best military defense lay in the fact that it was chiefly a wilderness. Jefferson was perfectly aware that the American Revolution owed its recent success more to the mistakes of European princes than to the wisdom and resolve of rebellious Colonial farmers and merchants. From the moment of discovery of the New World, American history was a function of European history, and this was still the case. Jefferson knew that America's best hope for survival lay in taking whatever advantage could be twisted out of Europe's troubles. War between France and Britain certainly impended, and the United States must somehow find a way to take advantage of that, although it was by no means clear whether neutrality might not be nearly as ruinous as an alliance with one side or the other. Nor was it clear that the citizenry of Jefferson's revolutionary republic could agree upon neutrality or upon an alliance. The interests of the New England merchants and tradesmen were not those of the Southern planters, and the interests of the Americans living,in the western territories beyond the Appalachian Mountains were different from both of these.

The map of North America was not reassuring. The Atlantic seacoast of the United States was indefensible against British sea power. The northern border of the republic was open to British attack from Canada. Spaniards were ensconced in Florida; along the Gulf of Mexico they were in possession of New Orleans and of the west bank of the Mississippi River, and they were in unknown strength in the unknown lands west of the Mississippi. Nor were the Spanish friendly: they had just closed the Mississippi and the port of New Orleans to free American trade. Jefferson's minister to Madrid had protested that this was in violation of the Spanish-American treaty but he was unable to obtain the slightest answer from the Spanish court. The Spanish empire was in a state of decline, but Spanish dollars were still common specie in North America, and Spain was still far more powerful than Jefferson's republic, which was for the most part confined to the Atlantic coastal plain.

There were growing numbers of Americans living between the Appalachians and the east bank of the Mississippi, and since the Spanish had put an end to free trade of those crops and goods upon which the livelihood of the westerners depended, the Americans in the western lands were full of schemes. They planned variously to ally themselves with Spain or to become Spanish subjects or to establish a separate nation of their own or to launch an attack down the Mississippi to capture New Orleans or, having taken New Orleans, to turn west to attempt the conquest of Mexico. Harebrained as such schemes might be, they had their advocates not only in the western territories, but also in the ranks of Jefferson's political enemies, the northern Federalists, and even in the brilliant and formidable person of Jefferson's great rival in the Republican party, Vice President Aaron Burr.

So there was danger of war with Spain in the south and the west, political dissension within the republic, and imminent war between France and Britain in Europe. Nor did Jefferson enjoy the option of doing nothing. Nor did he have much room to maneuver because, among other reasons, he presided over a nation of revolutionaries who had got into their heads the idea that a free people could do as they pleased. The westerners might start a war with Spain whether the Federal government wanted one or not.

The Mississippi question was the sorest, most delicate one of all, but even as the situation worsened, Jefferson heard that Napoleon had, by secret treaty, apparently reacquired for France the port of New Orleans and certain territories in the Mississippi River basin that France had earlier ceded to Spain. If this were true, then the muddle was worse than ever, for an adventure on the Mississippi by American filibusters would be an attack upon France—and Napoleonic France was infinitely more dangerous than the decadent Spanish empire. To complicate Jefferson's problems still further, if Napoleon owned New Orleans, as it seemed he might, and if he attacked Britain, as it surely seemed he would, then the British would just as surely attack both up and down the Mississippi River. They would do this not only because every European war also brought war to the European nations' possessions in the New World, but also because the British were still very far from conceding the possession of North America to the Americans.

One option open to Jefferson was to ally the United States with the British; to marry ourselves, as he put it, to the British navy. Unfortunately, this could not only prove to be a baroque means of committing political suicide (for his fellow Southerners were pro-French and anti-British to a man), but it would be potentially ruinous to the United States should the British improve upon such an alliance to the point of recovering their lost colonies. Not a few powerful New England merchants were more than willing to have their states rejoined to the British Crown, and were actually plotting to this end. They regarded Jefferson as an insane, atheistic Jacobin, and they were more than distrustful of all Southerners and of all their works and ways.

An equally dangerous option was to ally the United States to France, for wholly apart from the fact that pro-British New Englanders might not stand for this, it would invite a British attack upon the United States. Nor would an ultimate Napoleonic victory be an unmixed blessing. If Napoleon had reacquired former French territories in the Mississippi basin from Spain, then France obviously meant to reestablish herself in North America. French bayonets along the Mississippi might not always be friendly ones, nor would a French presence in Canada be more comfortable than a British presence there.

Jefferson's best hope was to discover whether it was true that Napoleon now held title to New Orleans and to the formerly French lands along the Gulf Coast east of the Mississippi. If he did, then Jefferson should try to make some sort of deal with Napoleon, to secure some kind of right or claim to free passage down the river, and to free trading rights at New Orleans. This would at least defuse the explosive plans of the would-be filibusters. If the United States could acquire a freehold of its own on the Gulf Coast, even if it were served by southern rivers other than the Mississippi, Jefferson would be well content. Best of all, he thought, would be to buy New Orleans from its owner before a British fleet seized it the moment a European war erupted. This would not necessarily put an end to British ambitions in North America, but it might at least cause the British to postpone whatever designs they might have till they first settled accounts with the French.

As the leader of only one segment of opinion in a nation of armed men who refused to recognize their own military weakness, Jefferson was willing to buy time and hope for the best. George Washington's advice, to have nothing whatsoever to do with European quarrels, was simply inapplicable. Europe was not remote: there were British, French, and Spanish on the borders of the United States. Jefferson was not an ardent pacifist; he was an ardent revolutionary. One of his best hopes was that his nation could grow strong while the European nations bled themselves white. Then he would drive them all out of the entire Western Hemisphere: he envisioned a single, great republic in both North and South America, composed of intelligent and well-educated farmers. But dreamer and revolutionary though he was, Jefferson was also an utterly practical politician. As such, at this point of time in 1803, he could only try to find some temporary solution to an exceedingly dangerous problem and, beyond that, try to find some way of wrenching profit for America out of Napoleon's murderous intentions. He could not allow his thinking to run further ahead than that.

The handsome genius who was First Consul of the French was burdened by none of Jefferson's problems. His idea of a constitution was that it should be short—and obscure. Political dissension did not exist for him: he was dictator, served by a terrifying secret police and worshiped by his army. For Napoleon, it was all rather simple. He would be master of Europe and, after that, master of the world. Since the British opposed his plans and sought to create combinations against him, he would attack Britain. But wars were expensive, even for dictators. If Napoleon had a problem, it was where to find the money.

It was just here that Napoleon bethought himself of the American ministers in Paris. They had been dangling on at court, trying to sniff out the truth of his secret pact with Spain, fairly jittering with anxiety, and humorlessly prating away about shipping losses and their natural right to navigate wilderness rivers. Talley-rand had been amusing himself by suggesting that the Americans would have to pay him a bribe before conversations could begin, by inventing complicated and graceful evasions of their nasal queries, and by telling them charming lies. But now, Napoleon thought, why not make use of those remote and contentious people? And the idea came to him that made him laugh and that left Barbé-Marbois gaping with stupefaction.

Briefly put, Napoleon would offer to sell the Americans land he did not own, in return for a great deal more money than the Americans actually had.

They were trying to buy New Orleans? Very well, he would not only offer them New Orleans, but the Floridas as well.

They wanted a right to float down the Mississippi? Bah—he would give them the whole river.

He would give them all the lands the Mississippi River drained—including all the lands drained by its tributaries. In sum, he would give them the entire tract that had been called Louisiana in the days of Louis XIV: all the property north of the Gulf of Mexico and west of the Mississippi to the Shining Mountains (wherever they were) and north to Canada (wherever that was).

Because this vast territory had never been systematically explored, no one knew how large it was, nor what kinds of terrain it included, nor what natural products it contained, nor what kinds of animals or men might live there. For all anyone knew, there might be in that unknown region such savage cities of golden splendor as the Spanish had found in Mexico and Peru centuries earlier. Possibly it was contiguous with China. No one knew.

At any rate, it would cost Napoleon nothing to sell a title he did not own, although it would cost the Americans a horrifying sum to buy it. But buy it they would, for the offer would be so dazzling they could not possibly refuse.

Where would they get the money?

Napoleon would insist they borrow it from a British bank. Thus he would permit the British to pay him money he needed to make war on them. But more than this, he would be paid twice. First he would collect the money from the British and launch his attack. Then, after his victory, as the ruler of Britain he could collect both the principal and interest that the Americans would be paying in annual installments to the British bank. Nor was this all: After his victory, and when France had regained Canada, Napoleon's veteran armies could attack down the Mississippi and win Louisiana back for France.

Of course there might be trouble with Spain, for Napoleon's secret treaty with Spain forbade his conveying Louisiana to any third nation. But it was not he who would have trouble with Spain. He controlled the destiny of that nation in Europe; Spain would not attack France. If the Spanish fought the Americans in the New World, Napoleon could not care less.

Finally, Napoleon reasoned that if worst came to worst and he failed to defeat Britain, and if the Americans took full advantage of the opportunity he was giving them, then Napoleon could console himself with the thought that he would at least have weakened Britain to the extent that he would have created a rival to their power in the New World. He was well aware that he was offering the Americans the title deed to a continent. The title might be clouded, but perhaps the Americans might make it good. It did not disturb Napoleon that the boundaries of Louisiana were, at best, quite obscure. Instead, he thought they ought to be; it was all the better for his schemes that such should be the case.

If this had been a private matter, it is inconceivable that any bargain would have been struck. No reasonably intelligent, honest man would go nostril-deep in debt to buy a property he had never seen, and which was entirely undescribed, and doubtless inhabited by warlike savages. He would be even less likely to buy such a property from a man who had a reputation for devious, dishonest, violent, and criminal behavior. He would be still less likely to buy such a property from such a man if he well knew that his purchase would at once embroil him in a fight with its actual owner—his larger, better-armed, and unfriendly next-door neighbor.

But this was not a private matter, and even though the Louisiana Purchase was the most stupendous real-estate transaction in all history, as well as being one of the least savory, it was not simply a real-estate transaction. Nor were the partners to the bargain ordinary men. American or French, they were all dangerous radicals and conspirators. Each had been treasonous to his king. They were men of wiles and ruses. They were patriots now only because they had come to power instead of having gone to the guillotine or the gallows. They were adventurers who had dreamed of power and whose dreams had come true.

The Louisiana Purchase can be understood only in terms of dreams, revolution, and adventure. The man who offered to sell the keys to a continent was an adventurer, and he was offering other revolutionary adventurers an opportunity to make a dream of their own come true. Purchase of the Louisiana territories seemed to promise a giant step toward fulfillment, and so far as Jefferson was concerned, a much safer step than one he had had in mind.

Politic as he was, anxious and fearful as he was, Jefferson had nonetheless completed plans to send military spies into the terra incognita of Louisiana. His spies were to discover who lived in the lands between the Mississippi River and the Pacific Ocean; to measure the distance between; to survey the terrain; to keep accounts of the flora and fauna; to learn whether the Spanish or the British were present in those unknown regions and, if so, in what force. The spies were to conceal themselves, or at least to conceal their identities and purposes if apprehended; and above all things, they were to search for the fabulous Northwest Passage. Just what use Jefferson intended to make of this military intelligence can be inferred easily enough—although when he might have been able to act upon it is quite another matter. In any case, the Lewis and Clark expedition, in the form of a covert military reconnaissance into lands nominally belonging to a nation with whom the United States was then at peace, was poised to set forth before the negotiations in Paris began. If Jefferson's political enemies had known his secret intentions, they might have revised their estimate of him as a timid man. Cautious he was, as he ought to have been, but he was as ready as anyone to make the American Dream come true, by force if necessary.

The dream itself (which is by no means yet dead) was an amalgam of dreams that had disturbed and inspired Europeans for time out of mind. The first ingredient was an image of Eden as a beautiful, bountiful, and innocent garden. This was closely followed by the old dream of a return to a Golden Age, bound up with that of a Chosen People in the Promised Land. The fantasy also glittered with images of glory, wealth, and power; with blown trumpets and shining spear points and the religious ecstasy of a Crusade; with visions of high adventure upon the Northwest Passage to Cathay. The peculiarly American addition to it all, originally the brainchild of Tudor Protestantism, involved the creation in the Garden of Eden of the New Jerusalem—to be built along the more virtuous lines of the Roman republic.

Such a dream was by no means always in the forefront of every New Englander's mind as he pried stones out of his fields, nor was it the daily preoccupation of the Southern planter as he oversaw the toils of his slaves, and the western frontiersman, swatting mosquitoes as he pushed through the brakes of the Natchez Trace, may not have thought of his activities as being an adventure in Eden. Yet all three responded to the American Dream in their different ways. Their differences made for politics as each variously interpreted the same dream.

It was no accident that the dream, in fullest flower, was entertained only by Americans of English descent, so different from the other Europeans who came to the New World. But everyone who came carried a fragment of the dream with him, and to understand Napoleon's offer, how it came to be made and why the Americans leaped upon it, it is necessary to begin at a point of time no later than the Age of Faith in Europe. This is so because every thought that had effect in Europe had its direct consequence in America, and most particularly, every religious thought. The wars of religion were brought to America and fought out along the desolate seacoasts and in the savage wilderness during the Age of Faith; so were the revolutionary wars of the Age of Reason. Differing concepts of man's relationship to God, and of man's relationship to man, had everything to do with why the English first won the mastery of North America; with why the English, rather than the Spanish, French, Portuguese, or Dutch, became Americans in one generation, once they found themselves in the wilderness; with why the Americans could never build the New Jerusalem but divided among themselves along religious and political lines; with why the Americans were determined to move ever into the western lands when there was every practical reason why they should not.

The dream of Eden, which is central to the whole of this monumental story, hovered always just beyond reach. No sooner did any Europeans enter anywhere into what might have been the Eden of the New World, than they very soon made a hell of it, as did the Americans when it became their turn to try. But always, just beyond the edge of their settlements, lay new lands. Those who entered these lands for a few miles or so would often discover areas where the animals were so unused to human presence that the birds would not start up in sudden flight, nor would the bison do more than but look up curiously, and then resume their grazing. Eden was always just over the next hill, and there was all the land a man might want, his for the gardening; there he could be his own master, live as it pleased him to serve God—till the next man arrived, and the hell began. Montaigne observed that the traveler takes himself wherever he goes.

Yet the hope of Eden was never lost till the continent was filled, and in 1803, for all the clamor on the eastern fringes of North America, where red men of several nations and white men of several others pursued their lethal quarrels against one another and among themselves, the possibility of Eden still existed—west of the Mississippi. This was the promise that Napoleon Bonaparte dangled before the long noses of the Americans when he offered them the very heart of North America. To be sure, the Americans looked at the offer in terms of wars, national power, commerce, plantations, mineral wealth, and internal partisan politics, and they weighed all this against the staggering price, but the most compelling factor was the promise—so far unrealized—of attaining the Peaceable Kingdom. That hope of attainment was full and strong in the Age of Reason; in fact, it then seemed so imminent that men in the little republic began to think in terms of America's manifest destiny even though there was little outward evidence that any sort of destiny was in any way manifest. Even today Americans continue to dream of a Peaceable Kingdom, although they live in a far more dangerous world than Jefferson did, and they still believe they can somehow re-create an Eden in the continent they have rather thoroughly raped and polluted.

For all its potency, the American Dream lay beneath the surfaces of American life in Jefferson's time. The President crept over and around the perils and issues of his days as pragmatically as a blind man making his way along a strange st eet. Sometimes he sneaked to advantages in the firm belief that if the end was good, then so were any means used to attain it. He lied to the people, and to the United States Senate, in pleading for acceptance of Napoleon's cynical offer. After all, no more than anyone else did Jefferson know what lay out there past the Mississippi, but he did know he meant to have it for America even though this meant jettisoning certain principles upon which his political life, and that of his Republican party, had hitherto been predicated— and even though accepting Napoleon's offer would almost certainly mean war, the end of which could not be foreseen.

The core of it all is Eden, so we shall begin there at a point in time before the first European ventured into the garden, in order to indicate the nature of the prize awaiting a claimant.

It will next be necessary to discover who the Europeans were in order to make some sense out of what might otherwise seem to be their incredible blunders in the New World.

This groundwork laid, we can then venture into the Louisiana territories, where all the elements of American history converged. Today, American filling stations, and not French restaurants, are among the principal attractions of Omaha. America's acquisition of Louisiana was the point upon which all American history turned, but that acquisition was not necessarily inevitable. As Wellington said of another occasion, it was a damned close-run thing. Indeed, it was so close run that when the three courtly revolutionaries concluded their devious transactions in the candle-light in Paris in April in 1803, and congratulated themselves upon what Livingston called "the noblest work of our lives," the agreement they signed was not worth the sand they dusted over their signatures—and no one knew this better than they.

2

Spirits
in the Wind

Desperate in the glitter and reek of our cities, oppressed
by a feeling that all has not worked out as it should have in God's
country, there are those who plead for a return to a simpler time,
when America was beautiful, and man lived in harmony with nature. The same voices are likely to stress the brotherhood of man,
arguing that all races of man are more alike than they are different, and stating we must live together in amity: the principles
of the Founding Fathers must be put into practice. Then, it is
said, there is much we can learn from that unjustly treated people,
the American Indians.

This point of view is the most recent expression of immemo-
rial, wistful dreams of Eden and a Golden Age. Unfortunately,
the facts are ever unkind to such dreams. Man has never lived in
harmony with nature; when not nature's victim, man has ever
sought to be her master. Any efforts to arrive at harmony are
ours, not hers. Then, while it is very true that the races of man
are more similar than different, it is precisely for this reason that

the differences are significant—not the similarities. The Founding Fathers, furthermore, were not the practitioners of their own principles, the reason for this being that the distance between the real and the imaginary was just as great in their time as in Plato's, as in ours. Finally, there never was a noble savage, save in Rousseau's odd mind, and the American Indian was not a particularly successful competitor in his own environment even when he was alone in it.

But there was an Eden.

The North American continent was a Garden of Eden, particularly that fair part of it the first maps called Florida, then Louisiana. Hither, as if by chance, came different races and nations of men, each bringing with them such a mixed baggage of inimical religions, traditions, and turns of thought that each either failed to recognize or to act wisely upon the possibilities suddenly open to them. The story of Louisiana is the story of America, and it shows how and why the North American continent passed, almost by default, out of European hands and into the hands of a new kind of man born in a wilderness to quarreling parents.

The first men to inhabit Eden may have been aboriginal. We are not sure who they were, but we do know that men lived in North America for thousands of years, because stone weapons have been found amid the bones of prehistoric animals. Yet, for reasons no one has so far been able to explain, the laws of social evolution seem to have been held in abeyance here. Elsewhere, from the Stone Age to the Renaissance, men changed the shapes of their lives and the shapes of their lands. In the millennial process, powerful societies emerged and exterminated many animal species and killed off or bred out or reduced to social impotence the least capable of their neighbors. Civilizations and empires blossomed and perished in Asia, Africa, and Europe as the millenniums passed—but not in North America. Never, in all that slow time, did men here make the same progress from cave to castle; from totem to cathedral; from canoe to caravel. No one knows why not.

The mystery thickens when we consider the opulence of North America. Here were thousands of square miles of prairies and savannahs where the rich, dark topsoil was not several inches but several feet thick. There were virgin forests of fantastic extent, full of game and birdsong. The continent was well watered with clear lakes, streams, and rivers that glittered with shoals of fish. At seasons the skies would be literally darkened by migrating fowl, and plains black with herds of game reckoned not in the hundreds, but in the tens of thousands. Everywhere but on the deserts and highest mountain slopes were fruits, vegetables, and grains wanting only the slightest sort of cultivation to provide fare for enormous human populations. The continent, several times larger than all of Europe, stretching from a subtropical sea to the Arctic, was a treasure trove of all that man might find useful. Elsewhere in the world, given a similar range of climates and natural resources, men fitted themselves into every corner they could find, and left the land to go venturing on the seas—but not here. The people of the continent were vastly outnumbered by the bison. There were more elk and deer than people, and quite possibly more wolves. There were regions of North America, large as duchies, where the hunting lions, the great silvery-coated bears fishing in the streams, the beavers in the ponds, had never seen men. From the dawn of time until the arrival of the Europeans, the North American tribes remained deep in a Stone Age trance, living fearfully without notable increase, learning almost nothing from nature, and less from one another, in a wilderness largely unexplored, virtually unpopulated, and certainly untouched.

No one knows whether the people the Europeans found in the New World were the descendants of the prehistoric hunters. They may have been later arrivals, or a mixture of both peoples. They were certainly to some extent Asiatics, for all were born with the Mongolian spot and the epicanthic fold of the eyelid. Many of the tribes had a legendary memory of coming to the New World across a sea of ice, led by spirits who danced ahead of them down the wind. Such legends are a principal support of the theory that the tribes migrated across the Bering Straits from Asia during interglacial periods. But a land bridge could lead in one direction as well as the other. In any case, a passage in either direction took place so long ago that the American tribes had no specific memory of Asia—nor did the Asiatics have any memory either of their entering Asia, or of any tribes departing from Asia north and east over frozen seas. All that can be said is that the Asiatic tribes in North America did not evolve into societies in any way comparable to the nations that evolved in Asia or anywhere else, although they surely had time enough to do so. If they were not indigenous to the New World, they had at least lived long enough in it not only to have forgotten their origins in the Old World, but also to have developed, among themselves, dissimilar languages, physical appearances, and ways of life.

Among the most primitive were a few tribes who crept about, altogether naked, in the semitropical Eden that lies along the Gulf Coast from Florida to Texas. It may be axiomatic elsewhere that the size of any population will be determined by the available food supply, but that axiom might assume the population can recognize food when it sees it, will select such food as is most beneficial, and has the means to acquire it. But these coastal tribes nearly famished in a country fairly bursting with birds, game, fish, and fruits. They subsisted in large part on spiders, worms, lizards, and deer dung. They would wander to an area of walnut trees and live solely on walnuts until they had eaten them all; they would go to where prickly pears grew and gorge on pears until the pears were gone. They gathered oysters in tidal flats, but otherwise were virtually innocent of the arts of fishing. Like all the tribes in the New World, they had bows and arrows, but again like all the others, their archery was in no way to be compared in power, speed, accuracy, or discipline to that of the wild Welsh tribes of the tenth century, much less to that of the English long-bowmen of the Middle Ages. When the coastal people hunted game, their method was to start a circular fire in the forest, hoping to find roasted carcasses at the center of it, or at least game driven into a circle small enough for their archery to be effective.

North and inland, matters were somewhat better. Mississippi River tribes practiced a rudimentary agriculture, but they seldom stored a surplus that could be used as an adequate protection against periodic famine, much less used as the basis of a stable community capable of growing into a civilization. Again in a land of plenty, these tribes lived marginally, and all of them knew periods of starvation.

On the western plains, hunters walked after game for thousands of years until the Spaniards brought the horse into the New World, but the introduction of that useful animal did little for primitive hunters except to add speed and range to their hunting and warfare. The American historian, Francis Parkman, who lived with a wild western tribe and sought reasons why it should still be living in the Stone Age, learning nothing from the nineteenth century, sadly concluded that the minds of these people were "hopelessly stagnant." He said they seemed not to have the ability to reason and suggested that "No race, perhaps, ever offered greater difficulties to those laboring for its improvement." He seemed unable to decide whether these people were incapable of learning, too set in their ways, or simply too proud to learn from the white man. In any case, he said, they were "hopelessly unchanging in respect to individual and social development."

As if in obedience to the mysterious rule that states the people who live in the northern portions of any country are always more energetic and well-developed politically than those who live in the south of it, some of the tribes who lived in the northeastern and north-central regions of North America boasted a relatively intricate society. The Iroquois, based in central New York, exercised a political control over five other eastern tribes. Their western cousins and enemies, the Hurons, who lived around Lake Ontario and in the forests of western New York and Ohio, were dangerous friends to tribes lying farther to the west.

These people lived in palisaded towns, in houses built of poles and bark in the form of modern Quonset huts, whole families together in the same house. The interior of any house, on any occasion, would be full of fleas, dogs, dribbling crones, copulating couples, filthy, tattooed warriors staring at nothing, adults gambling, children wetting the earthen floor, the whole lot of them naked, all of them choking in the smoke of the cooking fires. Such is the picture of their domesticity, as painted by Parkman and early explorers. These people raised maize, which they cooked without salt. They were not particularly competent hunters. Venison was rare even though they lived in a kind of natural deer park; their principal meat was dog. They raised hemp and made twine from it; their weapons were of stone or bone; their armor consisted of greaves and breastplates made of woven twigs; they carried shields of bison hide. They made canoes of elm and birch bark. Their organization into something approaching a town life, their agriculture and their armaments all might bespeak a higher evolutionary stage than that achieved by tribes elsewhere; yet otherwise their lives seemed to have little more order or purpose.

Most of their days were exactly alike in their utter vacuity. The men went hunting or made war when and if the spirit moved them. At all other times they loafed, slept, simply sat and stared, or amused themselves if they could. Despite their agriculture, they knew starving times. Occasionally there were feasts when the men would not only glut but gorge themselves, sometimes to the point where death would supravene. The nubile girls lay with the men and boys whenever they pleased—without causing anyone the slightest jealousy. Once pregnant, a girl was married to one of her men, and at once became a drudge whose lot it was to fetch, carry, make, mend, cook, and tend to all else of life's work. In almost no time, the girl became, Parkman says, "a shriveled hag, hideous and despised, who in vindictiveness, ferocity and cruelty far exceeded the men."

Warfare was a principal activity, but a war party might consist of three men, or thirty. There were no troops operating under disciplined command; almost never would there be pitched battles or sieges of palisaded towns. The wars were essentially guerrilla operations that took the form of small ambushes, raids into cornfields, and footpath murders. Attacks were never delivered unless the attackers had the advantages of numbers and surprise—if not also the advantage of terrain. The most potent weapon was the stone club or hatchet.

The warfare of these Stone Age people was not waged for material gain, for the people had no idea of amassing surplus food, much less surplus artifacts. Nor did their wars seem waged for possession of territory. None of these people had a concept of individual ownership of land. Instead, they thought of the land as being free and useful to everyone—as free to all as the air they breathed and the water they drank. (By everyone, they included the animals as well as themselves. They thought animals were other people—different certainly from men, but just as certainly their close relatives.)

To be sure, a tribe might consider the country it inhabited to be *its* particular territory. But unless they conceived it to have some religious significance, they had no particular *reason* to defend it, because the continent was so empty that it would have been much simpler and less hazardous to move to another, uninhabited region. So one might *reason*—but reason has never had much to do with the acquisition and defense of territory, as Robert Ardrey among others has pointed out.

The military operations of the Stone Age tribes may have been as rudimentary as their cuisine, but they were nonetheless often pursued with sufficient efficiency, and over a long enough time, to result in the total extermination of one tribe by another.

What seemed to occur was that one tribe would make war on another not for gain, nor even for vengeance, but simply because making war and torturing prisoners produced feelings of great satisfaction. In this they were no more than human: of all the animals, it is only men who make war; only men who torture their own kind.

But warfare was not the only form of intercourse. When the eels were thick in St. Lawrence River marshes, neighboring but inimical tribes would regard the marshes as a neutral ground in order that all could share the slimy harvest. It apparently did not occur to one tribe to starve another into submission by denying the fishery to them, or to extort wealth or slaves from the other in return for limited fishing rights. Such concepts would remain unknown on the continent until the arrival of the more reasonable Europeans.

As Parkman and others observed, these primitive people had only dreamlike memories of the past, in which yesterday's events were often confused with their grandfathers' tales. They had no reasonable concept of a future; they did not inquire into the why of things, and so had next to no idea of cause and effect. They lived entirely in the present, largely at the command of their whims, dreams, and bodily desires—at all times fearful of sorcery. A hunter with a deer in view might abandon his purpose and race for home if he noticed an insect crawling on a twig and took it into his head that this was an omen of disaster. A leaf blowing in the wind, a sound in the forest, could be fraught with occult meaning. Dreams and reality were indistinguishable; a man waking from a nightmare could send a village howling in panic into the woods by recounting his terrors.

While neighboring tribes could be friendly, instead of inimical, joining together for play, feasts, hunting, and the formation of alliances against mutual enemies, there is little evidence of trade. After all, there would have been little to trade among people who produced no surplus of food or artifacts. Nor is there much evidence of far-ranging travel by venturesome explorers—it is almost definitive of tribal life that all the individuals of a tribe find their entire meaning and existence within the tribe. No one strays far from it. The punishment for murderers, for example, was often expulsion from the tribe—a sentence tantamount to perpetual solitary confinement in the wilderness, if not to death.

But there is striking evidence that some ideas traveled everywhere throughout the North American continent. The calumet, or peace pipe, was universally recognized as a sign of parley—on the East Coast, on the West, and throughout the lands between. If the gesture was accepted, then men would squat in a circle, each smoking the pipe in turn, after which they would try to speak in words or signs together. Sign languages differed, but not to the degree that some common meaning could not be conveyed.

More remarkable still was wampum. This was a design, woven from beads made from the purple and white shell of a shellfish found only on the shores of the Florida peninsula, yet used everywhere throughout the continent. The designs were normally worked into a belt, and they were mnemonic devices of simple pictures and symbols that could convey an understandable story, or message, to people who lacked a written language. The fact that beads made from Florida shells found their way to Maine and Oregon does not necessarily imply a constant intercourse, along well-known routes, among populations mutually acquainted. It does imply spasmodic, successive, and perhaps accidental contact, over the centuries, among a race of men who at least had some ideas in common despite the fact that their race was widely scattered over an immense landscape and broken into little groups who spoke quite different languages and followed quite different lives.

But the lives they all followed, be they variously hunters, fishermen, primitive agriculturalists, or wandering food gatherers to whom spiders were as welcome as walnuts, were not much more purposeful than the lives of the animals they believed to be their brothers.

Such, then, was the condition of the inhabitants of the northern continent of the New World: pitiful, and entirely vulnerable to the well-organized purposes of the steel-clad Renaissance adventurers who, as if by magic, would presently appear among them.

Far to the south, and unknown to the North American tribes, there lay another vast continent where Stone Age people, also apparently of Asiatic stock, stretched thinly from tropical to subpolar regions. The physiognomy and physiques of the southerners were generally different from those of the northerners, and specifically different from one southern region to the next, but in most significant respects their lives were equally aimless by European standards. Here, too, the laws of human evolution seem to have been held in abeyance—but with three startling exceptions.

In Mexico, in Central America, and in Peru, there were stone cities inhabited by people whose language, appearance, legends, customs, and accomplishments were so wildly different from all the other people in the New World as to suggest admixture with some other race, if not an entirely different origin. Indeed, the city builders themselves believed a racial difference set them apart from their primitive neighbors, and whereas some New World tribes might have had dim legends of crossing a frozen sea from the west, the Aztecs, Mayas, and Incas each had well-developed religions stating they and their gods had come to the New World from the east. The Aztecs believed their God, the feathered serpent Quetzalcoatl, lived in the sun, and would one day return to them. The Mayas and Incas believed that bearded, white-skinned gods had come from the lands of the sun, in the east, and had taught them the arts of civilization. They also believed these gods would one day return. They meanwhile awaited this joyous day amid an opulence and sophistication that was as startling as it was unique in all the world.

Mexico, the capital city of the Aztecs, had a population of some three hundred thousand souls by the time the Europeans arrived. Merely to feed such a number of people implies a high order of agriculture, an efficient road net and supply system, and an intricate social organization. But more than this, Mexico was a metropolis that included suburban villas with pools; city apartments that had penthouses and roof gardens; playing fields, palaces, temples, and jails. A wealthy Aztec on an average day could waken to the songs of his caged birds, dress in fine cloth, slip into jeweled sandals, and admire the capering of his chained monkeys while he breakfasted on the patio. He could descend into the stone streets of the capital to pass the shops of silversmiths, goldsmiths, and merchants, inspect the great variety of foodstuffs in the market, and look over the men, women, and children for sale in the slave pens. He could lunch on stuffed baked dog in the city and spend the afternoon in his favorite brothel. In short, he could —and did—live among splendors in no way inferior to contemporary European ones, and in a style that many a wealthy European might well have envied.

The city builders were a Stone Age people in that their tools and weapons were made of polished flint and obsidian, and in that they had not invented the wheel. But there the resemblance virtually ends. They learned to smelt gold, silver, and copper; they invented a mathematics that lacked the concept of zero but which was sufficient to enable them to chart the sun and stars. They devised a written language and a literature; they produced schools of painting, sculpture, and architecture. Their weapons might be stone hatchets, knives, flint-tipped arrows, and spears that were fire-hardened sticks, but the Aztecs had an army led by a warrior caste. They had a society representing all social orders from slaves to peasants to a middle class to an aristocracy; there were school teachers and civil servants. Binding all this together, and giving the state its reason for existence, was a highly organized religion presided over by a hierarchy of priests.

Spirits in the Wind

Central to this religion was the Sun's need of blood. Without daily quantities of fresh, hot blood, the Sun would die—and, of course, if the Sun died, the world would end. Specifically, the Sun needed human blood; wherefore there was a constant need of sacrificial victims. To acquire these, the military would set forth on expeditions, but even so, the need was so great as often to outrun the supply of prisoners of war. There was therefore a great category of crimes punishable by death—such as trespass into a palace room, or behaving in an unseemly manner, or being too proud, or committing a social error, or making a misstep in a ritual dance. It was necessary to create and expand such a list of crimes, because the supply of erring slaves, ordinary thieves, cheats, murderers, and rapists was, like the supply of military prisoners, often insufficient to meet the need.

At the hour of sacrifice, the victims would be paraded atop a pyramidal temple, naked save for feathers on their heads and at their wrists and feet, and compelled to dance. Then one at a time they would be thrown on their backs across a stone altar, where blood-caked priests would, with obsidian knives shaped like eagles' claws, dig out the living hearts that, still pumping, sprayed the priests, the altar, and the stone walls and floors with beneficial blood. The dismembered carcasses would be thrown to carnivores imprisoned in pits below.

No one is certain when the high culture of the Aztecs, Mayas, and Incas first appeared, nor why these people, alone of all others in the New World, were able to create such civilizations. One theory, based on the legend of bearded, white-skinned gods arriving from the east, holds that a Mediterranean people must have come to Central America in remote antiquity. Thor Heyerdahl's voyage in the papyrus raft *Ra II* suggests that such a seafaring could have been accomplished. Moreover, several features of the New World civilizations were similar to ancient Mediterranean ones. In Central and South America, as in the early Mediterranean world, men built Cyclopean walls of sawn stones fitted tight without mortar. Like the eastern Mediterranean peoples, they concerned themselves with the movements of sun and planets. Some of their carvings are similar to Phoenecian ones. Like several early eastern Mediterranean people, they used the form of the pyramid for sacred buildings. Their religion embodied the same principle that human sacrifice was necessary to resurrection: the daily blood offered the Sun could thus be set beside the ancient Mediterranean ritual slaughter of the Corn King which, with the passage of time, evolved in the Mediterranean world into the story of Christ.

Another theory, based on impressive evidence, holds that the city builders were influenced by and learned much from Chinese, Japanese, and Polynesian seafarers. Thor Heyerdahl thinks this was just the other way around with respect to the Polynesians, and undertook the voyage in *Kon-Tiki* to give his theory a plausible basis. It can at least be safely said that prehistoric men were capable of making long sea voyages, and there is no doubt that prehistoric men undertook long overland journeys, and so there is no reason to suppose the Aztecs, for example, had never had visitors from either east or west. Instead, it is probable they met with both, and their legends are quite clear on the point that the gods who taught them the arts of civilization and who promised to return to them came from the east.

But if the New World civilizations were of Mediterranean origin, they remained static for thousands of years while Mediterranean civilizations did not. To be sure, a terrifying religion, backed by the military power of a theocratic state, can certainly hold a populace in thrall for centuries, and in fact has done so in various corners of the world. But over a period of millenniums, such theocracies have elsewhere been overthrown. Perhaps the New World civilizations remained static because they lacked potent enemies or other contact with people different from themselves from whom they might have learned new values and patterns of thought. Yet if they lacked such enemies, and if there were no cultures in the New World competitive with their own, why did the city builders not extend their civilization throughout North and South America, establishing sovereignty over their primitive neighbors? No one knows the answer, nor does anyone know why the smelting of gold and copper did not lead the New World city builders to the discovery of iron and steel, nor why, having conceived the circle, they did not use the wheel. Perhaps, if these civilizations *were* of Mediterranean origin, the answer to the puzzles may be found in the legend that a few Mediterranean people found their way to the New World in remote antiquity, and taught all they knew to primitive Asiatic tribesmen. Whereupon, the godlike teachers died, or departed to try to find their way home, leaving behind them all the gifts they had brought, and the New World people were unable to improve upon the lessons they had been taught. Therefore, stasis ensued while the millenniums passed. Such a hypothesis would imply that the city builders were no more capable of human evolution than the wild tribes found elsewhere in the New World who were also apparently of the same racial stock. It does not, however, explain why this race might have been incapable of social evolution—if, in fact, it was.

Another theory says these strange and in many ways beautiful cities were not thousands of years old by the time the first Europeans came across them, but had been in existence only a few centuries. And, if they seemed to have many aspects reminiscent of early Mediterranean cultures, this was merely an interesting example of parallel evolution. Perhaps so, but if so, no one has yet explained why so, nor why such cities appeared only where they did. All that we know today is that these cities were mysterious, unique, fantastic of design and color, and veritable treasure-houses of gold, silver, copper, and precious stones.

We also know that their existence, and the existence of the whole New World, was entirely unknown to men elsewhere in the world until the Renaissance. Until then, the Western Hemisphere lay dreaming asleep at the dawn of time, the northern continent a wilderness sparsely populated by primitives in paint and feathers; the southern continent as much a savage splendor and equally underpopulated save for those small realms of gold where men built temples to the Sun, and waited the return of their gods.

As the New World lay dreaming between its two untraveled oceans, an entirely different race of men was dreaming quite different dreams in Europe and, what is more, was busily employing the techniques of reason to make these dreams come true.

3

Deus Vult

In the Year of Our Lord 1474, a most unusual man was presented to King Jao of Portugal.

A contemporary says that Christopher Columbus was tall, strongly built, red-haired, and freckled, and "affable although with a certain gravity." He had a reputation as a shipmaster, and more than this, a recognition among scholars as "a learned man of great experience . . . a skilled man, eloquent and a good Latin scholar, and very glorious in his affairs." This was no ordinary combination of talents, but what was absolutely unique about Columbus was his single-mindedness. He could think of nothing but "the grandeur and immortality of the wonderful deeds he would perform."

Columbus gravely explained that Our Lord had been particularly kind to him. "I received from Him," he stated, "a spirit of intelligence. In seamanship He made me abundant, of astrology He gave me enough, as well as geometry and arithmetic, and of ingenuity in mind and hands to draw this sphere and on it cities, rivers, mountains, islands and harbors, everything in its right place. In this time I have seen and studied all writings, cosmography, histories, chronicles and philosophy and other arts."

To the medieval mind, this statement was not a boast, but a fact. It was universally believed that all came from God. But in addition to his divine credentials, Columbus had mundane letters of recommendation. Paolo, the physician of Florence, had written to him that "I perceive your noble and grand desire to go to the places the spices grow"—by which Paolo meant he agreed with Columbus' theory.

Columbus paraded his evidence before the king. He had read the works of ancient Egyptian, Greek, and Roman geographers. He had read those of French and Italian contemporaries. Men in antiquity had suggested the earth was a sphere and had calculated its dimensions. This was a theory with which the best medieval minds agreed. Extrapolating on the basis of current astrology (by which he meant astronomy), Columbus had decided the world was a bit smaller than had heretofore been suggested. That the earth was a sphere was not the question. Any sailor suspected as much when he stared at the horizon's curve. The only question was as to size.

Well, as to that. Columbus told a story sailors had told him. They had sighted land west of the Canaries. He told of a pilot who had been blown west by a storm—and who had seen an island in the Atlantic before the storm let go its grip. Doubtless the island was the Japan that Marco Polo mentioned in his travels. More to the point, the body of an Oriental had washed up on the Irish coast—and if a corpse had come ashore so fresh as to be recognizable as an Oriental, then the Orient could be reached, as Seneca had long ago supposed, within a few days—by sailing west from Spain, given a fair wind off the coast of Iberia.

So Columbus wanted to sail west to India, where the spices grew and gold abounded. He was reasonably certain—well, at least certain enough to stake his life on it—that there would be no problems.

Deus Vult

He said he wanted "to see those princes and peoples and lands and the character of them and of all else, and the manner which should be used to bring about their conversion to our Holy Faith." He wanted to meet the Great Khan of China, who, on the basis of Marco Polo's manuscript, was the ruler of all the kingdoms of the Orient—an enormously powerful despot, richer and stronger than any European prince, and perhaps more puissant than all the princes of Europe together. He, Columbus, would find out how to convert this monarch and all his people to the Holy Church—and, naturally, do a little business as well.

Now, all he wanted King Jao to do was finance this holy expedition in return for ninety percent of the profits. In return, Columbus thought it only natural that there should be a little something for himself. He wanted the title of lord, the title of lord admiral of the ocean sea, the job of being viceroy and governor forever of all the islands and continents he should discover; the right to nominate any subordinate officers, and to retain for himself and his heirs forever one-tenth of all the wealth that he and they would find.

King Jao heard him out, and said he would take the matter under advisement. There, for the time, affairs rested.

The venture Columbus proposed was thoroughly consistent with European thought, character, and then-recent history, for in essence, the story of European man throughout Christian times had been that of his unceasing search for God and gold. Columbus' choice of King Jao was also a logical one in the context of then-current European affairs. Twenty years before, the Turks captured Constantinople and put an end to the Roman empire in the East. Islam now blocked the overland routes to India and China, with the result the Venetian and Genoese trade to the Levant was more in the nature of an expensive smuggling operation than an ordinary business. The merchant states of Italy were apprehensive of the Turk and meanwhile involved in mutual warfare: they were too busy with their fears and affairs to entertain

Columbus' dreams. In France, Louis XI was hoarding his pennies, desperately trying to create a military power and a diplomacy superior to that of his ominous vassal, the duke of Burgundy. In England, the steel-clad nobility was busily exterminating itself in the War of the Roses. In Spain, Ferdinand and Isabella had yet to drive the Moors from the land and win a joint throne. By contrast, Portugal was peaceful. More important, King Jao had an interest in exploration. Much more important, he had the money and the ships.

The ships were the most important factor of all. Not since the Viking dragons had Europeans designed ships that could keep the Atlantic. The galleys and merchantmen of the Mediterranean were essentially coastal day sailers, ill suited to live in Atlantic seas. But by the middle of the fifteenth century, Atlantic shipbuilders were producing designs that could not only live in the seas, but also keep them for months at a time. Such a design was the caravel. It had a long, deep wetted surface, masts higher than its length, and carried square sails on yards that could be trimmed. As a legacy from the Punic wars, these ships had forecastles in their bows, structures from which soldiers could fire missiles down into enemy ships, and similar but higher castles astern. In gales, these superstructures shook and groaned and contributed to yaw and pitch; the caravel wallowed in the seas and seemed always on the point of running her round bows under. But she could survive in seas whose troughs were deep enough to put her out of sight. With such ships the age of discovery could begin, and when Columbus went to Portugal, the Portuguese were already using them to nose around the coast of Africa—with the aid of compass and astrolabe.

King Jao was not only receptive to Columbus' dream, he acted on it at once. Why, he thought, give this Italian ten percent of the gain when he, Jao, could take it all? So he told Columbus the matter was under advisement, but this was a lie. In utter secrecy Jao dispatched a ship of his own west into the Atlantic to put Columbus' theory to the test. How far that ship sailed cannot be known. Perhaps a terrified master went fishing out of sight of land until supplies ran low; perhaps some real attempt at discovery was actually made. In any case, weather-beaten mariners returned to their king with report of failure. Whereupon, Columbus was ridiculed and bundled out of court.

Put not your faith in princes. On the other hand, none but a prince could give him a ship. Ten years later, Columbus was as steadfast as ever in his monomania. He applied to Ferdinand and Isabella, who by 1484 had established their monarchy. He put his faith in them for seven years before giving up to try at the English court. He got nothing from Henry Tudor, who was trying to consolidate his new power and bring some measure of prosperity to a devastated kingdom. Next he went to France: Charles VIII was not interested—he was contemplating war in Italy. Columbus went back to Spain, where his wish at last was granted. In addition to the concessions he sought, in event of success he would also receive three salaries simultaneously: as admiral of the ocean sea, as viceroy of the new lands he would seize for his royal masters, and as governor of those lands.

It cost nothing for Ferdinand and Isabella to grant titles, and it cost them practically nothing to give Columbus his ships. The town of Palos lay under royal displeasure and was therefore ordered to provide three ships and crews at its own expense. The sullen townsmen offered three caravels in very mediocre condition. The flagship, *Santa Maria*, was fifty feet long and eighteen wide; she carried stone ballast and was rated at one hundred tons. She would carry Columbus, a pilot, a first officer, a surgeon, and thirty-six men and boys. *Pinta* was half her tonnage, and the third ship, *Niña*, was smaller yet at forty tons. The men, and the boys who were to learn the sea and serve for women to the men, were chiefly fishermen from the little town. But they also included a man who spoke Arabic. He was brought along solely because of this skill. It was assumed that Arabic was a language spoken by the Chinese and Japanese they would shortly meet en route to India, because the Orientals were heathen, and the heathen Moors spoke Arabic. The linguist was also to translate letters written by Ferdinand and Isabella to the mysterious Great Khan.

Columbus said he sailed "with very many supplies and with many a seaman, on the third day of August . . . on a Friday." Actually, he put to sea with eighty-eight men and boys, in three leaky ships whose total tonnage, including ballast, was more hopeful than realistic, to venture into almost mythological realms "by way of the west, which down to this day, we do not know certainly that anyone has passed"—into unknown waters, guided not by a chart, but by a theory that was only in a general sense correct.

The expedition had this in common with the first voyage to the moon: It was a government-financed project based on the best information of the time, carried out in a vehicle theoretically capable of making the trip, commanded by an officer thoroughly conversant with the theory and competent to operate the vehicle.

Like the moon voyage, Columbus' adventure was an intelligent extrapolation on the basis of known and suspected factors, but just as no one on earth could know, for sure, what dangers might lie either in outer space or on the moon, neither did anyone in the year 1492 know for certain what the Atlantic might contain, or the lands beyond. It was always possible that the little ships might be devoured by sea monsters, that sirens might lure them upon rocks, that the far lands would prove to be the Devil's realm, thickly infested by his attendant demons.

Again like the moon voyage, the vehicle was cramped. A man of middling height could not stand erect in Columbus' cabin, and Columbus was tall. Forty men had to live in a fifty-foot ship: the overcrowding approached slave-ship severity. There were no lavatories; the bilges stank of urine and vomit. The water in the casks would shortly turn green and slimy; the diet of salt meat and wormy bread would sicken a vulture; the sailors would vary their fare by fishing, chewing on the leather rigging, pouncing on rats, and hunting cockroaches.

It was taken for granted that not all who went to sea in those days would survive even a placid voyage. For this reason the crew of *Santa Maria* included three criminals whose life sentences would be remitted if they ever came home again. Yet the over-crowding, the diet, and the hardships were acceptable to the crew because they were normal to all seafaring at that period. So too the first men in space accepted virtual immobility in their vehicle, the limitations of their diet, and the necessity of living in a bag with their own excrescences: such was the normality of their period.

Finally, like the lunar explorers in space suits, the sailors in the sugar-loaf hats, doublets, and ballooning knee britches of hempen cloth or leather were men of courage and faith. Courage among men has always been a known quantity, but the faith of modern astronauts was of quite a different order from the faith of medieval man. Modern man has faith in what he can prove, whereas medieval man thought he could prove what he already believed. Medieval man believed that everything in this world was put here by God, and could be explained in terms of God's revealed Word, as interpreted by His Church. Every object was therefore symbolic of something else. The thing to do was to under-stand the true reality of an object—which was concealed by its ostensible form. To a medieval man, a mosquito was therefore not simply an insect: it must be an imp or demon, an agent of Satan, put on earth to torment sinners and/or to test man's faith in God.

Columbus was a Renaissance man in the sense that he was one of the first men given to the modern turn of thought. But he was much more a medieval man than a Renaissance one in *most* of his thought, and so were most of his learned contemporaries. The Renaissance did not burst all at once on any man in the fifteenth century, nor did it come in any degree to everyone at that time. Not even in Florence, much less in Spain. From the fourteenth through the sixteenth centuries, most Europeans remained illiterate, work-stunned peasants, while most of the learned men of those centuries were still deeply committed to trying to force reality to disclose its true significance in God's plan: to prove the mosquito an imp, not to classify it as an insect. Their faith was a thing of passionate intensity, compared to which the spaceman's faith in his science is niggling skepticism. Only in terms of medieval faith is Columbus' voyage in any way understandable, for otherwise, the objectives of his expedition made no sense.

For example, Columbus intended to rule all the islands and continents he should discover en route to India, meanwhile converting the people he found thereon. It was presumed that the Great Khan was richer and more powerful than all the princes of Europe together, yet Columbus would see "what manner should be used" to bring this potentate and all his people to Holy Faith.

Logic might have suggested that eighty-eight men and boys were not a sufficient task force, but logic had no place in the grand design.

"This was the alpha and omega of the enterprise," Columbus explained, "that it should be for the increase and glory of the Christian religion, and that no one should come to these parts who was not a good Christian."

It also followed that anyone who helped his king and Church to bring light to heretics, infidels, and pagans was doing the work of God; if he slaughtered unbelievers in the process, he was doing God's work, too. Most important, it was believed that God would give those who served Him whatever strength was necessary to the task, and if one of God's soldiers was killed in the attempt, he would at once be lifted into heaven to sit in the elect circle of saints and martyrs.

Such was the reasoning that had supported the faith of the Crusaders: God would give them the strength to cast down or convert unanointed kings and bring their subjects to Holy Faith. If the Crusaders failed, well, that was because of their sins. But at the time Columbus received his commission from Their Most Catholic Majesties, one Crusade had been entirely successful. Ferdinand and Isabella's victory over the infidel Moors was proof that the anointed monarchs of Spain were without sin and in the Hand of God. Therefore God would prosper all their affairs, including the voyage to be made in His name.

Meanwhile, if eighty-eight men and boys seemed too small a power to seize islands and continents and convert the Great Khan and all his myrmidons, it should be remembered that God had wanted Gideon to have a smaller army.

All this was not just implicitly but passionately believed by those who lived in the feudal, medieval Spain of 1492. The Renaissance would not be felt in Spain for years to come, and when it was, the Inquisition would be the Spaniard's principal response. The ordinary Spaniard unquestioningly obeyed Church and Crown, and drew his strength from the certainty of his absolute belief.

It was this terrifying faith in potentially murderous nonsense that sent the first Europeans off on their westward passage of the Atlantic, wallowing over the great sea hills in leaky caravels. Off they went, with the cross painted on their sails, praying every hour, firing off guns to the glory of God and His saints, and *A HIGH-CRESTED HELMET WITH NO VISOR* thoughtfully taking with them morions, breastplates, crossbows, swords, and spears to help them do God's Will and grow rich.

4

Tales
for a Tavern

How different history would have been had the Spaniards realized they were being worshiped and acted the part of so many Christs. But their medieval minds would have recoiled from such blasphemy, and in any case they were rough men whose lives in Spain had been little less primitive, and far more savage, than those of the wondering folk who stared at them with fear and love. The Spaniards watched them narrowly, their hands upon their weapons.

They were like no people the Spaniards had seen. They had red-brown skins and dark, curiously lidded eyes and were virtually devoid of body hair. Columbus, whose theory led him to believe he had arrived on an island off the east coast of India, quite naturally deduced they were Indians. He also decided to call the island San Salvador.

The populace made reverent way for Columbus and his men. They watched their gods plant bright banners in the sand, and a cross before which the gods knelt. Obviously this had a religious significance; everything about the gods would have such significance.

Seabirds swung overhead; a soft surf sifted upon the wet sand. A light air moved among the sword grasses of the beach, and in the leaves of the brush beyond. It was too slight to stir the significant banners of Spain. The sun blared upon the circle of suspicious Europeans sweating in their steel. It fell warmly on the bare worshipers. The chief god, his red hair lit by the sun, called into a religious silence. Unknown to himself, as well as to his tiny congregation, he was announcing the beginning of time in a new world.

In exemplary Spanish, Columbus told the Indians they were now and henceforth for all time subjects of Their Majesties of Spain; that they were now under the protection of the Church and would be instructed in Holy Faith for the salvation of their souls. He said that he, as governor and viceroy, was taking possession of this land, and now, having heard these words, they must obey whatever commands were given them.

To Columbus and his men, it mattered nothing that the Indians quite obviously understood no word of this. What did matter terribly to them was that the Word, which was the Word of God, had been spoken in proper form. The Word having thus been spoken, the Spaniards passionately believed themselves now entitled to proceed with their pious task.

Where is the gold? Columbus asked.

Coins and metal were shown the marveling Indians; it was dismayingly clear to the royal accountant that these people had never seen metal before. Still, Columbus was otherwise delighted. He remarked upon the Indians' meekness, their undemanding generosity, and how they loved their neighbors as themselves. He perceived the Indians would give away anything they had for nothing in return—"even spices and gold, if they had any." More to the point, he noted that one or two Spaniards could easily round up any given number of Indians, who could then be "forced to do whatever may be wished." In short, enslaved.

For their part, the Indians found it only natural that their gods should want gifts, and they thereupon cheerfully gave them fruit, fish, baked dog, and, it is widely believed, venereal diseases.

On this first voyage to the New World, the existence of which he never suspected, thinking himself to be in Asia instead, Columbus gathered the impression that the island Indians had heard of gold and knew where it was, although they had none themselves and had never seen it until the Spaniards showed them some. He thought they were trying to tell him gold was to be found on the mainland to the southwest. Apparently, the Indians were merely advising him not to go north. They did not love their neighbors who lived in that direction. They were instead terrified of them, for the people who lived there were cannibals.

Columbus did not raise mainland on this voyage, but it was to Central and South America, and not to North America, that subsequent expeditions would go; the course of history had been determined by an imperfectly understood naked primitive who pointed south with his chin when asked a question he did not understand.

Storms, chance, and possibly an Italianate desire for revenge brought Columbus first to Portugal on his homeward voyage to Spain. He was greatly pleased to be able to tell the Portuguese king that he had found the westward way to India, just as he said he would. He said he had discovered, and claimed for Spain, islands off the Indian coast. With that, he bowed and left to tell the good news to his Spanish monarchs, and to claim his new titles, distinctions, and salaries.

His Royal Jealousy of Portugal immediately protested to Rome. Since 1455, Portugal had been receiving a series of grants from Peter's throne to sovereignty over all the lands it discovered, and to "lands to be discovered" along the coast of Africa "toward that southern shore and beyond even to the Indies." No matter that these papal grants were predicated on Portuguese venturings down the African shore; the point was that India was the ultimate objective, and the Portuguese king argued that Columbus could not claim for Spain what the Holy Father had reserved for Portugal.

Unfortunately for Portugal, the pope in 1492 was a Spaniard, Alexander VI. By papal bull in 1493 he granted the kings of Spain dominion over all the lands, not already belonging to a Christian prince, that had been or might be discovered west and south of a line drawn from pole to pole one hundred leagues west of the Azores, no matter whether such lands lay in India or not. Portugal was to have all those lands lying to the east and south of the line. Such was the Will of God, announced by His vicar on earth, yet the pious monarchs of Portugal and Spain each found His Divine Will unsatisfactory. So they compromised between themselves on a line drawn more than three hundred leagues west of the Cape Verde Islands, thus unknowingly guaranteeing a Portuguese future for Brazil when that land should be discovered.

While pope and kings religiously divided all the non-Christian world between two small Iberian kingdoms, including continents no one knew to exist, Columbus' sailors were meanwhile introducing their new diseases to Christendom, and thickly populating lands they had never seen with creatures of their imagination.

The wonders the sailors had seen were real enough, but descriptions of savages who lived on sandspits were insufficiently impressive to command the attention of tavern audiences. A sailor describing willing foreign girls was just a sailor talking. It was something else again when a sailor described an island where the women were so beautiful they made old men young again. That was better, but still not quite enough. So, in subsequent tellings, the island became a paradise filled with beautiful and willing women, but more than this, at its center the island had a magical Fountain of Youth: sip from it, and the years melted away.

No, the sailors admitted, they had not been there yet themselves, but they knew just where it was.

They knew where the gold was, too, although they had not been there, either. El Dorado, the Golden Man, lived there, in a palace built of solid gold. There was a kingdom out there where the ships were made of gold, and in golden cages feathered apes sang like nightingales.

What other beasts?

Well, the sailors said, there were unicorns, for example. And griffons.

Amazons?

Oh, yes, of course. There were Amazons, and giants, too. And pygmies, and apes that blew trumpets. Yes, during the voyage they had certainly seen all they wanted to see of sirens, dragons, and mermaids. Well, maybe they would like to see more of the mermaids, but no more dragons. Still, a dragon would turn tail if you held up the cross.

There were also seven enchanted cities, founded by the seven Portuguese bishops who had fled west over the seas when the Moors invaded Iberia. Each of these cities was now fabulously wealthy. Saint Ursula and her ten thousand virgins were miraculously alive and well in India. All the people out there will do anything a Spaniard asks; anyone's desires, whatever they may be, are immediately satisfied. Any man can have a fortune simply by asking for it.

The stories grew even more exciting, but these tavern tales of marvels did not set all Europe adventuring. For one thing, few people heard them. For another, more people then as now would rather hear of adventures than attempt them. Tavern audiences, moreover, do not set policies for princes. In due course, subsequent expeditions were sent forth, for Columbus' account to the throne was sufficiently interesting to warrant further investigation; gold might be discovered at any point, and there was certainly a potential source of free labor to develop whatever other resources the new lands might be found to contain. But just as important to Columbus and to the princes who set him forth again was the fact that the Indians were heathen. And to rescue them from this plight was to do the work of God on earth.

5

Gold and Blood
in the
Kingdom of Satan

For the first twenty-one years after Columbus' touching on San Salvador, the Spanish gradually made themselves at home in the Caribbean, first searching south as Columbus advised, then turning west across the Gulf of Mexico.

They were not, however, the only Europeans to venture across the Atlantic in those years. In 1497, five years after Columbus' first voyage, England's Henry VII cautiously dispatched John Cabot on a voyage of discovery. He found, Hakluyt tells us, a "land which no man before that time had attempted. . . . The soile is barren in some places, & yeeldeth little fruit, but it is full of white beares, and stagges farre greater than ours. It yeeldeth plenty of fish, and those very great, as seales, and those which commonly we call salmons: there are soles also above a yard in length; but especially there is great abundance of that kinde of fish which the Savages call baccalaos."

Now, no less an authority than Samuel Eliot Morison says that the story of French sailors being on the Grand Banks of Newfoundland earlier than Cabot or Columbus is an "unverified myth" of later date. The implication is that the French lied about this, but it is, as a document in the royal library at Versailles states, quite remarkable that Cabot found the savages calling a fish by its Basque name. Surely, someone must have taught it to them at least the day before Cabot came blundering onto that coast, looking for the way to China. It does seem quite possible they may have learned it years earlier than that, particularly in view of the fact that the French believed their Norman, Breton, and Basque fishermen had been pulling tuna and cod off the Banks for decades before Columbus set sail for the New World.

In any case, the French definitely were off that distant, icy coast in 1506, when Denis, a mariner of Honfleur, entered and to some extent explored the Gulf of St. Lawrence. Two years later, Aubert of Dieppe made substantially the same voyage. Other fishermen coasted north to Labrador, returning with the news that griffons abounded in that land. They had seen polar bears and walruses, which they recognized as ghosts and evil spirits, and found that two islands off the Newfoundland coast were inhabited by demons. They drew these islands on their maps. Isles of Demons, the legends read, and for the benefit of illiterates, the drawings clearly showed winged, horned, tailed devils in residence. Perilous though this strange corner of the world might be, in 1518 Baron de Lery put a party ashore on tiny Sable Island, off the Nova Scotia coast. This first French attempt to colonize the New World was an immediate failure. Its only survivors were a few cattle which, strangely enough, not only survived the following winter untended in the wilderness, but multiplied.

Except for Cabot's voyage, and another undertaken by his son in Henry VIII's time, and for those of the French fishermen, Spain's two future rivals in America were in no position to contest the field in 1518. England was still the least of European nations, and France was bogged down in profitless Italian wars, and both took care that their mariners stayed well north of the Spanish fleets in the Caribbean. Both gave thought to the papal bull of

1493, the bull that divided "the lands to be discovered" between Spain and Portugal. The French particularly looked for any evidence that could support claims of discovery *prior to 1493,* of any continents and islands to be found west in the Atlantic. England, soon to break with Rome, would base its claims to North America upon Cabot's discoveries and on the allegation that Cornish fishermen had been on the Grand Banks years and years before either Cabot or Columbus sailed across the Atlantic Ocean.

The Spanish meanwhile established a headquarters at Santiago di Cuba and bases on Puerto Rico and Santo Domingo. These were military bases, not colonies. Like all sailors, the Spanish ones were not interested in trying to scratch out a living ashore. Nor would the soldiers accept other than military employment. They were medieval troops who, in return for risking their lives in battle, expected the royal quartermaster or the local populace to provide them with food and all other necessities. Fighting was for soldiers; work was for peasants. In addition to their board, keep, and minuscule pay, the soldiers also expected, as a matter of right, a share in the proceeds of conquest.

Self-enrichment was, however, only one purpose of the Spanish explorations in the Caribbean. To do God's Will on earth was still at all times the alpha and omega of the enterprise, although the ordinary Spanish soldier might not have seemed in all ways the ideal missionary. "Most of the Spaniards who come over," Captain General Hernán Cortés complained to Madrid, "are of low condition and manner, and vicious with various vices and sins, and if they were to be free to move about in Indian towns, they would sooner convert them to their vices than attract them to virtue." They were, however, exactly the sort of men to carry out the official Spanish policy with respect to the people the Spanish called the Indians.

This policy was written out in the form of a directive from their Most Catholic Majesties of Spain. It was called The Requirement of 1513, and it was to be read aloud, in Spanish, to each new group of Indians the Spaniards might encounter.

The requirement began by sketching the history of the world. It then dwelt at length upon the crucially important subject of apostolic succession, in order to prove to the Indians that what was about to happen to them was not only legally valid, but divinely inspired. It was the Will of God, as revealed to His vicar on earth and carried out by a duly anointed monarch.

One can imagine a village of hopeful but completely mystified Indians gaping on, wondering if these strangers were gods or men, while a royal notary stood before them, flourishing a parchment and droning along in a language the Indians had never heard before. What they could not know was that the notary was reading them the law, demanding that they yield themselves to the Spanish Crown at once, and accept the teaching of the Church. If they should do this, the requirement stated, then no hostilities would ensue.

No doubt the notary would look up and smile encouragingly at this point, while the puzzled Indians stared blankly back at him.

But if, having now been legally warned (the notary would continue), the Indians should not comply forthwith, the Spanish soldiery (and here the notary might nod toward the brutal pikemen clad in armor) would immediately fall upon them "with fire and sword."

Reading on, the notary would promise the Indians:

"We shall take you and your wives and children and make slaves of them, and as such sell and dispose of them, as their Highnesses may command; and we shall take away your goods, and shall do all the harm and damage that we can, as to vassals that do not obey."

The Spanish would thereupon look closely at the Indians, and if the people gave any sign that the Spanish construed to be

[49]

uncooperative or hostile, the slaughter would begin. If, however, the Indians seemed to the Spaniards to be docile and compliant, they were assumed to have chosen peace and conversion. In either case, whether it be that of women and children surviving a massacre or of a tribe apparently desirous of conversion, the result was the same. It was slavery. The innocent thing about it all was that the Spaniards, officers and men as well as their priests, utterly and profoundly believed that bringing these people to God, by force or terror if necessary, was an act of infinite mercy: they were saving the Indians' immortal souls from eternal torment in hell.

This holy policy had been pursued long before it found formal expression in The Requirement of 1513, but its practical effects left much to be desired. For one thing, the slaves died. They died in droves. Some Caribbean islands were virtually depopulated. No one could have then known the Indians had no natural resistance to diseases carried by the immune Europeans. Worse, not much work could be got out of the Indians. The naked primitive could not grasp the theory of working to accumulate a surplus for himself, much less for his master. Next, the beautiful islands were not productive of much the Spaniards wanted, anyway. Nor were the subtropical jungles the Spanish found along the southern Gulf coast. Furthermore, the Indians the Spaniards met seemed to be growing increasingly inimical. News did not travel fast among the scattered tribes who lived on islands and in jungles, but word of the Spaniards' behavior spread slowly before them like a stench, and now, twenty-one years after Columbus' first voyage, when the Spaniards came ashore, they were much more likely to be met by showers of stone-tipped arrows fired from ambush than to be welcomed on the beach by crowds of marveling worshipers.

It is impossible to say how long the Spanish would have remained in the New World, in view of the fact that all their explorations there, from 1492 to 1518, failed either to locate India or to turn up gold. True, they felt a holy duty to pass among the heathen with fire, sword and the cross. No doubt sailing strange seas and raising hitherto-unknown shores was exhilarating in itself. There was always the possibility of discovering the lost tribes of Israel on the next island. But ships cost money; men must be paid something; it was expensive to supply their New World bases with horses, cattle, swine, seeds in jars, barrels of wine, figs, raisins, olive oil, cloth, forges, iron, nails, tools, manacles and beads for the Indians, crossbows and bolts for the crossbows, powder, shot, guns, swords, pikes, and armor. In view of this drain upon the royal treasury, there might have come a time when, despite all the commands of faith and adventure, the Crown would no longer have been willing to finance further expeditions into realms so unproductive of treasure. Colonies could have been profitable, but in the early years the Spanish thought in terms of discovery and conquest, not in terms of colonies. So the expense went on until, in 1518, God saw fit to reward His children for the efforts they were making in His behalf. In that year, a Spanish ship reached the shores of Yucatán, and the Indians there had gold.

They had crowns made of gold, and masks and sandals of gold, and golden earrings, and jewelry made of gold in the shapes of lizards, dogs, ducks, and snakes.

This was no traveler's tale: the Spanish ship returned to Cuba with the precious artifacts aboard, and with the report that the Indians of Yucatán said the baubles had come to them from people who lived in a great city set among mountains far inland to the west. The Spanish did not doubt this in the least: China lay in that direction and the workmanship of the golden ornaments indicated a high state of civilization.

The good news, and the golden toys, were at once dispatched to Spain, where the Emperor Charles V now sat upon the throne. The order was given. Twenty-seven years after Columbus' first voyage, Spain was now to put the first large European expeditionary force ashore on the mainland of North America. Hernán Cortés commanded it.

The force consisted of two chaplains, two greyhounds trained as war dogs, and 508 men at arms. Thirty-two of the soldiers were crossbowmen and thirteen were musketeers. The others carried pikes, lances, and Toledo swords, and their number included artillerists to serve four falconet cannon that fired two-inch, pound and a half iron balls. The troops' defensive armor consisted of steel morions, breastplates, gauntlets, and greaves, and a kind of hard-finished, stone-stiff cotton armor that was not only rustproof, but was considerably lighter than the steel, somewhat cooler, and just as protective against stone arrowheads and the Indians' fire-hardened wooden spears. There was also cotton armor for the expedition's sixteen horses, who were to prove to be the Spaniards' most uniquely effective weapon of all. One hundred sailors were to put the task force ashore.

When the ships first touched the mouth of the Tabasco River in 1519, swarms of warlike Indians appeared. Years ago these Indians had greeted a Spanish ship, thinking the crew members to be legendary gods returning from the east. But the Indians had immediately learned how wrong they were, and now they wanted nothing more to do with the Spanish.

With this knowledge in mind, Cortés ordered the falconets fired. Pursued by lightning, thunder, and smoke, the Indians fled howling into the brush, and Cortés pushed cautiously inland after them.

The Indians, however, had not run away in abject terror. They had gone to summon their entire power, and when Cortés reached the site of modern Tabasco, he and his five hundred men collided with an army of no less than twelve thousand ululating savages. The chronicles say the battle went on for several days until the horses were brought up from the beach, and a cavalry charge was laid on. If so, the engagement could not have persisted hour after hour, night and day, hand to hand, because no matter how well-armed and courageous, five hundred men would shortly have become exhausted and been overrun by a force twenty-four times their number.

This well-disciplined force, drawn up in good order, protected by armor against enemy missiles, possessed of weapons superior in range and killing power, and of small arms infinitely superior to stone axes for close-in work, was apparently able to hold its perimeter against weak and sporadic attacks that occurred only during daylight hours and were never resolutely pushed home. The Spaniards' morale was excellent, fortified by their absolute belief in God's aid and the certainty of going to heaven if killed; by the effectiveness of their armament; by the knowledge they were past all human help and must conquer or die.

Matters hung in suspense for several days of this first pitched battle between European troops and Stone Age tribesmen, the Indians unwilling and unable to throw themselves en masse upon that armored infantry; the Spanish knowing they must hold their ground within a defensive perimeter. Two Spaniards had been killed, and several wounded, but as far as military considerations were concerned, the command was intact and as potent as ever. But it was immobile. And it was surrounded. It would shortly be faced with the choice of starvation, or cutting its way back to the ships, if it could not take the initiative.

Sixteen horsemen do not seem to constitute much of a cavalry, but they were the key to the battle. Once arrived from the beach, they charged in echelon through the Indians' encirclement, turned, and rode down the line, the trained horses rearing to add their descending weight to the power of the sword cuts, and the Indians fled. They had never before seen horses. They were demons, ridden by demons.

When all was over, the Indians were reported to have lost eight hundred warriors killed by the Spanish cavalry and infantry. They could only watch from a distance while the Spanish cut the fat from Indian carcasses and used this, together with a red-hot knife, to cauterize their few wounds.

With the aid of a translator, a peace was made. The Indians gave their allegiance to Charles V, their faith to the Spanish God, and their women to the victorious soldiers.

They also made gifts of food and cloth, and most important of all, they gave Cortés golden jewelry. It had come from a place called Mexico. So had the golden ornaments that had been sent to Spain a year ago. Mexico was the mysterious city that Cortés sought.

Far off in Mexico, the Aztec Emperor Montezuma was startled by confusing rumors of the battle at Tabasco. Since this was the very calendar year prophesied in ancient legends when the Plumed Serpent Quetzalcoatl would at last return to His people, and since the rumors from Tabasco were horrific with accounts of fabulous monsters, the devout prince who sat upon the golden throne of Mexico quite naturally supposed the Great God Quetzalcoatl had indeed returned—but that He had come in wrath. It was equally possible that the sea had thrown up demonic sorcerers or some strange unheard-of breed of invincible warriors accompanied by unimaginable beasts. The reports were at least clear on one point: be the newcomers Quetzalcoatl and Company or demons or superhumans, they spread slaughter before them and they were headed straight for Mexico. So the snakeskin drums boomed, and feathered victims danced on the blood-slimy stones atop a pyramid before their hearts were offered to Quetzalcoatl to appease His wrath if He had returned in anger and to enlist His aid against the savage monsters if He had not in fact reappeared upon the borders of the empire.

Then the Spaniards arrived. They were not gods, but strange and terrible men of supernatural powers who had come for gold. One of Montezuma's secretaries wrote, "Like monkeys [the Spaniards] seized upon the gold. It was as if only then they were satisfied, sated, and gladdened. [They] thirsted mightily for gold; they stuffed themselves with it, and starved for it, and lusted for it. . . ." In the court of Montezuma, where their unwelcome guests were entertained, a feeling grew that the Spaniards were perhaps more disgusting than they were terrifying. Montezuma was willing to give them all the gold they could carry away if only they would go. He was also perfectly willing to have them all slaughtered if only a safe opportunity for killing them could be found.

For his part, Cortés knew he must keep his troops under the tightest of control if the Spanish were to get out of this splendid, barbaric city alive: they must behave as guests should, no matter what they thought of their hosts. He could always return with a larger army. True, he and his five hundred had defeated twelve thousand Yucatán primitives, but three hundred thousand infinitely more sophisticated Aztecs might very well prove to be more Indians than five hundred soldiers could handle. It did not seem the time or place to read The Requirement of 1513 to Montezuma and the populace. He did bring up the matter of religion with the emperor, only to be told, "If I had thought you would insult my gods, I would not have shown them to you. Please do not say another word to dishonour them."

Here was the sticking point. Cortés and all his men devoutly believed themselves to be in the kingdom of the Devil. The human sacrifices of the Aztecs were, to them, ghastly travesties on the sacrifice of Christ. The Aztecs were equally horrified by the religion of the Spaniards, when they perceived what it was. They sacrificed men to keep their God alive; the Spaniards apparently believed that God had been sacrificed to save men. Aztec and Spaniard each believed the other's religion to be blasphemy. There could be no way around this point, although Cortés lingered on in Mexico to try to find some way of establishing a relationship between the Spanish and Aztec thrones on a diplomatic

[55]

basis; to find some temporary accommodation that would suffice until a Spanish force could be assembled that would be sufficiently strong to destroy, utterly, this kingdom of Satan.

While Cortés lingered there, word of Mexico's golden splendors filtered back to Santiago di Cuba, and Diego Velásquez, the royal governor of the Spanish in the New World, immediately ordered one Pánfilo de Narváez to proceed to Mexico to enter into secret negotiations of his own with Montezuma. With Aztec help if necessary, Narváez was to capture or kill Cortés, and take over command of the expedition: Valásquez intended to get the gold and glory for himself.

But in Mexico, Cortés heard of Narváez' mission and arrival at Vera Cruz. Leaving a company behind under the command of a lieutenant, Cortés returned by forced marches to the beachhead. There, he bribed some of Narváez' men and surprised the rest in a night attack. Narváez was blinded in one eye and taken prisoner.

During Cortés' absence, however, the Spanish lieutenant in Mexico decided in the name of God to destroy an Aztec altar, and when the horrified Aztec priests objected, the Spaniards butchered the priests. At last the Aztecs recognized the Spaniards for what they were: neither men nor gods, but devils. The war drums called; the little Spanish company was beleaguered, and Cortés hurried to the rescue with his troops, reinforced now by Narváez' men, and by Indian tribes he invited to join in the ruin of Mexico.

In the course of the brief and terrible events that followed, a few Spaniards were taken prisoner, and made to dance on temple floors before their hearts were given to the Aztec God, but Cortés and his men exacted a ghastly revenge. The superiority of Spanish arms, discipline, and tactics certainly had much to do with the victory which both the Spaniards and the Aztecs regarded as miraculous. The Spaniards were convinced that God aided them, and the Aztecs soon believed it futile to oppose men possessed of magical powers. But while military superiority and a mutual belief in magic might go far toward explaining why a ridiculously small number of Spaniards were able to crush the will of an Aztec army to resist, they might not entirely explain how and why the Spanish went on to destroy the Aztec civilization.

It is a biological fact that whenever two subspecies of the same animal species meet, the dominant one will at once begin to kill out or breed out the other. A modern theory is that all the races of men on earth are subspecies of homo sapiens. So, if the theory is as true as the biological fact, then what happened in Mexico (and everywhere else in North America where European men met Stone Age Asiatics) was simply beyond human control: Evolutionary law decreed extirpation.

Those who, for political or humanitarian reasons, find such an explanation abhorrent, may prefer to dwell upon the vulnerability of the poorly armed, naïve savage to the potent rapacity of the well-armed and sophisticated European. In such case, the matter could be considered thus:

If the Europeans were not the dominant race in the biological meaning of the word, they were certainly the dominant race in every other meaning of it. Mexico held what the Spaniards wanted, so they took it from a people whose religious, political, and military structures were comparatively insubstantial when they were not nonexistent. The Spanish policy was religious warfare. In an incredibly short time, they exterminated and/or bred out the Stone Age people, reducing the survivors to social impotence. They did this in God's Holy Name and gave Him thanks for the victory. The gold was sent to Spain.

6

Put Them All to the Knife

By midpoint of the sixteenth century, New Spain consisted not merely of Caribbean island bases, but of two viceroyalties, Mexico and Peru, each boasting a university and each divided into bishoprics. But for all its outward form, New Spain was not a Spanish colony. It was rather a prison farm dominated by Spanish soldiers, in which Indian and black slaves tilled the fields and worked the mines for the Spanish Crown. There were black slaves because not enough work could be coerced from Indian ones.

Virtually no Spanish women came to the Americas. The youth who were instructed by the priests, attended the universities, and who became the middle class, were mestizos, or mixed-bloods, born to Spanish soldiers and Indian mothers. Some became priests, teachers, and administrators to the Indians; others were given lands and placed in charge of Indian and black labor; some were shopkeepers, but none was accorded social equality by his father. They were often hated by the Indians beneath them, and always faintly despised by the Spaniards above them in the social scale. Still, the Spaniards accomplished more among the Indians than any other Europeans ever would, and the slaves of New Spain gave their masters an incredible amount of treasure.

Peruvian and Mexican mines were producing half a million pounds of silver and ten thousand pounds of gold each year, and this fantastic wealth enriched the Spanish Crown beyond all contemporary comparison in the sixteenth century and directly brought about the ruin of all Spanish hopes in both the Old World and the New.

The first of three reasons for this unlooked-for result was that the American gold enabled the Crown to rule as an absolute despot over a Spanish society virtually unchanged from medieval times.

Elsewhere in Europe during that glorious century when Leonardo painted, Erasmus taught, and Machiavelli tried to give princes a little practical advice, the once-feudal societies of the Middle Ages were evolving into modern Renaissance states. Outside of Spain, kings sought to limit the power of their feudal barons by creating standing armies of their own. When, as the Tudor kings of England did, they curried favor with the fast-emerging merchant class, raised members of that class to positions of power at court, and borrowed money from them to hire royal mercenary troops, they enhanced the power of that new middle class—perhaps unaware that they were creating a power that would one day be inimical not only to the baronry but also to royalty. Some princes, particularly those of northern Europe, also sought to limit the wealth and power of the Church in order to enhance their own, and these princes were more than willing to listen to intellectual priests who argued for reform of Holy Church. When Martin Luther nailed his theses to the church door in 1517, German princes protected him. Luther's teachings, and those of Calvin and Knox, and Henry VIII's defiance of the pope, were all portentous of a new age, and emergent Protestantism not only found bases of political power in the Lowlands and

[59]

in northern European kingdoms, but economic bases of power as well. The Protestant heresy (as the Spanish called it) was particularly congenial to the rising middle class of merchants, and these people sought strength in combination. A stock market opened in Antwerp in 1531; a Hansa League of northern seaports, including London, established mutual trading conventions; and in 1540 Henry VIII made an alliance with Dutch and German states as much for wool-trading reasons as for political and religious ones.

Little of what was taking place in Europe was reflected in Spain, however. The Spanish kings, first the Emperor Charles V and then his son Philip II, had no such need as other princes had of cultivating trade and manufacture, or of placating a rising middle class or anyone else. The treasure fleets from America brought them gold, which they transubstantiated into armadas and armies whose dour peasant soldiery was devout and ferocious beyond all European standards. Their soldiery gave the Spanish kings dictatorial power, and the Church gave them its blessing. No quarrel between Church and State plagued Spain. The Church loyally told the king he was divinely appointed to rule over men, and the king loyally gave the Church gold from America. Both Church and Crown recognized the threat to their positions posed by the rise of Protestantism, and their fear of it bound them even closer together. Ignatius Loyola's answer to the Protestant heresy was his *Spiritual Exercises,* and in the year the English king allied himself with the Protestant north, the Society of Jesus was founded. The Jesuits were to be the militant soldiers of Christ, sworn to eternal war against heresy.

Together with the Spanish monarchs, the Spanish Church tried to hold back the dawn. As far as the European Renaissance was concerned, Spain was a comparative dungeon. Her religion spoke of pain and death rather than of hope and life. Nowhere but in Spain did the priesthood cling so close to the motto of the Church of Rome, "Always the same." New thought was rejected. All during the sixteenth century, any Spaniard who dared think in new categories could expect torture at the hands of the Church, followed by a fiery death at the hands of the State. The Church smelled devils everywhere. Monks, Inquisitors, spies, and informers haunted the land, and no Spaniard could know what another might have said secretly against him. This in itself was a fair guarantee against improvisation, invention, and individual enterprise, but a poor country made even poorer by such repression was made poorer yet by arbitrary restrictions on commerce, by senseless prohibitions and unfair taxes capriciously imposed. Spain was a textbook example of all the ills of dictatorship. In no other European country at the time was there such a multitude of beggars, nor was there another land on the continent where the poor stood in such overwhelming proportion to the rich, and with such a distance between them. For all this, Spain glittered and glared with military power. Gold from America fed those armadas and armies, yet the maintenance of those large and costly armaments was otherwise ruinous to Spain, because it was an inflationary factor. Armies do not after all produce wealth, but consume it; if a nation's economy is stagnant, as Spain's was, the armies will consume everything while prices rise and the poor become poorer. Moreover, the American treasure was itself an inflationary factor, for as gold and silver became more available, the price of specie fell, with the result that all other prices rose. The kings of Spain could not have understood such matters. Their national policy was to keep Spain firmly in the feudal Middle Ages, and their foreign policy was to use the fantastic treasure of the New World to wage unceasing religious warfare against heretics in Europe and pagans in America.

Some idea of their single-minded zeal may be deduced from the fact that the Emperor Charles V, who was not only king of Spain but also the Holy Roman Emperor, spent thirty-five years in warfare against Protestant states before abdicating all his thrones at once to become a monk. He gave Austria, Hungary, and Bohemia to his Hapsburg brother Ferdinand, who became

Holy Roman Emperor. All the rest went to his son, Philip II, whose zeal bordered on the pathological. It was Philip who built the Escorial on the bleak hills outside Madrid—a royal palace that was a penitentiary formed in the shape of the gridiron upon which St. Lawrence was slowly roasted to death in 258. In a cell in the depths of this morbid structure, Philip lived in a fearful religious ecstasy, lost in that peculiar Spanish trance of cruelty, pain, and death. He was a gnome of a prince, brooding over reports of all that took place in his realms like an i-dotting, t-crossing clerk, but he also happened to be the most powerful man in the world.

Through marriage, he had added Portugal to an empire that included Spain, the Netherlands, the Free County of Burgundy, Milan, the Kingdom of Naples, Sicily, Sardinia, the Baleric Islands, Tunis, and North and South America. Virtually every ship found upon the Mediterranean and Atlantic oceans belonged to him. Through a dynastic marriage, he put forth a claim to the throne of France. He was, for the duration of his own unproductive marriage to Mary, daughter of Henry VIII, the king of England as well. He was king there in name only, and not for long, but Philip never forgot the English and he was determined to settle accounts with those heretics. He inherited, and carried to a point of fury, his father's belief in a Great Crusade to extirpate heresy wherever it might be found. He had no use for gold save as a means to this holy end, toward which the Church forever encouraged him. In 1557, the Church particularly called his attention to North America.

"It is lawful that your Majesty, like a good shepherd, appointed by the hand of the Eternal Father, should tend and lead out your sheep, since the Holy Spirit has shown spreading pastures whereon are feeding lost sheep which have been snatched away by the dragon, the Demon."

So begins a priestly remonstrance to Philip.

"These pastures," the remonstrance continued, "are the New World, wherein is comprised Florida, now in possession of

The Demon, and here he makes himself adored and revered. This is the Land of Promise, possessed by idolaters, the Amorite, Amalekite, Moabite, Canaanite. This is the land promised by the Eternal Father to the faithful, since we are commanded by God in the Holy Scriptures to take it from them, being idolaters, and, by reason of their idolatry and sin, to put them all to the knife, leaving no living thing save maidens and children, their cities robbed and sacked, their walls and houses leveled to the earth."

The remonstrance is in every way remarkable, particularly because the Florida of the document is not simply that low-lying peninsula where Ponce de León sought the Fountain of Youth and the River Jordan in 1513, and where on his return nine years later, he was killed by Indians. By 1557, the Spanish knew they were not in the Indies, but in an unexplored hemisphere, and by Florida they meant *all of North America,* exclusive of Mexico. The remonstrance is furthermore remarkable for its insistence that there were walled cities waiting to be robbed and sacked in Florida, when for the past forty years no evidence of any such cities had been found there, whereas there was much evidence to suggest the northern continent was a wilderness populated only by scattered and quite primitive tribes.

[handwritten margin note: MEXICO, THEY CALLED "NEW SPAIN"]

Herein lay the second reason why the treasure of Mexico and Peru proved ruinous to Spain. Since marvelous cities had been found and plundered in the south, the Spanish presumed such cities could be found in the north. The gold rush was still very much on, not only because Church and State decreed it, but also because the ordinary Spanish Conquistador dreamed of enriching himself in New Spain so that he could return to live like a grandee in Old Spain. Consider Francisco Pizarro: he had been a swineherd in Spain, but after the conquest of Peru, who could call Pizarro a swineherd now? One Conquistador, asked why he did not claim broad lands for himself, have them farmed by slaves, and grow quietly rich thereby, shortly replied that if he had wanted to work hard, he would have remained in Catalonia. To

[63]

be sure, the Spaniards knew as well as any other Europeans of their time that land meant wealth, and land in America lay all about them—as much as or more than anyone could ask, and there for the taking. But these men were not farmers; they did not intend to stay in New Spain longer than was necessary to make their fortunes. They were soldiers who were much more interested in taking gold away from someone who had it than they were in mining it themselves.

Nor were these men explorers. The techniques of sending out small reconnaissance parties were certainly available to them in the sixteenth century, and so were those of mapping and measuring the land. So they could have gone about the exploration of North America in an orderly way, particularly inasmuch as time was no object to them as it might have been had other Europeans been then competing with them for possession of the Western Hemisphere. But instead of sending out small search parties capable of living well off the land while they surveyed it, the Spanish kept sending out small armies which, though small, were still too numerous to live on the uncultivated natural products of that land. Armies were sent out because the Spanish expected to find walled cities full of armed savages awaiting them.

Thus, in 1528, Pánfilo de Narváez set out with four hundred men and eighty-two horses in four ships and a brigantine to invade the North American mainland. He was the same Narváez who had been blinded in one eye, captured, and four years later released by Cortés; he had now obtained the king's ear and was commissioned as grand constable of all the lands he would conquer in Florida. A gale threw his squadron on the shore of what is now the state of that name, and here he divided his command. He and his troops would march west along the Gulf Coast while offshore the ships paralleled their march. The ships and men would meet in the harbor of the River of Palms, the present Rio Grande. Two years later, the ships turned up at Vera Cruz. They had never found the river, had never seen the expeditionary force since they had put it ashore, and it was not till five years after that, that anyone learned what had happened. Then, four emaciated wretches limped into Mexico, the sole survivors of the expedition. Their spokesman was Alvar Nuñez Cabeza de Vaca.

He had a tale to tell of a fabulous golden city called Apalachen, which, he said, turned out to be nothing more than forty abandoned Indian huts, where the expedition found a few jars of maize. A second city, also recommended to them by Indians they had captured in Florida, proved to be another little cluster of huts with a patch of pumpkins nearby. Cabeza de Vaca otherwise described palmetto thickets, a wet tangle of trees ghastly with festoons of gray-green moss, and jungles roaring with insects. He spoke of Indian ambushes; of Spaniards dying of fevers; of starvation and eating the horses; of the survivors of the march inland returning to the Gulf of Mexico and there fashioning five leaky longboats that were all lost in a storm save the one he and three others were aboard. After shipwreck and enslavement by a primitive tribe, he and his friends at length escaped and walked across what are now the Texas plains and through the Southwest deserts where, he said, they found Indians living in mud villages, raising corn, and making ornaments of turquoise. They had seen "very great mountains" shining in the west, and, crossing these, had come out upon the Pacific coast where they had fallen in with a Spanish force raiding along the coast for Indian slaves.

Cabeza de Vaca told his story in all its horror, but what his audience deduced was that there was a city of gold in Florida called Apalachen; that there were other cities there, in a desert land, where the cloth was better than in New Spain and where armies of savage archers fired arrows whose heads were made of turquoises and emeralds.

Inspired by the story of Cabeza de Vaca, which lost nothing each time someone else retold it, the Spanish began to search the southwestern wastes for the fabulous Seven Cities of Cibola, and failing to discover these metropolises, they turned east in search of an even more magical place called Quivira. It was situated on a river six miles wide, and the river was filled with fish bigger than horses. Rowboats with sails plied this water, each boat propelled by forty oarsmen. Golden eagles decorated their prows, and in their stern sheets great lords dressed in silks reclined under canopies to dally with maidens and to eat from silver tables. Naturally Quivira was filled with gold, so much gold that there were not enough wagons in all Europe to drag it away—but much, much richer lands and cities lay beyond Quivira. Looking for these cities of Florida, the Spanish by 1541 reached the middle of Kansas. Hernando de Soto in that same year found the Mississippi River.

Two years earlier, De Soto had landed 620 men on the shore of what is now Tampa Bay. The landing was a pomp of blown trumpets, a sheen of lances glittering in the sun, a thing of pennons fluttering, and rolling drums. High Mass was celebrated, and the expedition was solemnly declared to be under the protection of God, for Whose Sake alone it had been undertaken. This having been pronounced, the trumpets flared, and with the cross before them, the Spaniards moved inland, bloodhounds baying and men singing. They had brought the bloodhounds for the purpose of hunting Indians and brought monks to save the Indians' souls; they had loads of jingling manacles to snap on captive wrists.

And off they went on their pious way to look for Apalachen, which by now had been identified as the home of El Dorado, the Golden Man who lived in a city of solid gold. It was always important to the Spaniards to wish to convert the rich.

Two years later, having wandered about in what is now Georgia, Alabama, and Mississippi, what was left of the expedition reached the great river that was apparently the one to which the stories of Quivira referred. They crossed the Mississippi above the mouth of the Arkansas River, still in search of El Dorado's golden capitol, but meeting no one but Indians who, as the chronicler said, "were as furious as mad dogs." Wherever they went with their bloodhounds and manacles, the Spanish kept meeting with this sort of Indian. They put the fear of God into the savages, but the wild men of Florida kept on shooting back. The expedition still pressed on, their clothing now consisting of horse and other animal skins, and of mats and kilts made of woven vines, and no one blew any trumpets or rolled any drums as they trudged onto the Great Plains to find great herds of bison and the warlike hunters who preyed on these herds, together with the wolves, the lions, and the grizzly bears. Here, they turned back. When they reached the Mississippi River again, De Soto sickened of a fever and died. Three hundred eleven men, almost exactly half the original number, all of them sick and starving, scarecrow figures in their matted beards and lugubrious costumes, at last shuffled into a tiny Spanish outpost on the Gulf Coast.

With forty years of this kind of experience behind them, dating from Ponce de León's first voyage to the time that priestly remonstrance was delivered to Philip II in 1557, one might think it would have occurred to the Spanish to work out new approaches to the problems presented to them by what was, quite obviously, a tremendous continent devoid of any populace other than those found wandering after the bison or growing pumpkins in river bottoms.

But the Spaniards were their own prisoners, prisoners of their prior success, and so believed the stories they told themselves about Quivira, El Dorado and the rest of it. They were the prisoners of the Church: if priests said North America was the Promised Land, currently in the power of the Demon, where idolaters lived in cities, then this must of course be true. They were also the prisoners of their own political system. As Cortés had complained, the court in Spain allowed commanders in the field no freedom to make on-the-scene decisions. They could make recommendations, and months later, after their messages had sailed across the Atlantic, been acted upon, and sent slowly back across the ocean, the commanders could expect to receive detailed instructions as to how to handle a situation which, by this time, either no longer existed or had evolved into a quite different and more serious problem. Worse, the orders sent from Spain were to be followed without question, and worse still, they were the bureaucratic productions of swarms of clerks who had no personal knowledge of conditions in the New World, but who were at once swollen with a sense of their own authority and with a fear of their royal master, who read every word of every report.

Finally, the Spaniards were the prisoners of laziness. They would willingly undergo unspeakable hardships searching for golden cities to loot, rather than endure far more bearable burdens in the process of discovering and developing the real wealth of the New World. The Holy Spirit had indeed led them into the Promised Land, but they failed to recognize it when they looked about. Instead, little armies of emaciated, sunburned men, starving, utterly lost, praying and fighting, made their proud and hapless way across the oil fields of Texas, the cattle lands of Kansas, the hot, fertile Mississippi valley, looking for El Dorado in the richest country on earth. Of course the oil, the cattle, the rice, cotton, fruit, corn, wheat, sugarcane, and all such else lay in a future the Spaniards of the sixteenth century could not imagine, but the fact that they could not imagine it is the central and excellent reason why North America held no future for Spain. They were Conquistadores. Unfortunately, there was nothing for them to conquer in Florida, and a law of diminishing returns began to make itself felt. The cost of maintaining armies in the field, supply fleets and treasure fleets and armadas to protect those fleets, and fortified bases to supply the armies and armadas, and a vast bureaucracy of clerks and administrators to superintend all this, began to rise while the price of gold and silver fell and while no other golden cities were found. Still, the expensive search went on.

The third reason why the treasure of Mexico and Peru proved ultimately ruinous to Spain was that it was attractive to others. For all that Spain was the first military power in the world, on the high seas as well as on land, there was no lack of daring men to raid the treasure fleets and their depots in New Spain. English towns and syndicates of English merchants fitted out fighting ships whose mariners sailed "on thirds." That is, the crew could keep one-third of the loot it seized; the rest went to those who sponsored the venture. The piracy was often a semi-official one in that royal warships went aventuring with the tacit knowledge and consent of the Tudor monarchs, Henry VIII and Elizabeth I. Indeed, when Henry VIII ordered construction of a new class of fighting ships that would be longer, lower in the water, faster sailing than the Spanish galleons, and armed with guns of longer range, he did not have defense of the realm solely in mind. The English pirates were joined on the high seas by those from the Protestant Lowlands, by freebooters from Catholic Portugal and France, and by men of no religion who owned no masters but themselves. True, it was treasure they all were after, but when an English squadron fell upon the galleons, furious religious hatreds were the reason why the victors gave no quarter to the vanquished; the wars waged by Charles V and Philip II against Protestants in Europe found their echo at sea.

The harm done by these piratical attacks could not, however, be reckoned in the loss of Spanish ships, but rather lay in the ever more costly efforts the Spaniards made to elaborate their defenses. Having laid exclusive claim to the entire Western Hemisphere, the Spaniards tried to make it good. They first forbade their own subjects in New Spain from trading with those of any other nation, and thereby shut themselves off from a commerce that might have been beneficial. Next, they sought to seal off the ocean approaches with squadrons fanning out from Spain to intercept foreign ships debouching into the Atlantic from the English Channel. Other squadrons guarded the approaches to the Caribbean and to Spanish harbors on the Pacific coast of America, and still other squadrons convoyed the treasure ships. The Spaniards fortified their bases not only in the Caribbean, and along the southern shore of the Gulf of Mexico, but also along the Pacific coasts of South and Central America, Mexico, and California.

They tried to be safe everywhere at once in the Western Hemisphere, meanwhile waging holy war in Europe, and establishing themselves in the Orient with a base in the Philippines, and it was all a bit too much. The Spaniards did effectively dominate the Caribbean, although they could not exert an absolute control over it, but they could not dominate the immense distances stretching north along the entire eastern seaboard of North America, toward which their first great rivals, the French, were presently sailing. Nor could Spain prevent the English, the French, and the Dutch from developing maritime powers of their own, any more than she could stamp the Protestant heresy out of Europe. But Spain tried. She put forth all her enormous military power—power sapped by distances too immense to be bound together by the communications systems of the day; by impossible directives sent to commanders by a theocratic bureaucracy; by a gathering feeling of frustration on the part of those commanders as they sought to comply and as one project after another miscarried; by inflationary factors that provoked a law of diminishing returns, and then at last by a diminution of the flow of treasure as the gold and silver mines began to work out. At midpoint of the sixteenth century, Spain was still the first of nations, but she was also quite sick. Her brilliant sunlight made her shadows all the darker.

7

The Two
True Faiths

W HILE the Spanish searched rather than explored the southern regions of North America, looking for magical cities in total ignorance of the real wealth that lay all about them, the French made sporadic efforts to find a way of their own to the fabulous riches of the Orient.

The story of French intrusion into the New World properly begins in 1523, when Francis I was king of the French. He ruled a nation whose vitality had been drained by the pointless wars his two royal predecessors had lost in Italy. He was nervously aware that whereas France was nearly bankrupt and almost without an army, his neighbor, Charles of Spain, was growing hugely powerful on the marvelous plunder of Mexico. Francis reflected upon the voyages his Breton and Norman subjects were regularly making to the fisheries off a cold, mysterious coast. Possibly a Northwest Passage to Cathay could be found—a route that would stay well clear of the Spanish military bases far to the south, and that might also prove to be a much shorter route to Asia than the immense voyage Magellan had made across the Atlantic and then across the incredible vastness of the Pacific.

So in 1523, Francis dipped into the shrunken treasury of France to subsidize a voyage of discovery, to be made by one ship commanded by Giovanni da Verrazano, a Florentine sailor in the service of France.

In due course, Verrazano found himself off the coast of what is now North Carolina, at about the site of Wilmington. He sailed north, carefully mapping the shoreline, sometimes coming ashore to be entertained, if not worshiped, by wondering savages. He coasted north, entering New York harbor by way of the Narrows, made around Staten Island, sailed past Long and Block islands, and thence to Newport. But the farther he sailed up the New England coast, the more repellent the coasts became—and the more repellent the Indians. They would, however, trade with Verrazano, although they would not allow the French sailors to get close to them. From overhanging cliffs, they lowered baskets on cords of vine, making clear by signs they wanted fishhooks and knives of steel in return for furs. Here was certain evidence of prior acquaintance with Europeans—and when the trade had been completed, the Indians capered on the cliffs, making faces and jeering at the white men before vanishing into their forests. Just once on this coast Verrazano's men tried to land, only to be pelted with arrows and stones.

After mapping the continental coast from the 34th to the 50th parallels, Verrazano returned to France to report that he had penetrated inland to a depth of several miles at sundry points, and his charts provide the earliest known description of that shoreline. He wanted to colonize this part of the New World for the same pious motive the Spanish held: to bring the blessing of Christianity to the Indians. Fingering the strange, luxuriant furs, certain French merchants were eager to colonize that country, too, but the political situation at the time permitted no such luxury.

Still, Verrazano managed to sail for America again, this time to be intercepted by the Spaniards and hanged for a pirate.

The troubles that afflicted France at the time of Verrazano's voyage were part and parcel of the general difficulty Europe was experiencing in the second decade of the sixteenth century, when medieval feudal societies were evolving into the beginnings of modern states, but together with purely political problems, there was one supremely important matter that was to complicate all others.

It was the time of the High Renaissance, and when Europeans opened their eyes during that age, the first thing they saw was the Holy Church that explained and dominated the world around them and offered them the only path to eternal life after death. Now, in the light of rediscovery of the thoughts of early Christian and pagan philosophers, it occurred to some thoughtful priests to compare the wealth, power, practices, and doctrines of the medieval Church with the poverty, simplicity, and teachings of Christ. This led them further to inquire into man's proper relationship with God. What neither the questioners nor the orthodox churchmen doubted for a moment was the absolute importance of knowing what that relationship was. All were agreed there could be only one True Faith; that any deviation from that Truth was heresy, doubtless inspired by the Devil and leading only to hell. Some read Scripture one way, and some another, but on the crucial question of who was right, the Church replied that only the pope and his prelates could know the true answer, for the pope was Christ's vicar on earth. The questioners could object with their own arguments on the text and with the observation that the behavior of certain popes, cardinals, and bishops was more scandalous than pious.

If this theological discussion could have been kept within church walls, all might have been quite different. But it became a public one as priests addressed their congregations and when, thanks to the invention of movable type, Bibles were printed and could be read by the educated among the laity. By 1534, when Francis I of France commissioned a second voyage of discovery under the command of Jacques Cartier, a seaman of St.-Malo, Luther's heresy had the German states in an uproar, and Calvin's heresy had begun to infect France. The heretics' point of view was that they, alone, expounded the one True Faith; that it was the Church that was really the Whore of Babylon, the Agent of the Devil. The Church's view was that the Protestant heretics must be identified, hunted down, put to the question, and burned.

Except for a relentless hunt for heretics in Spain and France, the horrors of religious war had not begun to unfold at the time of Cartier's voyage. It was however felt by the French Catholic clergy that the Church might recoup its losses to heresy in the Old World by gaining converts in the New. Therefore the French clergy supported the king's dispatch of Cartier into an area the papal bull of 1493 had reserved exclusively for Spain. In this it would seem the French Catholics were Frenchmen first, and Catholics second, but then the French clergy had always been jealous of what it called the Gallican liberties and could always argue that French sailors had been fishing in the northern reaches of the New World before the bull was issued.

Cartier passed the straits of Belle Isle, entered the Gulf of Chaleurs, planted at Gaspé, claiming this realm for God and his king, and, certain that he was on the high road to Cathay, sailed up the St. Lawrence River to the shores of Anticosti Island. The following year, in 1535, he went up the St. Lawrence as far as the present site of Montreal, where there he found a large, palisaded village—indeed, almost a small city—of log, pole, and bark huts the Indians called Hochelaga. All during Cartier's progress up the river, the appearance of the Frenchmen amazed and delighted the naked savages, who clearly had never heard of, much less seen white men before, and although these Indians had no such legends as the Aztecs had, they greeted their visitors as supernatural beings. The French had the wisdom to heal the Indian sick by the laying on of hands, and making the sign of the cross. The Indians offered the Frenchmen food and women, and the French gave presents in return. Nothing was more propitious than this amicable meeting, although Cartier would have been better pleased had his hosts been able to point out the way to China. At Hochelaga, however, they did take him to the top of Mont Reale, from whose height he had a superb view of the wide, shining river that glittered as far as could be seen into the interior of a fantastic forest of conifers and hardwoods. It was a forest that covered the earth from one horizon to another—one that the Frenchmen could not know extended over thousands of square miles in every direction.

As summer drew to an end, Cartier returned down the St. Lawrence to the site of modern Quebec where his ship's company built a fort of logs. Having offered the Indians no violence, the French received none from them. Instead the Indians brought them fish, pumpkins, and furs, and seemed willing to be converted to the true religion.

For a time, all went well; there is scarcely a better climate in the world than the Canadian summer on the St. Lawrence, nor a place of greater beauty. There is first of all the great river, still a Mediterranean blue today, which would have been air-clear in that century and alive with sturgeon, muskellunge, pike, and bass. Great gray rocks line this river, which runs in a fault of rock from the Great Lakes to the sea, and above the rocks are junipers, cedars, fir and pine, birches, maples, oaks and ash. For the first time the French would have seen immense flocks of geese and ducks making Xs of their wings overhead, and great blue herons flopping low through the air just above the water. The forests would have then been filled with game and predators strange to Europeans. Perhaps the Frenchmen marveled at this paradise.

But the wet winds shortly arrived, and the leaves turned brown and blew away and the trees became skeletons and the snow began to come. Nothing could possibly have warned the

French of what to expect of the Canadian winter; there is nothing in Europe to match it, nor could they have fully appreciated whatever the Indians might have tried to tell them. For that matter, the Indians might not have known what to tell them, for it seems they did not know, themselves: they knew that winter was a starving time, but not how to prepare for it.

The cold came, and then the bitter cold. The great river froze deep from bank to bank, the snow fell deep and drifted. The cold came into the fort to stay the winter with them, despite the fires roaring on the hearth, and the food supply diminished at an alarming rate. The Indians, too, began to starve, and no longer came naked through the drifting snow to bring the white men gifts of fish. Men's teeth loosened in their gums and fell out; scurvy was upon them. The diet now included bark and scraps of shoe leather boiled in whale oil, and still the snows came. And the winter stayed on. When it came time for the chestnuts to bloom in Paris, the starving Frenchmen at Quebec looked weakly out upon a glittering world of snow and ice. When at last the river ice broke, groaning and crashing, and the rains began to melt the snow, the company had been decimated by malnutrition and scurvy. The death rate among the Indians must have been at least as severe.

As the ice left the river, the prayerful survivors made preparations to depart; when the ship was ready, Cartier invited an Indian chief and several of his principal men aboard—and imprisoned them below and set sail. They dropped downriver while dismayed savages ran along the riverbank, calling to them, begging for the return of their chief and his lords.

It was at least to Cartier's credit that the French did treat their captives with civility if not with respect: they wished to present them to the king. They had a story to tell in France: a story of pumpkins, mosquitoes, and muskrats; of beavers and bears and forests through which a magnificent river led; a tale of unbelievable winter and hardships. But the tale they told instead was of a land full of gold and rubies, wherein there lived one nation of men who were white, like the French, and of another land they had seen where lived a race of men who hopped about on but one leg. They had seen a country where the people lived without eating; they had also seen demons, of course. In the telling, the settlement of Hochelaga became a fabulous city; the captives who had survived the seafaring were exhibited as its great lords. China lay just a bit farther than they had been able to journey before winter caught them; Cartier was anxious to return.

Six years later, Cartier was back in Canada, this time with five ships and a commission from Francis I that said, "We have resolved to send him again to the lands of Canada and Hochelaga which form the extremity of Asia towards the west." He was ordered to discover, settle, and convert the Indians, who were described (as it now seems, inevitably) as "men without knowledge of God or use of reason." In order to bring the benefits of True Faith and reason to these unfortunates, the prisons of France were emptied of thieves, robbers, and other felons. They were to serve aboard the ships and then become the colonists.

In addition to being given their freedom, the convicts could look forward to further rewards: a share of the profits. One-third of all the wealth the expedition should acquire would be divided among the men, one-third was to be the king's share, and the other third was to finance the costs of the adventure.

When his informants told him the French were sending a squadron to the New World, Charles of Spain was furious. So far as he was concerned, all of Florida was a province of Spain by right of discovery and by the order of God as expressed in the bull of 1493. He demanded of the king of Portugal that they hold a Council of the Indies and make war on the French if Francis I would not recall Cartier and renounce any further pretensions in the New World. But the Portuguese had no desire to go to war with France on behalf of Spain; besides, their fishermen were on that northern coast themselves. For the moment, Charles V was unwilling to go to war alone. He filed his claim and waited for a better time.

Cartier's squadron pressed on to Quebec, where irate Indians wanted to know what had happened to their chief and his chieftains. The Frenchmen tactfully explained that they were desolated but unfortunately by the Will of God some had died of natural causes but the others were living as great lords in the house of the king. In fact, they had all died, but the French saw no reason to say so. They made the Indians presents of cloth and steel implements and a bit of brandy, and the relationship was resumed.

It was a relationship quite different from the Spanish one. Like the Spanish, the French regarded the Indians as squalid primitives whose habits were often filthy. But the Catholicism of the French was far more supple, more practical, and less arrogant than that of the Spanish. The French priests were inclined to think the Indians were naïve, not corrupt, and they sought to win the Indians to the True Faith, not beat them into it. Perhaps if the French had found a Mexico in the forest, their treatment of the Indians might have paralleled that of the Spanish, but they were not looking for Mexicos there. The French dreamed of golden kingdoms, too, but the thrust of their exploratory effort was to find a Northwest Passage to those Asian lands. So scouting parties searched along the forest waterways, and gave presents to the Indians in return for food, furs, and directions.

A settlement was made at Hochelaga. Prayers were offered, a fort was built. During the ensuing winter, one-third of the expedition died of scurvy while watching the snow drift above the high sides of their icebound ships, and saw the masts, spars, and cordage turn to webs of ice. It may have occurred both to the officers and their jailbirds that the only jewels in Canada would prove to be crystals of ice. They had already discovered that if the St. Lawrence River led directly to China, a breakneck rapids closed it to shipping some leagues upstream from Montreal.

While the first Frenchmen starved and froze along their Canadian riverbanks in winter, and were deviled by black flies as they followed the watercourses west through the forests in the spring, certain other beginnings of American history were made in Europe as the emergent modern nations were drawn into two hundred years of what has been called religious war.

Yet the war was more complicated than that. While a religious concern was of central importance to all thoughtful men in the sixteenth century, it was not always the dominant factor in their disputes, nor in any country save Spain was a religious concern the only and all-sufficient reason for waging war. In other realms, political, dynastic, economic, social, and mercantile factors were always present, now and again becoming the dominant ones, even to the point where a French Catholic king could make an alliance with Protestant heretics and Moslem Turks to defend his realm from the Spanish Hapsburgs to the west and the Austrian Hapsburgs to the east. Except in Spain and Austria, two nascent political divisions began to form in every European nation at this time along the lines of religious difference. Insofar as the name applies, on one side there was the Spanish party, standing for ultramontane Catholicism, absolutism, and reaction. On the other, there was the Protestant party, representing a deviant religion, and standing for limited monarchy and social change. This division was barely discernible as a political one at the time, and there were no political parties in the modern sense of the word, but a beginning was made.

In Protestant countries, for instance, not everyone was a Protestant, and the Catholic community—whose members would certainly include a number of the military aristocracy still strong in the old faith—was a potentially subversive one. In England, during the rule of Elizabeth, Catholics put Crusaders' crosses on their military garments, put themselves under the duke of Norfolk, and rose in revolt against the Protestant queen. The pope obligingly excommunicated her in order that her subjects could kill her in good conscience, and Philip II sent the Catholic rebels money and advice. If Elizabeth had not been promptly successful in putting the rebellion down, Philip would have sent Spanish troops. Not without reason, the English identified the Catholic cause as the Spanish one.

In Catholic kingdoms such as France, it was the Protestant community that was potentially subversive, yet there was what could be called a Spanish party that was opposed by many French Catholics, including members of the clergy. At this time the kings of France had almost as little real authority in their nominal realm as the Holy Roman Emperor had over the hundreds of German principalities. There were in France some three hundred autonomous towns, regions, and holdings, each with its own laws and feudal privileges. Moreover, neither the French kings nor the French clergy had ever had too great a reverence for Rome: the clergy insisted on its Gallican liberties. The autonomous towns and institutions of France, the French clergy, and the kings of France, therefore, all had reasons of their own for opposing any attempt to create in the kingdom totalitarian central authority, directed by Rome. Yet it was Spain's devout intention to create just such an authority in every kingdom. In France, the ultraorthodox or reactionary Catholics were viewed as the Spanish party, if not identified as such by name.

The atomized structure of France was conducive to the growth of Protestantism. At first the Huguenots, as the French Calvinists were called, were hunted down and burned at the stake. They were, for the most part, unwarlike city burghers, and there was little they could do but dissemble, worship fearfully in secret, or flee to Switzerland or the Lowlands to escape persecution. But as martyrdom perversely begat converts, and as Protestantism gathered bases of political and economic strength outside of France, and as it became increasingly clear that Protestantism was at least the ally of economic and political freedom, a Calvinist underground spread in France, and no less than one-third of the military nobility joined it.

Those of the warlike nobility who became Huguenots included lords who had reasons of their own for competing with Church and Crown for the revenues of their ancestral estates and power over their peasants. But the larger number were younger sons, young men deprived by law of primogeniture from any patrimony, and who by reason of their noble birth were prevented from engaging in a profession or trade. These youth were acutely aware of their anomalous position in the social order, and just as aware that they had nothing to offer the world but their ambitions and their swords. Perhaps they sensed Protestantism's implicit challenge to that social order. Perhaps both lords and younger sons felt that the age-old concept of a European community united under Rome was a thing of the past if it had ever really existed and, thinking of themselves as Frenchmen in an age of emergent national feelings, distrusted the power of Spain. Since sane men never have but one reason for doing whatever they do, it would be ridiculous to presume they acted out of religious conviction alone. But religious conviction was also there, if not at the root of the matter, and the devout Huguenot was just as ready to vandalize a cathedral and slaughter Catholics for the glory of God as any Inquisitor was anxious to see him burn at a stake.

It must not be thought that the religious, social, economic, or political matters we have been discussing were of the slightest concern to most of the people of Europe in the sixteenth century. It was an agricultural age, most people were peasants, such affairs were not their concern—they merely felt the consequences. If the lord of a village were a Catholic, his people were Catholics. If he were a Protestant, they became Protestants at his order. In England, matters were a bit different, for in addition to the English peasantry, there was also the class of English yeomen, and because the English were islanders, it was easier for them to feel a sense of national identity; together these factors heightened the English political awareness. But it is generally true that what was done in Europe in that century was done by a few men: by men who ruled as princes, noblemen, as the councilmen of free cities.

In France, the spread of the Huguenot heresy among the nobility was of crucial importance, for it permitted the Huguenots to come more out into the open. It was after all one thing for Inquisitors to seize upon a terror-stricken and rabbitlike bourgeoisie, but quite another thing for them to try to lay their hands upon a cold-eyed, contemptuous, fiercely mustachioed warrior baron, particularly when he stood on his own lands, surrounded by his brutal men-at-arms. The result was, that by the time the first Frenchmen were poking about in Canada, the accession of noblemen to the Huguenot faith, and the accession to that faith of the bourgeois oligarchies of the free towns, had reached such proportions that there was the distinct possibility of civil religious war—and the intrusion of Spanish troops into French affairs. No one saw this more clearly than the admiral of France, Gaspard de Coligny.

De Coligny was a nobleman, one of the great officers of the realm, serving a king who loathed heretics, yet De Coligny was himself a Huguenot. His office was a tribute to his attainments and prestige, but his remaining in it would indicate not so much a loyalty to his king as it would his loyalty to a national concept: the concept of France. As a patriotic Frenchman, as a military man, and as a Huguenot, De Coligny feared both the power of Spain and the possibility of civil war as being potentially disastrous. He was therefore very ready to listen to a proposal put to him in 1555 by a Knight of Malta, one Nicolas Durand de Villegagnon.

De Villegagnon told Admiral de Coligny that he, too, was secretly one of the elect of God. He suggested it would be to the best interests of the Huguenots, the French Church, and the French Crown, to settle Huguenots in the New World. De Coligny at once saw this would remove the Huguenots from persecution at home and embarrass the Spanish abroad. Henry II of France was willing to listen: the Calvinist underground was an obvious threat to monarchy. Moreover, it was clearly in the interests of France to dispute the Spanish claim to the New World, and if *only Huguenots* were sent there, the possibilities were interesting. If the Spanish emperor reacted violently, Henry had an excuse: he would disown them; they were not Frenchmen, but heretics. If the Spanish slaughtered them all, Henry could, with a perfectly straight face, thank his brother of Spain for such a Christian service. But if these heretics by some good fortune should be able to establish themselves, possibly discovering such cities of gold as had enriched the Spanish Crown, then, eh bien, Henry would remind them they were still Frenchmen (heretics though they might be) who owed allegiance to the Crown.

The French clergy took a simplistic view of the proposal: to send heresy abroad would relieve France of its presence. Calvin, too, was enthusiastic. He imagined the New Zion could be built in the New World.

So De Villegagnon, whose idea this originally was, was put at the head of an expedition that included Catholic Norman and Breton seamen, Huguenot burghers, certain adventurous younger sons of the military aristocracy, and Huguenot elders and ministers. Off they went in two ships in August, but instead of fetching up in a part of the New World claimed by Spain, they found themselves in November in the lovely harbor that is now Rio de Janeiro—in Portuguese Brazil.

They built a little fort in which they all seemed to go slightly mad. De Villegagnon first turned into a Caligula, ordering men lashed for imaginary offenses, and then he decided he was not a Huguenot, but a Catholic Knight of Malta after all. He gathered together the Norman and Breton sailors, and those who like himself had decided to revert to the old True Faith, and they drove the Huguenots out of Fort Coligny and into the forests.

Then they sailed back to France before the Portuguese, having heard of the French intrusion into their realm, arrived in Rio de Janeiro harbor. The Portuguese pulled down the fort, slaughtered all the miserable heretics they could discover, and left. If any Frenchmen escaped, they must have lived out their lives in the forests as slaves to the Indians. In any event, no trace of any such survivors was ever found.

Despite this disaster, the French dispatched a second Huguenot expedition to the New World in 1562. It was probably De Coligny's doing, for strictly speaking, there was no king of France at this time. In 1559, Henry II died, succeeded by his girlish, fifteen-year-old son Francis II, who lived but a year. Francis was followed by his younger brother Charles IX, but what power there was in France was now divided between two camps. At the head of a reactionary Catholic party was the duke of Guise and the cardinal of Lorraine; at the head of a Huguenot faction was Henry Bourbon, king of Navarre (a small independent principality on the Spanish-French border), and Admiral de Coligny. Between the two parties stood Henry II's widow, Catherine de' Medici, loathing the Protestants but fearful of the duke of Guise, and meanwhile trying in her Florentine way to pit one faction against the other in order to maintain a balance of power until her royal children could look after themselves. Civil war plainly threatened, and in the context of the times it might seem foolhardy for the French to have provoked Spain. Nonetheless, a ship sailed, bearing a mixed company of sailors, soldiers, and Calvinists. The presence of the military would indicate the expedition was more in the nature of an armed reconnaissance than a simple attempt to put a colony ashore; the implication is that the French were looking for an area that would prove reasonably safe for future colonization, and were meanwhile prepared to fight their way out of trouble.

The ship arrived off the mouth of the St. Johns River in Florida after a tumultuous three months' crossing; one can imag-

ine everyone's relief on escaping the Atlantic to enter the sub-
tropics in April; to find themselves floating quietly in the warm
sunlight on fresh water, surrounded by a vast solitude broken
only by the "boyling and roaring through the multitude of all
kind of fish" that played about the anchored ship.

They were not long ashore when they became aware of the
silent presence of naked Indians, thoughtfully regarding them at a
respectful distance. Friendly signs were made; the Indians
strewed a bit of ground with what the French thought were laurel
boughs; the Frenchmen and the Indian braves sat on these to hold
a parley while the women and children watched. Through signs,
and through leaps of the imagination, the French concluded that
the Indians were trying to tell them that the wonderful land of
Cibola, with its seven cities stuffed with fabulous riches, was only
twenty days away by water. Plainly, these Indians had at least
heard of Spaniards—but if they had heard of the Spaniards, one
might well wonder why the Indians greeted the French with
signs of friendship.

The tales of Cibola had their immediate effect: visions of
gold, silver, and jewels danced in French heads, and the bulk of
the ship's company sailed away to look for a land that not only
was not twenty days away by water, but also, if it had an existence even in myth, would have been two thousand miles west
overland. Thirty Frenchmen elected to remain behind. They
built a log fort, and for a time lived in friendship with the Indians
who, as Indians had often done elsewhere on first meeting with
white men, gave them food and women. The two races were,
however, too far apart for a fully shared friendship to develop.

Meanwhile the Frenchmen made no effort to cultivate the
land, nor were they competent at hunting and fishing. Like the
Spanish before them, the French sailors and soldiers knew only
their narrow trades, and they began to starve and quarrel among
themselves. Their appointed leader, like De Villegagnon in Brazil, turned into a monster—it would seem there is something in

savage solitudes that provokes this sort of response among civilized men—and so his men murdered him. They then built themselves a fright of a boat and put to sea for France. During the terrible weeks of calms and storms that followed, the thirsting and starving few survivors were at last driven to cannibalism. When they sighted land, it was the English coast; a bark put out, and took them prisoners to Queen Elizabeth.

During the time this unlucky expedition had been sailing to disaster, religious civil war had broken out in France, but a precarious truce was patched together. The kingdom was plainly falling apart, yet in 1564 the French sent still another expedition into the southern regions of the New World, this one a squadron of three ships of not much more combined tonnage than Columbus' original fleet. Like its immediate predecessor, this expedition arrived in the St. Johns River, where a substantial log fort was built, and a treaty was made with the aborigines that called for the French to help them wage war on a neighboring tribe, presumably on the theory that their new friends would lead them to the plunder of a savage kingdom—and off they went into the marshy waterways to make the acquaintance of the alligators, water moccasins, rattlesnakes, and insects.

They found themselves wandering through endless miles of bleak pine barrens, scratching their way in and out of palmetto thickets, wading under a hot sun up to their necks in the high grass of savannahs, sinking up to their armpits in swamps, and working their way about the knotty knees of huge cypress trees that dripped with tangled webs of Spanish moss.

Of course the Indians they had set off to defeat proved to be as poor and primitive as their Indian allies—and it shortly appeared that their allies had no stomach for fighting, but hoped the French would do it for them.

So the French made their disgusted way back through the swamps and thickets to the open country where their log fort stood beside the river. Here, a familiar story was repeated. The

Indians withdrew; the French soldiers proved unwilling and incompetent to feed themselves. The garrison was near starvation when Sir John Hawkins, first of the English sea captains to enter the slave trade, appeared in the river mouth with his squadron. The Frenchmen had eaten all the maize they could buy from the Indians, and were trying to make bread from acorns and fishbones found on the riverbank; they were eating sorrel, roots, leather from their boots and fittings. The plight of the French astonished one of the Englishmen, John Sparke, who was quoted thus in Hakluyt's *Voyages*:

"This hardnesse not contenting some of them, who would not take the paines so much as to fish in the river before their doores, but would have all things put in their mouthes," they began to steal food from the Indians, "whereby there grew great warres betwixt them and the Frenchmen." Sparke thought the French would have perished "had not God sent us thither for their succor."

"Notwithstanding the great want that the Frenchmen had," Sparke wrote, "the ground doth yeeld victuals sufficient, if they would have taken the paines to get the same; but they being souldiers, desired to live by the sweat of other men's browes." The French, he said, had been in Fort Caroline for fourteen months, and he was astounded by the fact that although there were "deere in marvellous store, with divers other beasts, and fowle, servicible to the use of man," and that "the commodities of this land are more than are yet knowen to any man: for beside the land it selfe, whereof their is more than any king Christian is able to inhabit, it flourisheth with medow, pasture ground . . . as better can not be in the world," the French made no attempt to grow maize themselves, nor to hunt the deer or the birds. They had, however, made themselves twenty hogsheads of wine from the local wild grapes, and they did kill and eat snakes.

Sparke made two pregnant observations—pregnant because Hakluyt's *Voyages* were closely studied by his contemporary merchants and ministers of the Crown. The first was that farmers might live in amity with the Indians, because if they had crops of their own they would not have to steal food from the aborigines. Second, Sparke said if there was any gold in Florida, it was so scarce that the costs of mounting an expedition to get it would be more than the value of the gold, whereas the real wealth of the land lay in its ability to produce thousands of pounds worth of foodstuffs and livestock annually. "And because there is not the thing [gold] we all seeke for, being rather desirous of present gaines," he said, "I doe therefore affirm the attempt [to cultivate the wilderness] to be more requisit for a prince, who is of power able to go thorow with the same, rather than for any subject." In short, Sparke envisioned the establishment of royal agricultural colonies.

While Sparke made his observations, the English sailors brought food and supplies ashore for the French, and Sir John offered to give the Frenchmen one of his ships, so that they might sail home. The good knight was in a generous mood, for he had captured a cargo of blacks in Africa and sold them to the Spanish. He told how the Spanish in the Caribbean had refused at first to trade with him, until he trained his cannon on them, whereafter he had received a good price for his goods.

The French were properly impressed and grateful, and they might have accepted Sir John's offer of a ship had there not, just at that time, appeared another flotilla off Fort Caroline. It was a French one, carrying three hundred Huguenot men and women to be colonists in the New World. Sir John sailed away, and no sooner had the newcomers been welcomed and thanks offered to God for His timely help, than another shape appeared out of the sea.

It came at dusk, a great, vast ship whose battle lanterns struck highlights upon the steel helmets of the soldiery and illuminated the Crusaders' crosses on the sails and the dreadful banner of royal Spain.

The French, mindful of their women, asked for quarter, and the Spanish commander granted it. But the French would have to evacuate their fort. The French agreed. But without their weapons, the Spanish said—and the French agreed to this, too. They were required to leave the fort in small, successive groups. In the morning, the first group of Frenchmen was marched away over the dunes, where, out of sight and earshot of the fort, Spanish soldiers waited for them. No one was shot. It was all done with swords and pikes and knives. The killing went on all day. The Spanish commander had not broken his promise because, to his devout mind, promises given heretics were not binding.

News of this holocaust filtered back to France, whereupon the dowager queen, Catherine de' Medici, and her son Charles IX protested to Philip II. The Spanish emperor shortly said the New World was his, and that the French had invaded it. The French replied that North America belonged to France, alleging their fishermen had discovered it in 1465—a claim the Spanish ignored. France was in no position to pursue a quarrel with Spain, but the interesting point is that Catherine and Charles should have remonstrated with Philip II over the slaughter of a few hundred heretics. The late Henry II might not have done so. But it was important to Catherine to try in all ways to assert the rights of the French Crown, precisely because the power of the Crown was so feeble. The quarrel was over the rights of kings; it was composed on grounds of religion: Philip and Catherine and her son agreed that Protestantism was the common enemy. A suspicion therefore arises that Catherine's protest to Spain was merely pro forma; that it was not intended to be taken seriously by Spain, but was intended for internal French consumption—that it was Catherine's effort to assuage the indignation of an already rebellious Huguenot community. But an expedition led by a French nobleman, Dominique de Gourgues, was soon fitted out to avenge the honor of France—a step it is difficult to imagine being undertaken without royal knowledge or consent.

This time it was the Spanish who were slaughtered to a man. In his attack on Fort Caroline, De Gourgues had the enthusiastic assistance of those Indians who, for all their trouble with the French, had now learned a thing or two about the Spaniards. If the Indians had had their way, the wounded Spaniards who had been taken prisoner would not have left this world by so simple a means as choking to death at the ends of French ropes.

8

God Sent
a Storm

FOLLOWING the events at Fort Caroline, the further adventures of Catholic and Protestant Europeans in the New World waited upon the outcome of a general war. It erupted in 1566 in the Netherlands and led to combat at sea between Spanish ships and Protestant privateers. There was also war in eastern Europe, where the Spaniards were waging a Crusade against the Turks.

In the course of the latter struggle, the Spanish won an impressive naval victory at Lepanto in 1571—and in the flush of this victory, the Spanish commander, Don Juan of Austria, brother of Philip II, had a talk with Pope Gregory XIII. Between them it was decided that Don Juan should proceed to the Netherlands, there to mount an invasion of England, kill Elizabeth, put Mary Queen of Scots on the throne, marry her, and then as king of England, Don Juan was to slaughter the heretics of that island and bring the surviving English back to the bosom of the Mother Church.

The pope meanwhile was also conducting negotiations with Philip II, Catherine de' Medici, and Charles IX of France: he wanted them to plot the destruction of the Huguenots. Catherine agreed, and when the Huguenot King Henry of Navarre came to Paris to be married, bringing with him a train of Huguenot magnates, Catherine was ready with a little plan of her own for his nuptials. On St. Bartholomew's Eve, Huguenots were pulled from their beds and put to the knife. Three thousand of them were slaughtered in Paris alone. Admiral de Coligny was butchered in his nightclothes, but Henry of Navarre, who was, after all, a king, was given the choice of instant death or of changing his religion. He promptly embraced the True Faith.

Philip II shouted with laughter when he heard this good news, and in Rome, Pope Gregory XIII jubilantly exclaimed it was "more agreeable than fifty Lepantos." He had a medal struck to commemorate the event, and commissioned Vasari to paint a picture of the slaughter.

But there was no jubilation in France, where Henry of Navarre, escaping from Paris, put himself at the head of a Huguenot army, declaring himself a Calvinist again. Civil war raged in France for the next thirty years. Philip II sent Spanish infantry to help the Guise party, both sides hired German mercenaries, and the Protestant commercial cities in the north of France appealed to Elizabeth of England. They reminded her they had once been ruled by English kings, and offered to become English again if Elizabeth would deliver them from the Catholics, particularly from the Spanish. For her part, Elizabeth was entirely aware of Spanish intentions against England: she was well served by an admirable forerunner of the British secret service. So in 1585 she did what she could—she sent Leicester and six thousand troops to France and warships to raid Spanish shipping. At this, Philip II, who had war on his hands in eastern and western Europe and on the high seas, began to plan the invasion of England and to equip an Armada.

France meanwhile knew only unrelieved disaster, for be the soldiers Spanish, German, Dutch, Belgian, English, or French, none of them had adequate logistical support and all of them lived partly on what they could capture or steal. The mercenaries changed sides whenever this seemed advantageous to them, and fire, slaughter, and atrocity followed in the wake of Protestant armies as well as in the wake of Catholic ones.

There was not war everywhere all of the time in France and the Lowlands, but there was always enough disruption and destruction to render ordinary life uncertain, and trade and commerce chaotic. Given these conditions, one might think the New World not only remote in geography, but also the furthest thing from any European's mind. But, despite all the moil, there were in those years no less than one hundred fifty French ships off the Newfoundland coast each season, and two hundred others variously belonging to the Portuguese, the English, and the Spanish, all of them fishing for cod and trading with the Indians for furs and walrus ivory. Inland along the St. Lawrence, the French maintained missions and trading posts, and such was the French presence in Canada and off the coast that even the Spanish were disgustedly admitting the French ruled in those parts. The French were calling that part of the world New France.

It is fascinating to speculate as to what might have been the fate of Europe, New France, and of all the Western Hemisphere had Philip II been able to concentrate on one enemy at a time, and had he been able to accept facts instead of trying to force facts to conform to his pious dreams. But instead of concentrating his enormous military power to defeat his enemies serially, he sought to be victorious everywhere. Perhaps his Crusader's faith prevented him from appreciating facts that were perfectly obvious to others. For example, the Armada Catolica that sailed in 1588 against England was an overwhelming force that, used intelligently, should have been able to accomplish its mission. The plan called for the prince of Parma, the Spanish commander in the Netherlands, to load his army on barges. The Armada would meet the barges off the coast and escort them to England. Parma's troops, together with those aboard the Armada itself, comprised a force more than sufficient to have defeated the English forces then available.

But there were not enough barges in the Netherlands on which to embark an army. And, as Philip's sea captains tried to tell him, even if there had been barges aplenty, they would not be suitable for Channel seas: this was not a river crossing, but a sea voyage. Against competent advice, Philip sent his Armada forth to perform a task that plain fact said was impossible; he sent it out at the wrong time and under the command of a man who knew nothing of the sea, who was not a warrior, and who had begged Philip to please appoint someone else.

The English ships inflicted relatively minor damage on the huge fleet which proceeded up the Channel to its impossible rendezvous with Parma, and then on to its desultory fate of storms, rocks, and shoals. The great majority of the Spanish ships eventually returned to Spanish ports, some of them battle-scarred but all of them storm-damaged, their complements of soldiers and sailors decimated by deaths due to exposure, disease, thirst, and starvation. The crucial importance of the Armada's fate was that both sides saw in the disaster the hand of God. To the English and to Europe's Protestants, it appeared that God had sent the winds that blew the Armada to destruction. To the Spanish, it seemed that it had not pleased God to give them the victory.

While the English in their sober moments realized the Spanish fleet had been driven away by the weather, not by themselves, their experience with the Armada was generally intoxicating. It first confirmed them in their belief they enjoyed God's protection. Next, the threat of Spanish invasion gave them an even keener sense of national unity than they had known before. Third, the fact that their ships had come out of the action virtually unscathed gave them a confidence in their naval abilities which, if exaggerated, was to stand them ever afterward in good stead. Fourth, their experience in a fleet action taught them that, while their fast ships had an advantage, those ships would have to carry heavier guns if they were to sink great ships instead of merely damaging them. Finally, their experience of the Armada transformed the English awareness of the importance of sea power into a preoccupation with it. Under their great privateers, Sir John Hawkins and Sir Francis Drake, the English had successfully raided Spanish shipping and Spanish towns, but it was now realized that raids were one thing, and fleet actions another, but that the safety of the realm required the English not merely to put fleets to sea, but entire armadas superior to the navies of their enemies. For their part, the Spanish learned no such lasting lessons; the war continued.

In the following year, King Henry III of France, who had succeeded his brother Charles, was killed by a Catholic assassin sent by the duke of Guise—and the duke was killed by a Protestant one. It was thereupon discovered that, by right of blood and law, the throne of France now belonged to Henry Bourbon, king of Navarre and head of the Huguenot party. The problem was that the Catholic party would never accept a Protestant king. Henry knew this, and he was also aware that the Huguenots, while powerful, were nonetheless a French minority. He wished, however, to be Henry IV of France rather than Henry of Navarre, and so, to the consternation of the Protestant community, he calmly changed his religion once again, reportedly with the remark that Paris was worth a Mass. His reconversion to Catholicism disarmed the Catholics, who though suspicious of his sincerity could do nothing but accept his legitimate claim to the throne; the Huguenots, though equally wary of Henry's sincerity, could at least hope he would not entirely forget them. For nine years, Henry IV patiently worked to repair the spiritual and material damage done by thirty prior years of war, and in 1598 he paid his political debt to the Huguenots by proclaiming the Edict of Nantes. The edict gave Protestants a right to hold offices, a right to worship as they pleased in their homes, and the right to fortify their cities. Under this accommodation, the French could (for a while at least) stop killing each other.

In the same year that Henry IV proclaimed the Edict of Nantes, Philip II died. All of his Crusades had come to nothing. The victory of Lepanto had not been decisive; the Turks not only recovered, but went on to take Tunis. The decades of warfare in Europe saw Protestantism entrenched rather than exterminated; the enterprise of England had miscarried; the French were still poaching on Spain's preserves in the New World. When Philip died, Spain was still incomparably the strongest military power in Europe and on the seas, but, while other nations were finding strength in political and economic ways, Spain continued to remain in the eleventh century in these respects. Her most intelligent men continued, as in medieval times, to enter the Church; her political structure remained feudal; her military power was still predicated on the uncertain arrival of a treasure fleet. With the disaster of the Armada, something went out of the Spanish confidence, and with the death of Philip II, Spain lost a directing force. She now began the long descent into the abyss that is her current residence, and insofar as the New World was concerned, the sum of all her efforts was to ensure that, when the French and English arrived in North America, they would bring with them their ancient national distrust of one another, the mutual animosity of French Catholics and English Protestants, internecine religious quarrels of their own, and a common loathing of Spain. In time, all this emotional baggage, together with dreams of riches, national glory, and political power, would accompany the French and English who ventured into the interior to meet, in the Mississippi River basin, what was left of the once imperial power of Spain.

9

A Quarrel
of Princes

In between New Spain and what the French were optimistically calling New France lay one of the larger continental masses of this globe, but no one knew this to be a fact as the seventeenth century began—not even the Spanish, who had blundered about in some of it for more than a century. Instead, it was widely supposed that this land mass might be a huge island, or perhaps a screen of huge islands, and that China lay immediately north and west of it. Insofar as the first English and French explorers were concerned, China was the goal and North America was an obstacle in the path.

They were still excited by Marco Polo's reports of the wealth of Cathay, but Islam still blocked the overland route from the Near East, and New Spain blocked a possible route by way of the Caribbean ocean. As early as 1527, a British spy in Seville, one Robert Thorne, had penetrated the mysteries of Spanish navigation at the considerable risk of his life, and using Spanish charts and the mathematics of his day, Thorne correctly informed London that the shortest route to China lay in a great circle drawn north from Scotland. It would also be safer than venturing near Spanish possessions, he said.

At about the same time, French mariners had come to an identical conclusion, by means of the same mathematics, and moved by the same fears of Spain—but with the difference that while the English set out northeast and opened a trade with Russia, the French set out northwest, trying to find a Northwest Passage to the Orient through, or above, the North American continent. The English later followed, and although both the French and the English subsequently established themselves in North America, the search for the Northwest Passage continued up to and past the time of the Louisiana Purchase. Indeed, Thomas Jefferson as a boy had been brought up on dreams of the fabulous passage, and as President, he acted upon them. No small reason for the purchase was Jefferson's hope that Louisiana would at long last provide the answer to the ancient mystery, and that America could find and claim the passage for herself, and so come upon the wealth of Cathay.

While the search for the way to China was always an ultimate objective, both the French and the English gave more immediate attention to the establishment of settlements on the continent that barred the way. The seventeenth century was four years old when Henry IV of France appointed Pierre du Guast, Sieur de Monts, to settle and govern La Cadie, or Acadia, which was defined as all that part of the New World lying between the 40th and 46th degrees of north latitude—or roughly from about the present site of Philadelphia to a point above Montreal. The object of the expedition was to convert the Indians and establish a royal monopoly of the fur trade. Samuel de Champlain was the commander of its two small ships and their company of seventy-nine convicts, adventurers, Huguenot ministers, and Catholic priests. They landed on Cape Breton Island. Two years later, James I of England by royal patents awarded to a company of mercantile speculators all of the New World lying between the

34th and 45th degrees of north latitude—or from about Charleston, South Carolina, to Montreal. The object of this venture was in no way religious. It was simply to find gold, and a ship was loaded with what could be turned up in brothels, gambling houses, and taverns. With a few exceptions, the ship's company therefore consisted of prodigal sons, bankrupt and debauched gentry, alcoholic tradesmen and disreputable servants, all of them looking for a way to mend their fortunes. This somewhat raffish lot was put ashore on the banks of the James River in Virginia; it is from such sires that today's First Families of Virginia largely derive.

[handwritten annotation: OUR AUTHOR MUST HAVE BEEN DENIED MEMBERSHIP IN THE FFV!!]

The two royal grants to almost exactly the same territory were certain guarantees of 150 years of war between the French and English in North America—a war that was in great measure a continuation of the religious wars of the Age of Faith. The grants also guaranteed wars that both nations would have with the Spanish, who still claimed the entire North American continent as their preserve, and still knew it by the name of Florida. The grants were otherwise significant in that both the French and the English put ashore in North America very much the same kind of men the Spanish did.

In each case, the officers of French, English, and Spanish expeditions were adventurous noblemen who hoped to find opportunities for riches that, for one reason or another, were denied them at home. The men they commanded came largely from prisons or from the ranks of a brutal mercenary soldiery. In sum, the first white men in America were the sort for whom there is little place in a civilized community in a time of peace. They were also for the most part urban animals ignorant of the arts of survival in a wilderness. That so many of them did survive, adapting themselves to a life among the aborigines, strongly suggests they were the survivors of hardships in Europe that were not less arduous than the different ones they endured in America. None of these men was a colonist, in the sense that colonists are groups

[handwritten annotation: THE AUTHOR'S CREDIBILITY HAS GOT TO BE SUSPECT!]

of men and women willing to work together to build a new life for themselves in a land far from home. They were simply armed adventurers, put down in terra incognita, bidden to see what they could find there that might be wanted in Europe.

But the Spanish, French, and English adventurers were each different from one another in respect of their attitudes toward the natives of the New World. The Spaniards intended to convert and enslave them, which they did. The French came to convert the Indians and trade with them. The settlements of New France were wilderness missions and trading posts: whereas it was useful to the Spaniards to organize the Indians into a society that would produce what the Spaniards wanted, it was useful to the French to allow the Indians to remain themselves in order to procure the furs the French wanted. The English view was entirely different. They had no particular desire to convert the Indians, nor had they any other use for them. What the English wanted was land, and once they got it from the Indians, they wanted the Indians to stay out of it. Like the Spanish and the French, the English wanted to find gold, and like the French, they wanted to find the Northwest Passage. But they were ready, to an extent neither of the Latin nations were, to turn the land into account by working it for themselves. From the very beginnings of their Elizabethan probing into America, the English saw that English colonists could create profitable plantations in the wilderness. And for all that the English distinguished among their social classes and sent their share of scoundrels along with the gentry, the English proved far more able than the Latins to take root in America.

It was the French, however, who first explored the wilderness, sensed the possibilities of empire, appreciated the strategic significance of the waterways, drew up a coherent continental plan, and gave the name Louisiana to the heart of North America.

The story of France had many strange if not unfortunate beginnings. When in 1604, for example, Samuel de Champlain took his two small ships and ill-assorted company of seventy-nine convicts, adventurers, Huguenot ministers, and Catholic priests to settle in La Cadie, the voyage was enlivened by religious discussions among the rival clergy that ended in fistfights. One can imagine the ironical sailors cheering from the rigging as the learned divines pounded one another on the tilting decks, tottering for balance as they swung and dodged, their collars ripping, rosary beads flying about, their faces suffused with righteous wrath as each sought to grapple with the Devil. These diversions continued when the victorious Frenchmen came ashore to build the little log fort they called the Habitation del'Isle Saincte-Croix. Here, a priest and a minister happening to die upon the same day, the sailors bundled them into the same grave to see if the two clergymen could lie in peace together.

The short fall and long winter were by no means so amusing. Blizzards soon shrieked through the bare, empty forests; pack ice grated and groaned in the tides about the island rocks and cut the company off from mainland and denied them, too, the possibility of escape by sea. It proved difficult if not actually impossible for the Frenchmen to wade through snow drifts in below-zero weather to cut and drag in all the wood they needed to melt snow water and keep themselves warm. It was so cold in their ill-built fort that their cider and wine froze in the casks and had to be chopped up and served by the pound rather than issued by the pannikin. Here, in infinite squalor, a wretched clot of unshaved, hairy men in stinking clothing lapsed into hopeless apathy about their half-tended fires, and scurvy soon appeared. By the time the ice at last broke up, thirty-five of them were dead, and that was the end of that adventure.

But it was by no means the end of the adventure of France in North America. Two years later an expedition of merchants and traders established themselves at Port Royal. Having learned from the experience of others, they arrived early enough to set out garden truck, plant winter wheat, and make friends of the Indians. The Indians, overjoyed by the taste of bread, but even more by that of wine, which quickly made them drunk, helped the Frenchmen to fish and hunt, and a description of that winter is one of gastronomic adventure. The Frenchmen vied with one another in the preparation of trout, sturgeon, ducks, geese, plover, caribou, deer, moose, hares, and bears. Everything went into the pot, including otters and beavers. It would seem that, for the first time, Europeans were doing something not only right, but well in America; they had laid in supplies for the winter, there was plenty of wood, the fires burned brightly upon song and feasting in the long nights and shone on the happily muzzy faces of the Indians. But then the Frenchmen did something wrong. They had hoped to traffic in furs, but it appeared that traders from the offshore fishing boats had got there before them, and the Indians and the French hunters could not turn up as large a supply as the merchants wished. So Indian cemeteries were looted for the furs wrapped around the bodies, and no amount of wine could buy back the former friendship of the natives.

Still, in these early years of the seventeenth century, a few Frenchmen were beginning to learn to live in the Canadian forests; their relationship with the Indians was excellent as compared with the Spanish; there were trading posts as far inland as Montreal. Champlain meanwhile searched for the Northwest Passage, and, acting on the advice of one of his men, who turned out to be a pathological liar, he looked for it up the Ottawa River and then west until he came out upon Lake Huron.

While Champlain was threading the waterways, emerging from the forest to gaze upon the largest body of fresh water he— or any Frenchman, probably—had ever seen, and no doubt wondering all the while as to the size of the land mass that apparently blocked his way to China, he was also careful to make friends of the Algonquin and Huron Indians he met along the Ottawa and St. Lawrence rivers. So far, so wise. Unfortunately, however, Champlain allowed himself to go so far into friendship as to form a military alliance with these people against their relatively powerful and certainly bloodthirsty traditional enemies to the south-east—the Five Nations of the Iroquois. One kind of wisdom might have suggested he should have made friends with the Iroquois instead; another kind would have led him to be the friend of both. Perhaps Champlain thought by championing the weaker tribes, he could create a balance of power. In any case, he and a handful of Frenchmen put themselves at the head of a small army of their allies and took to the warpath. Like the Tabasco Indians who met Cortés, the Iroquois were initially defeated by armored Europeans who fired guns at them. Iroquois braves taken prisoner were tied to stakes and set afire by their delighted Huron enemies. But the power of the Five Nations was not broken by this skirmish in the woods; it was hardly scratched. The significant result of the battle was that the Iroquois never forgot it. It was, as Parkman says, "the beginning, and in some measure doubtless the cause, of a long suite of murderous conflicts, bearing havoc and flame to generations yet unborn"—for the territory of the Five Nations included lands into which the first white colonists would soon intrude, and when they did, they would find the Iroquois waiting for them.

In France, meanwhile, an even more tragic mistake was being prepared for export to America. For some time the Jesuits had been intriguing with Henry IV for permission to establish a base in New France. At first the king saw nothing wrong with this: his views of religion were pragmatic if not downright satirical, and he would have been pleased to send all the Jesuits in France anywhere they wished to go, so long as it was several thousand miles away from France. But he shared a view with many French Catholics that the Jesuit order was the original creation of the Spanish, and that these black-robed soldiers of Christ were so many secret agents of Spain, whose real interest in going to New France was to regain it for the original claimant, the king of Spain. So while Henry had reason to wish the Jesuits out of France, he also had reason to keep them out of New France, and no one agreed more with him on this point than the Huguenot merchants trading in Canada. But then in 1610, everything changed when Henry IV, one of the wisest rulers the French ever had, was murdered by a crazy Catholic assassin. France passed into the hands of the queen, Marie de' Medici, and her young son Louis XIII, both of whom were plastic in the hands of Cardinal Richelieu. Here was a prelate in the French tradition of being a Frenchman first and a Catholic second. As a French statesman he encouraged trade and commerce, blurred the line between bourgeoisie and nobility by selling patents of nobility to merchants and telling the nobility they could engage in vulgar trade without loss of honor and station. He forbade private warfare and ordered all fortified castles destroyed except those needed by the Crown and manned by royal troops; he pursued the policy of Francis I in trying to undermine the power of Hapsburg Spain to the west, and Hapsburg Austria to the east. As a Catholic, however, Richelieu not only allowed the Jesuits to go to New France, but agreed with them that all Huguenots and foreigners be barred from that land; that all immigrants had to be Catholic, and French. The effect of this policy was to guarantee that the religious wars of the Old World would be exported to the New.

The opening shots were fired by an English pirate, Samuel Argall. He had been commissioned in 1613 by Governor Sir Thomas Dale of the Virginia colony to seek out and destroy any settlement the French might have within the boundaries of King James's royal patents. Cruising off the Maine coast, Captain Argall found a French ship anchored off Mount Desert Island; a party had been sent ashore. He sailed up to the ship, gave her a broadside that killed some of the crew, and accepted the surrender of the rest. He sent them in chains to Virginia, and continuing his voyage, arrived at Port Royal and demolished that settlement.

Looking back on such events, Parkman was moved to say:

A Quarrel of Princes

"Here lay the shaggy continent, from Florida to the Pole, outstretched in savage slumber along the sea, the stern domain of Nature, or, to adopt the ready solution of the Jesuits, a realm of the powers of night, blasted beneath the scepter of hell. On the banks of the James River was a nest of woe-begone Englishmen, a handful of Dutch fur-traders at the mouth of the Hudson, and a few shivering Frenchmen among the snow-drifts of Acadia; while deep within the wild monotony of desolation, on the icy verge of the great northern river, the hand of Champlain upheld the fleur-de-lis on the rock of Quebec. These were the advance guard, the forlorn hope of civilization, messengers of promise to a desert continent. Yet, unconscious of their high function, not content with inevitable woes, they were rent by petty jealousies and miserable feuds, while each of these detached fragments of rival nationalities, scarcely able to maintain its own wretched existence on a few square miles, begrudged to the others the smallest share in a domain which all the nations of Europe could hardly have sufficed to fill."

Another view of the matter would see in the English attack on the French a sort of sublime impudence, or measureless confidence born no doubt at Agincourt, nourished by the long years of English victories in France, and more recently fed by the intoxicating sea victories of the Elizabethans. Simply, the English did not like the French, never thought much of them, and still do not.

But more important than their confidence in their innate superiority to Frenchmen, the English of the early 1600s also felt themselves to be the narrowly escaped objects of the machinations of Rome. So they were not content with their own inevitable woes, as Parkman put it, because they felt a call to a higher duty. It was not just for nationalistic reasons that they felt compelled to chase the Frenchmen out of King James's woods. It was rather because they utterly believed that foreign Catholics could not be allowed to remain in them. If this was the feeling of the predominantly Anglican community in Virginia in 1613, it was a matter of overriding importance to the Puritans who seven years later arrived in Massachusetts. In New England the most bitter of radical exponents would shortly confront one another: the militant Jesuits with their wild Indian cohorts, and the sanctimonious farmers who believed themselves to be the elect of God. Neither of them for a moment believed that the continent was large enough to share.

For that matter, the Jesuits did not think New France was large enough to be shared with other Catholics. They not only saw to it that Huguenots were expelled, but they planned to expel the Recollet Fathers, who were Franciscans. The Jesuits would (if they had their way) keep all Frenchmen out of New France except themselves, for their holy dream was to convert and domesticate the savages and rule over them as benign fathers. They envisioned a new nation where white fathers taught red children to love God, raise crops, manufacture goods, and engage in commerce, and devote the ensuing profits to the construction of churches, colleges, and forts. They pursued this dream with appalling steadfastness. By ones and twos they slipped into the forests, calmly accepting all the hardships that Canadian nature so overwhelmingly supplies, believing they were walking in the lands of Satan. To the extent that they were accepted into Indian communities, they enjoyed a remarkable success in remaining alive and in gaining nominal converts to whatever scraps of the True Faith the Indians seemed to understand. Many of them were terribly unlucky, but the martyrs' unshakable belief in gaining the Kingdom of Heaven sustained them while their hosts tied them to trees, tugged out their hair and beards, chewed off their fingers, and then slowly roasted them alive. Meanwhile, the majority of Jesuits who were not martyred penetrated deeply into the forests, and kept their maps and information as to the back country a black secret from all other Frenchmen. Their ostensible reason for this was entirely plausible: that the behavior of the grinning French fur trader among the Indians was something less than Christian, inasmuch as it so frequently involved getting the Indians drunk and subsequently wallowing in the sins of avarice and fornication. But the principal reason for their secrecy was the Jesuits' realization that withheld knowledge can be a source of power.

Strangely, the English attack on the French at Mount Desert Island and Port Royal did not provoke a war, perhaps because Richelieu did not want one in America when more serious European matters commanded his attention. The Thirty Years' War erupted in Germany in 1618, and Richelieu saw in it a lurid danger to France should the closely related Hapsburg rulers of Spain and Austria establish a rule upon the Rhine that, however Catholic it might be, would nevertheless be a Hapsburg one. Accordingly, this prince of the Church supported the Protestant side of the conflict just as a French king had done in the prior century: the Thirty Years' War was a belated continuation of the earlier war of the Counter Reformation.

Other matters were afoot; in an apparent desire to minimize their mutual difficulties, France betrothed its royal daughter, Henrietta Maria, to Charles of England—together with the promise of an eight-hundred-thousand-crown dowry. Then, the Huguenots in France were a problem. The Edict of Nantes had given them the right to maintain their own fortified towns, and so they constituted a sort of armed camp within the state. But Richelieu's ban on private armies and fortresses was squarely at odds with the rights granted the Huguenots in the edict. When Richelieu sought to press his point, the Huguenots balked, and in 1627, under the leadership of the duc de Rohan, they mounted a revolt against Richelieu and the king. It was based in the Huguenot city of La Rochelle, which Richelieu besieged. The burghers of La Rochelle appealed to England for help, and Charles I, despite his marriage and despite his personal detestation of Calvinists (whose religion he entirely understood to be a threat to the rights of kings), decided to send them military help. It would seem that if France feared a too-powerful Hapsburg empire on the Continent, so England feared the creation of a too-powerful French monarch across the Channel. The point that concerns us is that Charles's support of the Huguenots of La Rochelle took the form in America of another English raid on New France. A fleet, subsidized by English merchants, and containing among its crews former Huguenot settlers who had been expelled from New France and who were now returning in vengeance, was sent against Quebec.

The operation was enormously successful. The English fleet entered the St. Lawrence River and sailed as far as the trading post at Tadoussac, where they gained news that a French fleet was on its way upriver with supplies for the outpost at Quebec. The English accordingly ambushed and destroyed this fleet. They then amused themselves for months by cruising about the Gulf of St. Lawrence, capturing fishing craft, while far upriver the French slowly starved at Quebec. When the English arrived below the rock, the Quebec garrison was in no shape to repel them. Quebec, and New France, was surrendered to the English.

Nothing remained now but for the English simply to shoo the French out of Canada and back to France, and nothing at the time would have been easier to accomplish. At Quebec itself there were only 105 men, women, and children, and only two of the families had tried to establish farms there. The French settlements were absolutely dependent for their sustenance upon such French fleets as the English had destroyed. It would have been simplicity itself for the English to have deported the Frenchmen found at the trading posts, to occupy these posts, and collect the fur traders and wandering priests as they came straggling in out of the forests. If the English had only done this, much misery, past and present, would have been avoided.

But it was Charles I who threw away the victory. That feckless monarch was, in 1629, trying to rule England without Parliament, if not in defiance of Parliament, and he needed money. He told his ambassador to France to remind the French that they had paid only half of the eight-hundred-thousand-crown dowry of Henrietta Maria, but if they would now get up the rest of the money, he would give them back New France. Wherefore, for about a million of today's dollars, Charles set a stage in the New World for more than a century of the most ghastly sort of frontier wars, and for troubles in Canada which murderously persist to this day.

The return of New France to the French Crown was hardly a cause of joy to all Frenchmen. There were those in Paris who pointed out that Canada had so far been more of a rathole than a treasury, that the value of the furs was exceeded by the cost of acquiring them, that the territory was apparently deep in snow for half the year and was anyway a wilderness full of savages, that it was an area of such vast extent that to colonize it would be to depopulate France—that it was too costly to try to maintain colonies there in any case. For example, these critics said, observe the wretched plight of Spain and Portugal: their holdings in the New World were no longer productive, because the costs of administering them were a constant drain upon the royal treasuries.

Despite these objections, France persisted in the search for something valuable in America. At this time, when, incidentally, Richelieu's meddling in the Thirty Years' War in the Rhineland had now resulted in open war between France and Spain, the French were not yet interested in establishing colonies in New France. The Jesuits, who were now the only priests there, were entirely opposed to the idea. The merchants in France who traded in Canadian furs were interested only in furs. The territory continued to be operated as a kind of military-missionary-trading post, entirely dependent upon France for its supplies of arms, wine, powder, stores, and virtually all of its food. Insofar as the French had a policy at this time in the New World, they placed exploration first, trade with and conversion of the Indians second, and colonization last. It was not until the reign of the Sun King, Louis XIV, who ascended the throne in 1661, that serious efforts to plant viable colonies in New France would be undertaken.

Meanwhile the Jesuit missionaries persisted in explorations of their own. They kept hearing rumors from the Indians of great rivers to the west, of the Missouri that apparently went west; of the Mississippi that flowed south; and they wondered where these rivers rose, and, more importantly, where they emptied. Into the South Sea? Into the Sea of Virginia? Did the rivers flow to Mexico, Japan, or China? Together with their explorations, the missionary work went on apace.

While the Jesuits pursued their secretive researches and enjoyed their ecclesiastical triumphs, the French military commanders in the trading posts became uncomfortably aware of the rapidly increasing population of the English colonies. The English seemed uninterested either in exploring the wilderness or in improving the state of the Indians' souls, but they were certainly interested in acquiring land and farming it, and their communities were growing like so many amoebas. Despite the perils of climate, wilderness, and ambush by savages, English men and women were pouring into the New World: Puritans into New England and the West Indies, Anglicans into Virginia, English Catholics into Maryland. No less than twenty thousand Puritans came to New England between 1630 and 1640, and the French commanders regarded this as ominous.

Worse, there were also those among the English who, together with the Dutch moving up the Hudson, were entering into the fur trade with the Indians and who (even more ominously) were making overtures to the Five Nations of the Iroquois, the sworn enemies of the French and the most dangerous Indians of the forest. It, therefore, occurred to the more prescient of the French officers in Canada that the security of New France, as well as the viability of their settlements, depended upon the immigration of a populace of Frenchmen. Their thoughts turned to Normandy, where there was not only a surplus of peasants, but peasants used to the least comfortable climate of France.

In due course, Normans were rounded up, put on ships, and sent to New France, which accounts for the appalling French accents heard in Canada today, and this immigration was one factor in a geopolitical scheme that, forming quite slowly, found its first full expression in 1670 in the minds of two men: Jean Talon, royal intendant of Canada; and René Robert Cavelier, Sieur de La Salle.

The position of intendant was exactly similar to the Spanish one; he was an officer directly responsible to the king and independent of the king's royal governor. The French and Spanish governors were always testily aware that intendants were peering over their shoulders, and no doubt writing to the king behind their backs. This suspicious division of command responsibility was a major source of weakness in the governance and direction of the settlements planted by the Latin nations in the New World. But in Canada at this time, the formidable Frontenac was the governor, and the equally formidable Talon was the intendant, and their thoughts as to the future of New France marched as one with those of that entirely remarkable twenty-nine-year-old adventurer, La Salle.

La Salle had arrived in Montreal in 1666, at a time when the French were again involved with Iroquois wars, and he established a fortified residence of his own at La Chine, some leagues upriver from the town. The name of his seigneury, China, indicates the hopes of France and La Salle, and while at La Chine, La Salle began to hear from Indian neighbors stories of the Ohio. The name meant "The Beautiful River," and La Salle gathered that the Indians were telling him that it flowed to the sea. He also gathered that the Ohio ran south, and he wondered if, therefore, it led to the Vermillion Sea of shadowy rumor—a body of water which, no longer a rumor, we now call the Gulf of California. In any case, the notion of a river leading south through the wilderness to a sea was doubly intriguing to the young lord of La Chine. One possibility was that the route to China might go southwest rather than northwest. The other possibility was both complex and intriguing, and when he discussed it with Talon, it appeared that the intendant had been thinking along the same lines.

In the course of those duties which required him to follow all that took place in New France, Talon began to realize that, since the waterways were the most practicable highways through the wilderness, the French should seize them and control them as a first step toward barring all other nations from venturing into the unknown interior of what was, quite apparently now, a large continent. Having done this, the French should then occupy the interior. Now, La Salle's story of an Ohio that flowed to a southern sea permitted Talon and La Salle to arrive at a specific concept.

If France could control the St. Lawrence from its gulf to the Great Lakes, and then control the Ohio from its source to the southern sea, establishing forts along these waterways, several good things would follow. First, the English colonists could be penned up along the seaboard east of the Appalachian Mountains. Second, France would acquire a warm, all-weather port on the southern sea. Third, a southern frontier would be established against the Spaniards with whom France had recently been at war and who should always be regarded as a potential enemy. Fourth, by keeping the English to the east and the Spanish to the south, the French would be free to hunt for the Northwest Passage without fear of interruption—providing that a sufficiently large French population took possession of the drainage basins of these rivers and if enough French troops could be sent to man a linked chain of fortifications. Here was the first coherent continental plan. It was one that would certainly give the French supremacy in the New World, for if the plan was driven through to completion, France would hold a central position in North America from which she could subsequently attack the English from north, west, and south while French fleets attacked from the east, thus ridding America of the English presence. Afterward, the French could then turn their attention to Mexico.

But no one knew where the Ohio was or what the interior of the continent contained, and explorations could be expensive. But here was young La Salle, an apparently fearless man of magnificent physique, afire with Talon's dream and more than ready to be off at daybreak. It occurred to Talon that he need not use Frontenac's men nor the king's money: he could get La Salle and the Jesuits to do the exploring for him.

Talon's faith in the Jesuits would seem to be a monument to their powers of dissembling, for Talon apparently did not realize that the Jesuits loathed Talon, Frontenac, and men like La Salle even more than they detested merchants and traders. Such people, to the Jesuits, represented secular government, military occupation, and colonization of the wilderness, whereas they had their own dream of an empire—from which all Europeans other than themselves were to be excluded. In the event, when La Salle and a handful of lay adventurers set off to find the Ohio in 1671, together with a party of Jesuits, the priests went their own ways shortly after entering the forests. It would appear they might have been perfectly acquainted with the Ohio, but if they were, they did not say so.

The story of La Salle is the tragedy of a man of fantastic energies and indomitable will—brusque, single-minded, domineering to a fault, perhaps a little mad. But that part of his story important here is that he did come to the Ohio and at once realized why the Indians had given it that name.

He and his men paddled softly down clear, glassy water through infinite solitudes where the animals were so unused to the presence of men that deer would share their riverside bivouacs; where wild turkeys and passenger pigeons could be taken from their roosts in trees. The Frenchmen could be forgiven if they imagined that no men had been in this land before; neither they nor any Indians had knowledge or memory of whatever prehistoric race it was that once in the regions of Ohio had achieved a civilization high enough to have constructed mysterious earthworks and barrows here.

The voyagers dropped slowly down a silent river in whose deep shadows great fish glided; along the banks otters played on their mud slides. There were fishers and muskrats and beaver dams on tributary streams. The Frenchmen came to open grasslands dotted with herds of grazing deer and bison; to parklike meadowlands in the river valley. They could hear at night the voices of wolves and coyotes and the strange cry of the cougar. They would occasionally encounter innocuous Indians who were stark naked save for strings of beads in their ears and noses. The voyagers saw great flights of herons, ducks, and geese; crancs stood fishing in the river shallows, while far overhead eagles swung in their effortless, slow circles; below them, hawks hunted through the middle air. The river also entered deep forests of crepuscular light where the mosquitoes, deer flies, black flies, and no-see-ums billowed as dense as smoke. There was no protection. La Salle and his men had no mosquito bars, no repellent lotions, no insecticides, and no escape unless, like Indians, they sat in the thick smoke of a fire of wet wood or covered themselves with bear grease. In these forests, the insects were thick enough to drive cattle mad. But then the river would wind again, disclosing another land of open meadows where elk and woodland bison could be seen at the edges of farther forests, and where in the mornings the Frenchmen could see deer drinking near their camp, graceful in the morning mists rising from the river.

Here, surely, was where the French belonged—in a land far more fair, temperate, and fruitful than half-frozen Canada or, for that matter, France.

Then the limpid Ohio entered that great river the Spanish

had crossed, but had never understood. Spanish maps indicated the Mississippi as just another river emptying into the Gulf of Mexico. De Soto had not found El Dorado there, only misery and death, and the Spanish had turned their attention away from the interior of the continent to pursue their search for golden cities to the south and west. La Salle, of course, was not looking for gold but for an empire.

In that same year, far to the north, another Frenchman, Simon François Daumont, Sieur de Saint-Lusson, held his sword high in one hand, and a clod of earth in the other, and with what necessary pauses of breath we must imagine, shouted as loudly as he could:

"In the name of the Most High, Mighty, and Redoubted Monarch, Louis, Fourteenth of that name, Most Christian King of France and of Navarre, I take possession of this place, Sainte Marie du Sault, as also of lakes Huron and Superior, the Island of Manatoulin, and all countries, rivers, lakes, and streams contiguous and adjacent thereunto: both those which have been discovered and those which may be discovered hereafter, in all their length and breadth, bounded on the one side by the seas of the North and of the West, and on the other by the South Sea: declaring to the nations thereof that from this time forth they are vassals of His Majesty, bound to obey his laws and follow his customs: Promising them on his part all succor and protection against the incursions and invasions of their enemies: declaring to all other potentates, princes, sovereigns, states, and republics,—to them and to their subjects,—that they cannot and are not to seize or settle upon any parts of the aforesaid countries, save only under the good pleasure of His Most Christian Majesty, and of him who will govern in his behalf; and this on pain of incurring his resentment and the efforts of his arms. Vive le Roi!"

And so it would seem that Talon was leaving nothing to chance; while La Salle searched for the source of empire to the south, possession of that empire was claimed in the north. All of North America from Atlantic to Pacific, and from the Gulf to the Pole, was now French by proclamation. All that remained was to make this claim good.

10

No View
from Pisgah

As the English began to explore arctic waters in Tudor times, searching for the Northwest Passage, they carefully compared notes and collected all the information they could on the voyages of others. The lessons they learned are explicit in a compact drawn up to govern an expedition dispatched into the White Sea by Sebastian Cabot, son of John. Hakluyt entitled the document "Ordinances, instructions, and advertisements of and for the direction of the intended voyage for Cathay, compiled, made, and delivered by the right worshipful M Sebastian Cabota Esquier, governour of the mysterie and companie of the Marchants adventurers for the discoverie of Regions, Dominions, Islands and places unknowen, the 9. day of May, in the yere of our Lord God 1553."

At this time, the Catholic courts of the Latin nations were sending autocratic instructions to their explorers, whose relationship to their crews was that of master to man, but these English instructions were framed by the merchants themselves and speak with the very voice of Tudor Protestantism. The compact consisted of thirty-three rules to which everyone aboard, from cabin boy to master, was pledged to obey. One rule commanded them to treat any natives they met with kindness, remembering that if a person "may be made drunke with your beere, or wine, you shal know the secrets of his heart." Another forbade their cursing, quarreling, or playing cards, and a third told them to have "present in your mindes that you be all one most royall kings subjects, and naturals, with daily rememberence of the great importance of the voyage, the honour, glorie, praise, and benefite that depend of, and upon the same, toward the common wealth of this noble Realme."

It was all there: confidence, self-discipline, self-government, mutual dependence upon one another regardless of rank, decisions to be arrived at in council on the scene and at the time, Puritanical behavior, the feeling of being God's Chosen People, sharp business practice, a constant eye for anything that might yield a profit, a pragmatic willingness to conceal their true religion and pretend to honor local gods for the sake of safety and profit, and a constant sense of national duty. The relationship of Crown and subject was very clear: both shared in a common wealth. Unfortunately, God did not see fit to prosper this particular voyage, but the compact, rather than the voyage, was important. The concepts it expressed were revolutionary, and in acting on them once they gained a mastery of the sea, the English gained an empire, for the rules that applied to a company of Marchants adventurers at sea were also applicable to any other company put ashore in a wilderness to form a colony.

The notion of sending English men and women to establish plantations in North America probably began with John Sparke's observations of Fort Caroline in 1565. In any case, thirteen years later, Elizabeth granted letters patent to Sir Humphrey Gilbert for "the inhabiting and planting of our people in America." Nothing came of this, but the Crown had stated a policy. In 1585, Sir Walter Raleigh put the ill-fated Lost Colony ashore at Roanoke, Virginia. The colony apparently prospered for a time at peace with its Indian neighbors. But then for unexplained reasons, the colonists abandoned their fort, houses, and fields—and vanished. The next attempt at colonization had to wait till the Edict of Nantes and the death of Philip II of Spain brought a measure of peace to Europe, but the idea was always there. When the James River Colony arrived in 1607, the important fact about it was not that a rather raffish lot came to hunt for gold in Virginia, but that they were to establish a beachhead for a colony, whether gold was found or not.

There presently followed a phenomenon without parallel in modern European history. The population of England in 1600 was perhaps five million, but no less than half a million English men and women arrived in North America by the middle of the century. The populations of Spain and France were each several times larger than that of England, yet no such number (let alone such a percentage) of Spaniards and Frenchmen came to the New World, nor did the Latin nations send out anywhere near so many women. It was almost as if the English, the ultimate descendants of pagan Teutonic and Viking tribes, were mysteriously resuming their ancient westward migrations. A more prosaic explanation is that a sizable portion of the English people saw an opportunity to make money in America, while an even more sizable one was a body of religious fanatics who imagined themselves to be the Children of Israel and who were looking for a wilderness. But the reasons why the English came in such a flood, and the Latins in such a trickle, have more to do with their very different national characteristics, their different forms of government, and the different opportunities that resulted from two different wars.

Following the destruction of the Spanish Armada and the death of Elizabeth, England entered upon a period when she was able to pursue her own devices without undue involvement in European affairs. Alone of all the nations of Europe, England played virtually no part in the Thirty Years' War, and was not represented in the peace conference that ended it. During these years, the affairs of England centered around the rise of Parliament as the ruling instrument of government. The process was remarkably speeded when James I succeeded Elizabeth. His view of the power of the Throne was expressed in his book, *The True Law of Free Monarchy*, which stated that kings were anointed of God, ruled by divine right, and were responsible to God alone. He also detested Calvinists and promised "to harry the Puritans out of the land." Such opinions were utterly anachronistic in the England of that time, and equally unacceptable. When James sought to levy taxes on his authority, rather than follow Elizabeth's practice (and that of monarchs before her) of asking Parliament to raise the money, he was shortly disabused of his illusions. He discovered the greater power in England was not vested in the mystery of the Throne, but reposed in the hands of the landed gentry and the merchant magnates who were not only represented by Parliament, but who also happened to be its members, and who were not about to place their wealth at the disposal of an arbitrary king. They would tax themselves for the sake of their common wealth of England if need be—but since it was their money, and to a great extent their kingdom, they and not the king would determine the need. Nor would anyone allow, much less help, James to harry the Puritans out of the land.

What James seems not to have understood, but which Elizabeth certainly did, was that a kingdom consists of all of its people and their often diverse interests. Although she often claimed to be an absolute prince, she understood her role to be that of the ultimate arbiter of matters relative to the general welfare. She also understood that however much she disliked Puritans, they were part of her people, and more important, she sensed that there was an identity of interests among the forces of radical Protestantism, and those of manufacture, commerce, trade, political liberalism, and representative government.

If James was myopic about this, his son Charles I was fatally blind. First, Charles tried to rule without Parliament, only to find he could not. Next, as head of the Church of England, he sought to force the Anglican rite upon the Presbyterian Scots—and when they rebelled, he asked Parliament for funds to put down the rebellion. Far from doing this, Parliament embraced the Scots—not out of any love for them or for their Presbyterian religion, but to inform Charles that the powers of the king derived not so much from God as from the kingdom. The result was civil war that ended with Charles on the scaffold and with Oliver Cromwell as lord protector of the realm.

Here the story of England was crucially different from that of other European nations. Elsewhere, when kings were killed or deposed, a period of anarchy ensued while the disparate forces that had combined to overthrow the king each jockeyed for power. But in England, where Parliament had been sharing the governance of the realm prior to the civil war, it was merely logical for Parliament to assume full responsibility following the execution of the king. While this did not immediately occur and a period of Cromwellian dictatorship ensued, it was the end result. There was that in Protestantism that could no more abide dictators than it could abide kings, and there was also among the English a sense of common nationality that took precedence over intranational differences. It also appeared that the Stuart kings were not entirely wrong in supposing that a mystical power reposed in the Throne. The king represented the genius of the nation; he symbolized the past and all the powers that derived from the accomplishments of prior generations. Set above men, he could preside over their quarrels; he was in a way superhuman and therefore symbolized the transcendent hope any nation must have in order to endure. In sum, the English discovered that man cannot live by factions or elections alone, and so the monarchy was restored—with all of its mysticism and none of its power; with the point now established that Parliament ruled through the king, and not the other way around, and that in no event could a king rule alone. This working relationship between Parliament and Throne preserved a strong central government for England, meanwhile permitting the development of political and social liberalism and the further evolution of representative government. This was not only unique in Europe, but it also had profound significance for America: the half-million English who crossed the Atlantic in the first half of the century brought the seeds of independence with them.

Those immigrants came, however, in response to a sense of national purpose, as well as for whatever other reasons they had. Following the Parliamentary victory in the civil war, the merchants and magnates of England acquired a taste for empire. No one sat down at a desk to write it all out, and certainly not every plowman and barmaid in the land was caught up in the national dream, but a kind of unspoken consensus arranged itself in the minds of the Englishmen who mattered. The empire would be a commercial one, founded on salt water and guarded by warships, drawing its strength from new lands inhabited and developed by Englishmen. Such an empire would require a secure home base, but the means to security was at hand: Cromwell's New Model Army. Born during the civil war, it had become the best-disciplined and most modern military force in the world of its time. Spain, France, the Netherlands, Austria, and the German and Scandinavian states had hacked away at one another for thirty years, all of them weakening themselves in the process, but the English emerged from their brief civil war as the most potent land power in Europe—and well on their way to preeminence at sea.

The facts of the new English power were apparent to Philip IV of Spain and to Jules Cardinal Mazarin of France, who ruled in the name of the boy king, Louis XIV. At war with one another in 1657, Spain and France each sought an alliance with Cromwell, despite the fact that both nations had been at war with England in the recent past in Europe and in America, and despite the more important fact that both Philip and Mazarin equally detested Protestants, abhorred republics, and particularly loathed Protestant republicans who murdered God's anointed kings. But the New Model Army was most impressive.

For his part, Cromwell as an Englishman and as a Puritan had more reason to despise the Spanish than he did the French, but there was an economic matter to consider. So he agreed to help Philip defeat the French in the Netherlands if the Spanish would grant the English the right to trade freely in New Spain and to give English residents in Spanish possessions the right to own Bibles and profess the Protestant faith. When Philip indignantly refused these concessions, Cromwell listened to what Mazarin had to say.

The Frenchman promised the cities of Dunkirk and Mardyck to England if the English would help the French capture them, and the city of Gravelines, from the Spanish. An Anglo-French victory on this coast would cut the Spanish Netherlands off from Spanish supplies. Cromwell agreed; he sent six thousand armored cavalrymen to the Lowlands, and they promptly captured Dunkirk. Cromwell also sent a fleet to take Jamaica away from Spain, and it succeeded. At this point, Philip IV quickly sued for peace—not only because he was losing the war, but more because he learned that Cardinal Mazarin was seeking to arrange a marriage between young Louis XIV and the duchess of Savoy.

Here began a European tangle freighted with future meaning for America. To Philip's Hapsburg mind, eternally troublesome Lowland provinces and remote Jamaicas were far less important than a marriage of France and Savoy. Such a marriage would drive a French wedge between Hapsburg possessions in Italy and those in Hapsburg Austria. Mazarin proposed a solution: Spain and France could compose all their differences if the infanta of Spain, Maria Theresa, were to marry Louis XIV, who was after all her first cousin. The dowry would be £500,000, the first installment due upon the wedding day, but (and here Mazarin carried cleverness to a point of genius) with Maria Theresa retaining her royal Spanish rights in the Spanish Netherlands until the second half of the dowry was paid. Mazarin seemed to be suggesting that France would forgo any claims to the low countries if she received £250,000 in compensation. Actually, he was confident that Spain was now too nearly bankrupt to be able to raise the second half of the dowry, and that when Philip IV died, France could then take the Spanish Netherlands to satisfy the claim. The Spanish agreed to the marriage, and the Treaty of the Pyrenees was signed in 1659. Just how these Latin family events became crucial to American history will presently appear. For the moment, it is enough to say that Cromwell's taking Jamaica was followed by the establishment of more than twenty thousand Puritans in the Caribbean islands. The English also brushed the Dutch governors out of New York, and the English migration to the New World went on apace.

During the reigns of the Stuart kings, before and after the Restoration, this migration particularly took the form of English magnates purchasing or otherwise obtaining charters from the Crown that granted them lands in North America. Here was jam for the Crown, which could blithely take over wilderness territories no one had ever seen, in return for money and an extension of the realm. The magnates undertook to fill these lands with colonists who would produce foodstuffs and raw materials that could be sold in England and elsewhere to the profit of both the magnates and the Crown. In return, the colonists would buy goods manufactured in England—and here was jam for the manufacturers. The colonists were not to trade with any nation but England, and all goods bought and sold in the colonies were to move only in English ships—jam for the shipowners, and taxes for the Crown. The arrangement was not felt to be onerous on the colonists, for they would be established and initially supported at someone else's expense; they would have an opportunity to create better lives for themselves in the New World than they might have in the Old, and would furthermore enjoy the military protection of the Crown. The establishment of colonial trading monopolies was therefore seen as a system containing nothing but jam for everyone.

The general sense of empire was now assuming a rational form. In the next century, the colonial system would become a stated official policy. The entire arrangement was predicated on military sea power. Control of the seas was the key to it all—to the planting of colonies, protection of the colonies, enforcement of the mutually beneficial trading monopoly. For more than a hundred years, the Spanish had that key in their possession, but they had not fitted it into the right lock, and eventually let it slip through their fingers. By the middle of the seventeenth century, the French made no effort to seize the key, but the English saw it, knew at once what it was, and reached for it.

Much has been said about the English coming to America to escape religious persecution in England, but perhaps not enough has been said of the point that religious persecution in England, during and after Elizabeth's time, chiefly took the form of inconveniencing people—not of slaughtering them. The fact is, it was Crown policy to encourage colonization in America without respect to religion, which was a very different policy from that of the Latin nations. Moreover, the Puritans who came to America were very far from being religious refugees. They feared no one at home; they in fact became the Ironclads of Cromwell's victorious New Model Army. The Pilgrims who arrived in Massachusetts in 1620 were particularly fanatic; they unquestioningly believed that the Old Testament prophecies pertained solely to themselves, and they came to America to fulfill them.

The peculiar dream of this cult was that God had chosen them to reenact the Old Testament, story by story. So they were not merely the elect of God, as other Calvinists put it, but they were in fact the Chosen People whom God would lead through the Wilderness to the Promised Land where they would build the

New Zion. America was the Wilderness of Scripture. It was also the Promised Land, God's country. The Indians were the Lost Tribes of Israel, or so the colonists at first imagined, until having greeted the Indians in Hebrew, it appeared the savages did not understand that language. But the realization that the Indians were not Israelites did not shake the Pilgrims' faith in Scripture. They immediately seized upon the alternative explanation that had earlier occurred to the Spaniards and the French: the Indians were creatures of the Devil.

"It is reported in scripture," Governor William Bradford wrote back to England, "as a mercie to the apostle and his ship-wracked company, that the barbarians shewed them no smale kindness in refreshing them, but these savage barbarians, when they mette with them . . . were readier to fill their sids with arrows then otherwise."

So the Indians were disappointing, and warfare with them began almost at once. The Wilderness, however, was as wild as the most devout could have wished. "And for the season, it was winter," Bradford wrote, "and they that know the winters of that cuntrie know them to be sharp and violent, and subjecte to cruell and feirce stormes, deangerous to travill to known places, much more to search an unknown coast. Besids, what could they see but a hidious and desolate wildernes, full of wild beasts and wiild men? and what multituds ther might be of them they knew not. Neither could they, as it were, goe up to the tops of Pisgah, to vew from this willdernes a more goodly cuntrie to feed their hops; for which way soever they turnd their eys (save upward to the heavens) they could have so little solace or content in respecte of any ourward objects. For summer being done, all things stand upon them with a wetherbeaten face; and the whole countrie, full of woods and thickets, represented a wild and savage hiew. If they looked behind them, ther was the mighty ocean which they had passed, and was now as a maine barr and goulfe to separate them from all the civill parts of the world."

All this was regarded as a sort of divine obstacle course. As John Winthrop put it, "Wee shall be as a Citty upon a Hill, the eies of all people are uppon us; soe that if wee shall deale falsely with our god in this worke we have undertaken and soe cause him to withdrawe his present help from us, wee shall be made a story and a by-word through the world."

Never for a moment did the Puritans envision failure. In the words of a third, Francis Higginson, "That which is our greatest comfort, and meanes of defence above all others, is, that we have here the true Religion and Holy ordinances of Almightie God taught amongst us. . . . thus we doubt not but God will be with us, and if God be with us, who can stand against us?"

Here was a belief as devout and unquestioning as any Jesuit's, but, unlike missionary Catholicism, it was not for export. Far from wishing to convert others, the Massachusetts colonists wanted nothing to do with anyone else.

"I dare take upon me," wrote one Nathaniel Ward, "to be the Herauld of New-England so farre, as to proclaime to the world, in the name of our Colony, that all Familists, Antinomians, Anabaptists and other Enthusiasts, shall have free Liberty to keep away from us, and such as will come to be gone as fast as they can, the sooner the better."

This point of view was forcibly expressed in one of their earliest laws, passed in 1637. It declared that no one could set foot in Massachusetts Bay Colony whose orthodoxy had not been tested by local magistrates. This applied not only to visiting strangers, but to members of the colony as well. Protestantism might be inherently schismatic, but no religious contentions were allowed to vitiate the Puritan colony. Anyone who quibbled, dissented, or doubted the true faith was forthwith bundled out of Massachusetts. As Ward would put it, they were free to go elsewhere.

So religion was not an issue with the Puritans, in the sense they all saw alike in the matter. Nor did they have to speculate as to what might be the ideal goals to which a human society should aspire, for their reading of the Bible made all clear to them. Relieved of the dreadful burden of intellectual inquiry, they were free to bend all their thought, and considerable energies, upon the practical problems presented by the wilderness, the climate, and the Indians. Nor in the process were they badgered or instructed by the English government. The charter of the Massachusetts Bay Colony, granted them by King Charles I in 1629, empowered the Puritans to make any laws they wished to govern their affairs, providing that these be "not contrarie to the Lawes of this our Realme of England."

Here were Europeans absolutely different from any others who came to America. They sought no Chinas, northwest passages, gold, fur, or walrus ivory; they cared nothing for the conversion of savages, and unlike the Spanish and the French, they were told to govern themselves. They came to a wilderness with their wives and children, and ale in ballast, to build a New Zion where no one could smile or laugh on Sundays. They were at least suspicious, if not contemptuous, of everyone but themselves.

It appears that none of the English who came to America during the seventeenth century were the good friends of one another. Just as the Puritans of Massachusetts made it illegal for persons of any other faith to set foot in their colony, so the Anglicans who settled in Virginia passed a law in 1640 barring Puritans from theirs. Neither had any use for the English Catholics who settled in Maryland, and in time everyone would despise the Quakers who came to Pennsylvania. Religious animosities were the basis of ill will; political divisions formed along religious lines. During the English civil war, the Puritans were logically in the Republican camp; by equal logic, the Anglicans were in the king's. For religious reasons as well as for any other, each colony was jealous of its boundaries and rights. The relationship of the several colonies was not only cool, it was barely civil. Meanwhile, within any one colony, social distinctions proved to be just as important to the Englishmen in America as they had been when they all lived in England. The few gentlemen planters in Virginia were separated by a considerable chasm from the great bulk of that colony's population, who arrived as indentured servants—the latter men and women who, in return for transportation to the colony and a chance to mend their fortunes, agreed to hire themselves out in de facto slavery for a period of years. The jailbirds sent to the colonies to work out their sentences occupied the same social position in the New World they had in the Old.

Yet all the English who came to America soon discovered they had tasks in common, the first being their urgent need to clear the woods to create farms in order to feed themselves and, concurrently, to protect themselves from Indian and European enemies. As separate political entities, the several colonies approached these problems in their separate ways, and little as the colonies felt either the need or the desire to work closely together to accomplish what an objective observer would have recognized as common purposes, the colonies all did think of themselves as English. One reason for this was that the island people had long sensed a national identity; another was that by the middle of the seventeenth century, European minds were turning more to nationalistic considerations than to purely religious ones. For nearly two hundred years theological matters had commanded almost exclusive attention, but a secular age was now at hand. The emergent questions had not to do with man's proper relationship to God, so much as they had to do with man's relationship to the state, and the state's relationship to other states. The wilderness, and the isolation of the English colonies from Europe, helped to bring these questions to the fore, and thereby heightened the colonists' sense of their mutual Englishness.

An exception to this rule might seem to be the New England Puritan who, in his role as a latter-day Israelite, could indulge in the intoxicating certainty of his superior difference to everyone else. But even the Puritans were aware of their

Englishness and, like all other colonists, thought of themselves as loyal subjects of England. Charles I need not have feared they might pass ordinances "contrarie to the Lawes of this our Realme," because the Puritans shared with other Englishmen a jealous regard for the principles and privileges embodied in the English common law. True, the Puritans passed sufficient ordinances to ensure that, at one time or another, no less than one-third of the Puritan population was variously in jail, seated in the ducking stool, standing in the pillory, seated in stocks, or lashed to the whipping post, but evidence of guilt was found within the principles of English jurisprudence: it required twelve true men to hang a witch.

The recruiting advertisements in London depicted the colonies as broad lands bursting with good things, waiting only the hand of the husbandman to touch them in order to transform them into opulent gardens, but the appearance of the colonies at midpoint of the century must have struck new arrivals a sharp blow. The reality of the squalid foreshores, the jerry-built towns, the crazily tilted drafty log cabins sitting in tiny patches full of stumps and stones, promised nothing but an absence of all amenities and backbreaking labor from sunrise to sunset as far into the future as anyone could imagine. There was also the promise of danger. Each colony looked apprehensively out to sea. Whatever concerned the powers of Europe concerned their colonies abroad; the next sails to appear might be those of a Spanish warship, or a French. With even keener apprehension, each colony looked into the immediately adjacent forests. The burned-out cabins, the mutilated corpses, the horrific accounts of what happened to families captured by Indians, were staples of conversation from Massachusetts to Virginia. Without in the least deprecating the courage and accomplishments of those who met the tests that America provided, it is probable that many of the settlers survived because they had to—because they were marooned in North America with no way home; because like Dr. Johnson's man about to be hanged, their plight wonderfully concentrated their minds upon it.

They all bore arms all the time, including the time they spent in church. Their axes, knives, and muskets were the necessary tools that everyone, men, women, and children, had to use for the dual purposes of acquiring food and defending themselves against Indians. In Tudor times, the English had speculated that farmers could live in amity with the Indians, but they had not foreseen that the Indians' concept of land would be very different from the European. Europeans believed land could be owned by individuals. The Indians, however, could no more imagine land being owned than they could imagine air being owned. When dealing with Indians, the English thought they were buying land, whereas the Indians thought they were merely allowing the English to share in its use. The Indians' use for land was essentially as a hunting ground. They would never use a hunting ground as a place of residence, but as a game preserve. It made no sense to the Indians when the English felled the trees and cleared the brush from a good hunting ground: in fact, quite the contrary. Still less could they tolerate being ordered off the property. Two years after the *Mayflower* touched shore, the first Indian attacks on the Massachusetts colony began, and warfare with the Indians continued to be a staple of frontier existence for as long as there was a frontier in North America.

Necessity drove the colonists to all manner of invention; the lessons of make-do, do-it-yourself, or do-without were instantly driven in upon them as upon no other Europeans in America (or, for that matter, in Europe). Spanish and French soldiers depended upon supplies from their mother countries. But the English colonists were not soldiers; they were men, women, and children whose survival depended upon themselves. Individual independence was thrust upon them by the dangerous distances separating one farm family from another, and these same dangers, along with the routine difficulties of a pioneer existence, also thrust upon them the need to combine for such social purposes as helping one another to build cabins, clear land, and fight off Indian war parties. Given the conditions under which they labored and fought; given the lessons they had to learn, and the self-reliance they had to assume; and given, too, the implicit egalitarianism of their Protestant faith and that which could be found in the English common law, the artificial social distinctions quickly began to blur. No one for a moment believed that one man was as good as another, but everyone saw reason to believe that a man could be measured only by what he could accomplish. The colonists' meetings for common purposes therefore increasingly became assemblies in which individual competence, measured pragmatically, counted far more than the accident of gentle birth, formal education, or a royal commission.

Left to devise their own government within the general framework of English law, the Puritans of Massachusetts Bay Colony picked out a wary path in the selection of their leaders. They hoped to avoid the peril of anarchic egalitarianism on the one hand, and the danger of granting too much power to any individual (no matter how competent) on the other. It would never do, John Cotton said, to allow leaders "to effect more liberty and authority than will do them good, and the People good. . . . There is a straine in a mans heart that will sometime or other runne out to excesse, unlesse the Lord restraine it, but it is not good to venture it: It is necessary therefore, that all power that is on earth be limited." The profound significance of Cotton's remark is that he was not charged with heresy by his audience. He was not only refuting the theory of predestination, but was rather flatly saying that God could not always be trusted, but apparently no one chose to hear. Almost from the beginning, the conditions of pioneer life began to make the Puritans less Puritanical and much more practical: the New Jerusalem would need politicians. Thus, like the ax, the knife, and the musket, government was a tool that everyone had to learn to use to provide for the general welfare and common defense. Like those other tools, this one would have to be used carefully.

The English colonists learned, and thus survived. They not only survived, but multiplied. And, multiplying, they pushed inland into an apparent infinity of wilderness. The English did not explode inland, but nibbled their way into it, a few acres at a time, meanwhile creating an increasingly secure beachhead behind them on the Atlantic coast. In the process, they were becoming less English, although they were, not consciously aware of this. But a child born in America led a very different life from that of a child born and raised in England, and for this reason, when he was a man, he had a quite different view of himself and of society. He would think of himself as a loyal Englishman, but in England he would be considered an American, for his manners, attitude, and outlook on life would mark him as a stranger.

The progress of the English colonists into the interior of North America was glacial, as relentless as it was slow; but it led soon enough to a meeting with the French. The earlier meetings of Englishmen and Frenchmen had taken the form of English naval raids on French possessions, the most recent of these during the Huguenot wars that had involved France, England, and Spain. The Treaty of St. Germain in 1632 provided that each of these nations agreed to recognize the existence of each other's colonies in America, but not the boundaries—for no one could imagine what the boundaries might be in an unexplored world. The meeting that now took place between colonial Englishmen and Frenchmen in New York and New England was not a raid, but a gradual collision. The two sensed one another's presence and inched warily closer. When they met, a holy war immediately ensued. The French Jesuit missionaries and the dour Puritans were at least alike in the thoroughness of their bigotry. Each saw the other as the servant of the Devil and the enemy of God. The Jesuits incited, and sometimes led, their savage converts to war upon the New England frontier settlements, thereby arousing hatreds that are by no means dead in New England today.

II

Wars,
Whores, and
the Death of Dreams

T HE court of Louis XIV was the wonder of the world—a coruscation of gilded tables and chairs and polished floors, mirrors and crystal, silks and satins, where a thousand perfumed courtiers moved in a kind of dance, as rigidly stylized as a Balinese legong, all of them slowly revolving around the Sun King and drawing life from his merest glance, his slightest nod. If the Grand Monarch deigned to interest himself in orange trees in tubs, then everyone who wished to be anyone madly set out orange trees in tubs. When His Most Christian Majesty exclaimed over the delicate delicious little new green peas, then everyone exclaimed over the delicate delicious little new green peas. They ate them for breakfast; they served them for dessert.

In the year 1677, this court was not yet moved to Versailles, which was still under construction, but already it drew and reflected from the Sun King a light of such dazzling brilliance that the courtiers themselves were deceived as to one purpose of the glorious charade. Essentially, this was to draw the nobility away from their lands, the source of their wealth and power, and set them swirling about the king like so many iridescent moths about a golden flame. Like a Tudor monarch, Louis was anxious to reduce the power of his nobility while giving them the illusion they retained it. So he brought them to court and encouraged them to engage in rivalries of splendor, so as at once to have them under his eye, lead them into bankruptcy, and divert their attention from the realities of his reign.

Again like a Tudor, Louis believed himself anointed of God, king by divine right, and he also resorted to sundry secular ploys to keep himself upon the throne. He prudently refused to tax the wealthy, for fear that, if he did, they would want a voice in the affairs of the realm. He employed bourgeoisie as his ministers and officials, giving them the real power in the kingdom and feeling certain of their loyalty because he knew that they knew their power existed only at his pleasure, as, in fact, did their physical safety. These commoners elaborated a great bureaucracy that governed France, and New France, from offices in Paris. They helped the king devise schemes for raising money by annulling town charters and selling severely reduced rights back to the towns again; by having the Crown sell offices, including judgeships and military commissions; by selling new patents of nobility that not only brought in money, but also had the further effect of diminishing the prestige of the nobility by thus watering its stock; by devaluing the currency. Like Philip II of Spain, Louis XIV gathered all the details of government into the hands of a swarm of clerks over whom he presided. It was a bureaucracy that regulated prices, maintained quality controls over manufactured goods, subsidized trade and industries, regulated commerce, built roads and canals, and generated the money that Louis devoted to the huge expansion of *his* source of power, the French army.

This, too, like the glitter of his fantastic court and like the rationalization of French industry and trade, was another wonder of the world. Louis was the first European ruler since the Romans to dispense with feudal levies and mercenary bands and instead create a national army, put this army into a uniform, teach the troops to march in step and, in disciplined step, to perform military maneuvers, feed and house his troops in barracks, and establish graduated ranks in a chain of command leading up and down from the corporals of squads to the generals of armies. Louis stood at the head of this chain and held it in his fist. He was ever mindful of the recent Huguenot wars and the possibility of rebellion. He meant his army to be the only armed force in the state. He meant warfare to be an activity carried out only by the state— and by the state, he meant himself. Moreover, he fancied himself a warrior.

Louis came to the throne in 1661 to find France surrounded on three sides, to the east, northeast, and south, by a decadent Spain. Five years later, Philip IV of Spain died, and in the following year, Louis took advantage of the opportunity Cardinal Mazarin had thoughtfully prepared for him. He seized the Spanish Netherlands as compensation for the unpaid half of his Spanish wife's dowry on the ground that she retained her royal Spanish rights to this land as long as that dowry remained unpaid. He also sent his troops into the Franche-Comté on France's southeastern frontier, thus extending his realm as far east as Switzerland. At this point, the Protestant nations became thoroughly alarmed. Louis XIV's France, it seemed, was on the way to becoming the power that Philip II's Spain had been: ominous to Europe and ominous to Protestantism. England, Sweden, and Holland formed a Triple Alliance, and after brief hostilities, Louis was forced to compromise. The Treaty of Aix-la-Chapelle in 1668 recognized Louis' conquest in Flanders but required him to return the Franche-Comté to Spain, and the nations of the Triple Alliance undertook to guarantee Spain's possessions in the Lowlands. For the ancient Protestant enemies of Spain to take her part against France was an irony of history, but the politics of expedience were beginning to blur the politics of religion.

At this time, the emergent modern nations of Europe were

discovering that political self-interest and economic self-interest were closely allied, if not exactly the same thing. For example, two partners to the Triple Alliance, the English and the Dutch, were longtime allies and coreligionists, but they had been at war with one another in Europe, Africa, at sea, and in North America in the years immediately preceding Louis' venturing into Flanders. Their quarrel was over commercial rights. As a result of the war, the English took away from the Dutch the American territory called New Netherlands, consisting of the modern states of New York, New Jersey, and Delaware. The fact that they could so quickly become allies again against France and on the side of their old mutual enemy, Spain, could also be explained in terms of commercial advantage.

Louis, brooding over a momentary impasse, set about improving his army, and two years later, in 1670, he signed the secret Treaty of Dover with Charles II of England. Under it, Charles agreed to help Louis attack Holland in return for a bribe of three million *livres* a year, with another two million due on the day when Charles would become a Catholic. Louis next allied himself with Sweden, the other former partner of the Triple Alliance, and with certain minor German states. Then, in 1672, he invaded the Netherlands. Louis' reasons for starting this war have been variously charged to (a) his hatred of republics, (b) his venomous dislike of Protestants, (c) his anger that Holland had revolted from his father-in-law's Spain, (d) his recognition that Holland was the center of antimonarchical plots in Europe, (e) his desire to end Holland's dominance of European trade, commerce, and finance, (f) his anger with the Dutch for placing an embargo on French wine and brandy, and (g) Louis' intense desire to play soldier. Some of these reasons seem inconsistent; for example, if he hated Protestants, how could Louis ally himself with the Swedes? But it was just as apparently inconsistent for the Swedes to have allied themselves with Louis.

In the seventeenth century, a king still counted for something, and Louis' personal desires could have a decisive influence on events. But it also appeared that popular will was beginning to count for something, too, as well as popular religious prejudice and commercial considerations. In short, nations were beginning to act like single entities. In earlier centuries, warfare in Europe was almost in the nature of a private hobby indulged in by princes in which relatively small armies were involved in limited operations. In the seventeenth century, this was still the case, but a growing sense of nationalism was changing this situation into one whereby the energy of an entire nation of people would be mobilized against the energy of another; it would no longer be, for example, the king of France against the king of Spain, but the French against the Spanish. The rise of the merchant class to positions of political and economic importance in European nations led to a diffusion of power that once reposed entirely in the Throne. The more widely this power to govern was diffused, the more clearly the general nature of a nation's interests could be seen, and the sharper a sense of national identity became. The era of truly national wars was now drawing nearer, although royal passions and religious animosities would continue to be factors in them well into the nineteenth century.

Louis' invasion of the Netherlands in 1672 informed the other European nations that France was too powerful for anyone else's good, and so another strange alliance appeared. This time, Spain entered the war in defense of the Dutch, along with Denmark, Lorraine, Brandenburg, Trier, Mainz, and the forces of the Holy Roman Empire led by Austria. At the end of six years of war by land and sea, the Treaty of Nijmegen was patched together. In return for evacuating the Spanish Netherlands and ceding the city of Maastricht to the Dutch, Louis XIV regained the Franche-Comté and a part of Lorraine. Louis had by no means gained all he wanted, but France emerged from the war as the strongest power in Europe, and the Grand Monarch began to contemplate his next campaign. He would attack in the direction of Strasbourg; he wanted the rest of Lorraine and a border on the Rhine.

It was to gain the ear of this military monarch that Robert Cavelier, Sieur de La Salle, arrived in Paris from Canada in 1677. Life seems to have gone out of her way to strew obstacles in the course of La Salle, and those he now met were of that particularly formless kind found only in bureaucracies. The king was at war, but even if he were not thus preoccupied, he could not be seen without an appointment, and requests for an audience must be put through channels. The impetuous and impatient La Salle immediately met with this sort of thing:

One believes your business is urgent, M'sieu, but so is that of everyone else. If M'sieu will state his business? Ah, yes, but no, that is not the business of this department. M'sieu should see Minister A, instead. And Minister A refers him to Minister B, and so on through the soggy alphabet. But at last someone suggests that there is a man who is the lover of the mistress of Minister Z, and if he finds him, then he will speak to her, who will speak to him, who can speak to the official who keeps the royal appointment schedule.

La Salle's funds began to run out as he stayed at an inn in Paris, while each day he waded in this sort of bog. If he could not see the king, he at least wanted to see Jean Baptiste Colbert, the commoner who was the king's first minister and the principal architect of the military-commercial complex that was the France of Louis XIV. Colbert was a man of the new age who believed in mercantile theory as much as any London merchant; he believed in colonization and therefore was greatly expanding the French navy he had called into being. But Colbert was as difficult to meet as the king himself. In the end, La Salle could only write Colbert a letter and hope the minister would read it. The letter focused on La Salle's voyage down the Ohio to the confluence of the Mississippi.

"It is nearly all so beautiful," La Salle wrote, "and so fertile;

so free from forests, and so full of meadows, brooks and rivers; so abounding in fish, game and venison, that one can find there in plenty, and with little trouble, all that is needful for the support of flourishing colonies.

"The soil will produce everything that is raised in France," he insisted. "Flocks and herds can be left out at pasture all winter; and there are even native wild cattle, which, instead of hair, have a fine wool that may answer for making cloth and hats. Their hides are better than those of France. . . . hemp and cotton grow here naturally, and may be manufactured with good results; so there can be no doubt that colonies planted here would become very prosperous.

"It was knowledge of these things, joined to the poverty of Canada, its dense forests, its barren soil, its harsh climate, and the snow that covers the ground for half the year, that led the Sieur de la Salle to undertake the planting of colonies in these beautiful countries of the West."

La Salle's rather chamber-of-commerce opening gambit was designed to appeal to the merchant in Colbert, and it had the further virtue of being absolutely true, but La Salle had more important matters to discuss than that of making hats from bison. He wanted colonists sent to New France to provide the base of power for the continental plan that he, Frontenac, and Talon envisioned. By fortifying the mouth of the Mississippi River, France could close the southern access to the interior to both the Spanish and the English. This would also provide an all-weather port, which New France badly needed, for the St. Lawrence was frozen during the winter months. The inhabitants of the fort, and the seaport, could support themselves by trading in bison hides till the agricultural resources of the region could be developed. Frontenac also wanted forts established on Lakes Ontario and Champlain, and if Frontenac differed from La Salle, it was only in that he believed such forts were a matter of more immediate concern than one on the Gulf of Mexico, for he wished to hold the Iroquois in check and put a stop to the trade in furs which the tribes of the upper Great Lakes had begun to carry on with the Dutch and English in New York. Frontenac and Talon were aware of the possibilities inherent in the broad grasslands west of the lakes and hoped the route to China lay across them, but they first wanted the north country waterways fortified. Of all the British colonies in North America, only New York had an easy access by water into the interior, and the rate at which the British colonists were arriving and multiplying was frightening. Surely the British would pour into the western lands via New York if the French did not soon act to stop them; for this forts were needed, and in order to maintain and provide for the garrisons, a population of farmers and artisans was necessary. The life of New France could not safely depend entirely upon the receipt of supplies via the St. Lawrence River, which, when not frozen, could be closed by British action, as had occurred once before. In sum, to be viable, New France needed new Frenchmen.

These points of view reached and duly impressed Colbert, and so did something else that La Salle had to report. La Salle had returned to Quebec from his explorations of the Ohio and Mississippi valleys to find a conspiracy against him. His abrupt and imperious ways had caused some of his men to desert him during his travels. Returning to Quebec ahead of him, they gave a black account of his character and found Jesuits and fur traders quite ready to believe this. The Jesuits were willing to intrigue against anyone else who wished to colonize New France. The fur traders were opposed to colonization for quite different reasons. These men, the voyagers and coureurs de bois of romantic memory, were in fact adventurers, bitter younger sons of the minor nobility, and criminals who had been transported to New France because Old France had no place for them but jail. It would seem that the only time the fur traders cooperated with the French military commanders was when the Iroquois were on the warpath. Otherwise, they were men virtually impervious to discipline and

scornful of civilization. The forests offered them limitless opportunities to abandon all restraints; to live on an aboriginal plane of
utter lawlessness; some were more savage than the Indians with
whose women they coupled. Their last desire was to be subjected
to government. When La Salle returned to Quebec from his
Ohio expedition, one of them gave him poison. Suspicion fell first
upon the Jesuits, but La Salle himself felt the poisoner must have
been a voyager. As for the Jesuits, La Salle believed they were the
secret agents of the Spanish king. "They intend to make a new
Paraguay [free of all Europeans, save themselves] in these parts,
and the route which I close against them [by means of fortified
colonies along the Ohio and Mississippi rivers] gave them facili-
ties for an advantageous correspondence with Mexico. This
check," he wrote, "will infallibly be a mortification to them; and
you know how they deal with whatever opposes them. Nevertheless, I am bound to render them the justice to say that the poison
which was given me was not at all of their instigation."

Colbert could easily appreciate the situation. A handful of
soldiers, priests, and half-wild trappers squabbling in the wilderness and working at cross-purposes would never hold an empire,
much less build one. Colbert, of course, could see the opportunities La Salle described. He was also impressed by the reports sent
by Frontenac and Talon, and as the king's first minister, he was
in a position to act. But ministers are never entirely free; in politics, the area of the possible is often narrower than in many another profession. The Jesuits had an influence at court. Certain
Paris merchants had an interest in the fur trade. The treasury was
not a bottomless gold mine, and the king was involved in an expensive war. Perhaps even more to the point, who wished to leave
France? The answer to that question seemed to be, very few—
and only the sort of men who had gone out to America already:
priests and pirates. Otherwise no one seemed desirous of leaving
his snug French kitchen for a Canadian campfire. A considerable
body of French Catholics would gladly expel the Huguenots into

the wilds, although the Jesuits violently opposed this, but it appeared the Huguenots had no great ambitions to be pioneers. The Edict of Nantes had given them relief from persecution; many of them belonged to a prosperous middle class, and, as a whole, the Huguenots were far more interested in establishing what amounted to a political bloc in France than they were desirous of leaving France for anywhere else, America least of all. In the end, the likeliest candidates for transportation as colonists seemed to be peasants, prisoners, orphans, and whores.

There was also the problem of La Salle. All this talk of conspiracies and poisons and machinations of Jesuits, when coupled with his statements that his men had deserted him, at least suggested that La Salle had very meager abilities as a commander of men, if it did not suggest an unbalanced mind. There was indeed merit in the continental plan, but La Salle was not perhaps the most competent man to carry it out. In view of all the circumstances of the moment, Colbert temporized. Since La Salle believed the Mississippi flowed to the Gulf of Mexico, he should be encouraged to find out if it actually did. That would at least be the first step toward the accomplishment of any continental plan. But to what extent should this particular young man be encouraged? Colbert's solution was to obtain a royal patent for La Salle. It granted him the king's permission to explore in North America—at La Salle's own expense. Then, to provide him with a means of raising the money to spend, the patent also granted La Salle a monopoly on whatever trade he could turn up in those bison hides he so much admired.

With this royal gift in his threadbare coat, La Salle at once returned to Canada to find the money by a process that amounted to his selling shares in his monopoly of a hypothetical trade. For the next three years, La Salle found himself trying to accumulate sufficient furs to appease his stockholders; he was for that while an explorer on a treadmill. He built a ship on the Great Lakes and stuffed it with hides, but the ship and its cargo were lost on its way to Niagara. La Salle formed an alliance of Illinois tribes to fight the Iroquois; he was again deserted by some of his men and survived a subsequent attempt by twelve of them to murder him; he fought almost by himself to protect his life and fortunes; surmounted all manner of violence and intrigues and treacheries in the forests and in Quebec, till, in the winter of 1682, his fortunes no better or worse than ever, but still pursuing his steadfast dream, La Salle sold his seigneury above Montreal, obtained new supplies and the adherence of a small party of Canadians and Indians, and ventured down the Illinois River to its confluence with the Mississippi. It took the expedition three months to float down this great river till the wind turned salt and they could smell the sea.

At the mouth of the river, the land and water intermingled in a vast confusion of swamps, sandbars, bogs, and forests that grew out of water, winding water paths, canes, reeds, grassy hummocks, and mud flats. It was a little company of sinewy scarecrows who entered this wet mess, looking for a bit of high, drier ground. They were nearly famished. For days they had been subsisting on alligator meat. They beached their canoes among the bushes that grew on the skirts of an island and there, on a hillock, erected a log cross on which they inscribed the royal arms of France and the legend, "Louis Le Grand, Roi de France et de Navarre, Regne, le Neuvieme Avril, 1682."

Perhaps the greatest monument to the memory of La Salle is the fact that he had carried with him, through four years of the most perilous and unpromising adventures, those documents necessary to the occasion that had at last materialized. Extracting these from the hide-wrapped bundle of his belongings, La Salle held them out for his party to see and read his proclamation:

"In the name of the most high, mighty, invincible, and victorious Prince, Louis the Great, by the grace of God King of France and of Navarre, Fourteenth of that name, I, this ninth day of April, one thousand six hundred and eighty two, in virtue of my commission of His Majesty, which I hold in my hand, and which may be seen by all whom it may concern, have taken, and do now take, in the name of His Majesty and of his successors to the crown, possession of this country of Louisiana, the seas, harbours, ports, bays, adjacent straits, and all the nations, peoples, provinces, cities, towns, villages, mines, minerals, fisheries, streams, and rivers, within the extent of the said Louisiana, from the mouth of the great river St. Louis otherwise called the Ohio . . . as also along the river Colbert, or Mississippi, and the rivers which discharge themselves thereinto, from its source beyond the country of the Nadouessioux . . . as far as its mouth at the sea, or Gulf of Mexico, and also to the mouth of the River of Palms [the Rio Grande], upon the assurance we have had from the natives of these countries, that we are the first Europeans who have descended or ascended the said river Colbert; hereby protesting against all who may hereafter undertake to invade any or all of these aforesaid countries, peoples, or lands, to the prejudice of the rights of His Majesty, acquired by consent of the nations dwelling herein. Of which, and of all else that is needful, I hereby take to witness those who hear me. . . ."

His audience consisted of a few Canadian canoeists, a parcel of savages, a swarm of insects, and a few fluttering birds. But as it had seemed to the Spanish explorers of an earlier century, so it seemed to La Salle: since the proper forms had been observed, an empire had passed into the hands of a king anointed of God to rule over men. Whatever occurred from now on would be whatever God saw fit for the king to do—with the assistance, of course, of Colbert.

La Salle returned to France in 1684 to find the court had moved to the preposterous splendor of recently completed Versailles, where it was the king's pleasure to lead his courtiers, guidebook in hand, through the gardens—pausing at those precise locations where one could admire the mathematical perspectives. Mathematics and logic were the queens of science, and Versailles itself was a demonstration of precision. The gardens, the buildings, the minutely detailed and scheduled etiquette of the court, all obeyed an intricate and orderly pattern. But Versailles was also a military headquarters, as well as being an elaborate confection, and there was in its pattern a time for the king to play with his soldiers. His armies had captured Strasbourg and made good French possession of lands east to the Rhine. Louis now contemplated a resumption of his attempts at conquest of the Spanish Netherlands and Holland, to give France that northern coast. He was meanwhile further consolidating his power over all aspects of French life, and to that end, was planning to destroy the Huguenots' bases of power by revoking the Edict of Nantes which permitted them to rule themselves in Huguenot towns. So the mind of the king was turned upon France, and upon France's position in Europe, and not upon the creation of a New France in a domain several times larger than all of Europe. His interest in New France was not nonexistent, but it was minimal. Colbert, however, was much more interested—and perhaps sufficiently flattered by having one of the greatest rivers of the world named for himself to pay some attention to La Salle. Still, he did not wholly trust in La Salle's abilities to lead an enterprise. While he did agree to send an expedition to establish a fort at the mouth of what was now the River Colbert, it was no great force. Four small vessels were dispatched, under the joint command of La Salle and of a naval officer, Captain Beaujeu.

There are few ways more certain to guarantee the failure of an enterprise than to assign two commanders to it. La Salle and Beaujeu entered upon their violent disagreements before the little squadron was fairly out of La Rochelle. Even had Beaujeu been the most forgiving of men, he would doubtless have had difficulty with La Salle. In the course of this adventure, one of the four ships was lost in a wreck; another was captured by a Spanish warship. The expedition never found the mouth of the Mississippi, but entered what is now Matagorda Bay on the Texas coast, apparently because La Salle mistook the bay for the river mouth. Here, Captain Beaujeu left him; perhaps marooned him is more accurate. And here La Salle built a little fort and spent the next two years vainly trying to rediscover the Mississippi. In 1687, he was still trying to find the river, wandering around in Texas, when his men, tired and disgusted, at last murdered him. When a Spanish force ultimately discovered the fort the French were reported to have built somewhere on the coast, they found only a few dejected Frenchmen still alive and living as the virtual slaves of a nearby Indian tribe. The others had died of disease, starvation, and Indian arrows and clubs.

The melancholy end of La Salle and his expedition was not the end of La Salle's dream of a continental plan for New France. But the further pursuit of that dream had to wait upon events that began to unfold in Europe even as La Salle's expedition was sailing toward disaster. In 1685, Charles II of England died, and to the considerable dismay of many members of Parliament, and of the majority of Scots and Englishmen, Charles's brother, James II, succeeded to the throne. Their dismay arose from the fact that James was a Catholic who had fled to France during the Puritan revolution; who returned to England only to be subsequently exiled on suspicion of having been involved in papal plots against the kingdom; and who through marriage was believed to have close ties to Louis XIV and sympathy for that monarch's imperial ambitions. James had been allowed to return to England, and Parliament had narrowly refused to bar him from succession, but he was viewed with profound suspicion. This suspicion was buttressed when, in the year of James's succession to the throne, his friend and fellow monarch, Louis XIV, revoked the Edict of Nantes.

Louis' reasons were these: As an absolute monarch, Louis could not tolerate the existence of autonomous communities of Huguenots in his kingdom, particularly when the nature of those communities was antimonarchical and potentially rebellious. He was a devout Catholic who styled himself His Most Christian Majesty, and, as a Catholic king, he could not tolerate heresy in his realm. Moreover, the Huguenot cities were wealthy.

Revocation of the edict sent a thrill of apprehension throughout the Protestant realms of Europe, but one of terror through the Huguenot communities of France. St. Bartholomew's Eve and the wars that had followed were only too vivid a memory. Huguenot émigrés flooded into Holland to the protection of William of Orange, and some four hundred of them escaped to America, establishing a settlement in what is now South Carolina. The Huguenots naturally feared that the religious persecutions of an earlier century were to be resumed in all their horror, but Louis XIV was not contemplating the kind of Crusade-cum-Inquisition the Spanish kings had attempted. He did not intend to burn Huguenots but merely to put an end to their privileges and their sanctuaries. He meanwhile contemplated still another attack on the Lowland states to the north and on German ones to the east.

Louis' revocation of the edict, however, plus his intention to seize the property of his neighbors, all the more easily enabled the Holy Roman Emperor Leopold to create a new alliance of Catholic and Protestant powers against Louis. It was called the League of Augsburg and consisted of the Holy Roman Empire, Spain, Sweden, Bavaria, Saxony, the Palatinate, the Dutch Republic, Savoy, and England. The English accession to the league followed their disenchantment with James II, whose autocratic treatment of a generally hostile Parliament was one thing, and his trial of seven English bishops was another. Worse, he sought to keep Protestants from holding state offices. The last straw was the birth of an heir, James Edward Stuart, as the probable continuing link in a Catholic monarchy. When in 1688 war began between Louis and the league, the English deposed their Catholic king, disinherited his son, and called to the throne James's daughter Mary, who had been raised as a Protestant and had married the redoubtable leader of the Dutch, William of Orange. Once again, James II fled to France; William and Mary assumed the English throne, and England joined the league and entered the war. Like other members of the league, England had reason to fear that France was too well armed for anyone else's good, and that a triumphant France would be an overwhelming commercial antagonist. But unlike the other members of the league, England also had reason to fear that a triumph for Louis XIV meant the reestablishment of a Catholic monarchy in England and a religious civil war in the island kingdom.

The fact that the war lasted nine years is testimony to the potency of Louis XIV's France. The combined navies of the English and the Dutch defeated the French navy, but the French army held its own against the armies of the league until it was at last clear that no one could either win or lose the war. A peace was made at Ryswick, near The Hague, in 1697. Louis was obliged to give up most of the lands he had taken since 1679, with the exception of Strasbourg. He had to yield commercial concessions to the Dutch, recognize the independence of Savoy, and acknowledge William of Orange as the king of England. So far, the reign of the Sun King had been thirty years of intermittent warfare. Each time Louis attacked the Lowlands, alliances were formed against him, and each of his wars had ended less profitably than he had hoped. But this experience taught him nothing other than to increase his armaments. With peace made at Ryswick, Louis began to prepare for his next war of conquest. It was to prove the longest and most costly of all.

Each of Louis' wars brought battle to the New World—at sea in the Caribbean and off the North Atlantic coast, and ashore in New France and in New England. So far as the English colonists were concerned, the fighting never stopped; once begun, the French and Indian Wars, as the colonists called them, were really all one war. When French and English regular forces were not in the field, relentless guerrilla warfare persisted in the intervals of nominal peace. French army officers and Jesuit missionaries armed and led Indians against the English frontier farms and settlements, and for their part the English made allies of the Iroquois and struck back at the French and their Indian allies. These guerrilla operations followed the water paths through the forests, but while both the French and the English clearly understood the strategic significance of the water routes, neither side was able or willing to close them to the other. The French built a fort at Detroit to command the entrance to the Great Lakes; they placed forts on the Ohio River and on the upper Mississippi; they fortified the St. Lawrence River and Lake Champlain. But these forts were never adequately manned, armed, and supplied, nor did any colony of French men and women grow up around them. For their part, the English colonies not only failed to cooperate against their common enemy, but within any single colony there were endless disagreements. If a fort was built as an outpost in the forest, it would be abandoned as soon as word got round that a French force was no longer in the immediate neighborhood, and its garrison of colonial farmers would go home to their crops. The idea of maintaining a constantly guarded and fortified perimeter was at once impossible and far from their desires; the colonists' best defense was to repay French and Indian attacks on their settlements with similar raids upon their enemies. Nor did the colonists work easily with their governors. They were all loyal Englishmen, but they were particularly loyal to the idea that they should enjoy whatever rights of self-rule might have been granted them in their colonial charters, or of whatever such rights were implicit in their Protestant religion, or which they had appropriated to themselves in the course of their necessary responses to pioneer circumstances. If a royal governor broached a perfectly sound military plan, the colonists would typically fail to vote him the men and the money by way of demonstrating resentment at being governed by an appointed official, however good he might be. Then they would make a stab at carrying out his plan themselves, but in their own way.

During the wars of Louis XIV, neither Paris nor London understood the significance of North America. The attention of both governments was fixed primarily on Europe—a focus that was understandable, if myopic. When Louis made his secret Treaty of Dover with Charles II, he could very likely have bought New York from that friendly and money-starved king. Strategically speaking, nothing would have been wiser. For less money than the cost of a campaign in Flanders, Louis could have acquired a far larger area of potentially profitable land; the northern New England colonies would have been cut off from those on the middle Atlantic seaboard; the water gate to the west would have been closed. On the other hand, central New York was full of warlike Iroquois; a population of French would be required to take over the colony. For whatever reasons, Louis let the opportunity pass and concentrated on Europe, instead.

Nor did the English act more wisely. The Parliaments that placed England in alliances against France (despite the wishes of the Stuart king) did not take advantage of the opportunity to mount a serious invasion of Canada and expel the French from North America, nor did the English colonists. Parliament sent a few English warships and troops to help defend the colonies, but there was no thought of conquest: the Peace of Ryswick made no changes in territorial boundaries in North America.

Meanwhile, the guerrilla operations persisted, and the stomach-turning atrocities perpetrated by the Indians on both sides left a legacy of the most murderous hatred, particularly in New England. It was the Indians' custom to torture to death their prisoners of war—including, often enough, women and children. Both the French and the English found this custom utterly revolting. But only too frequently a lone European, in nominal command of a war party of Indian allies, would be incapable of controlling his excited savages in the moment of victory. It was all the French could do to persuade their Indian allies to enslave the English women and children instead of murdering them, and whenever they could, the French would offer to buy the captives from the Indians and then deliver them back to the English colonists in return for ransom. On not a few occasions, however, the French Jesuit priests saw to it that orphaned English children would be sent to Quebec to be raised in the True Faith for the salvation of their immortal souls, and this, to the New England Puritans, who had a True Faith of their own, was an infinitely more horrible fate than to be tortured to death at the stake. Both the Jesuits and the Puritans viewed the struggle as a holy war, with each devoutly believing the other to represent the forces of the Devil. The New Englanders saw the French as those who loosed fiends upon their helpless and innocent families; such was their bitterness that even today the New Englanders of Maine and Massachusetts despise French Canadians. One unfortunate population was caught in the middle of the quarrel—the Norman peasants who had been settled in Acadia, a province that included the modern provinces of New Brunswick and Nova Scotia. They wished only to be left alone to try to contend with their unpromising new land, and in fact tried to negotiate a separate treaty with the *Bostonais*, as they called the Massachusetts colonists. Unfortunately, the negotiations broke down when the English refused to agree to stop fishing off the Nova Scotia coast, and as the merciless raids continued upon the English frontier settlements, and as the English hatred of the French deepened as time went on, the Massachusetts colonists lumped the luckless and inoffensive Acadian peasants in with the rest of all that was French.

While both France and England passed up opportunities to contend for mastery in North America during the wars of Louis XIV, both began, following the Peace of Ryswick, to consider the significance of the Mississippi River. The French acted first. Even as it occurred to London to send an expedition to take possession of the mouth of the river, a French expedition landed in Biloxi Bay, an arm of the Mississippi Sound. It arrived in 1699 under the command of Pierre Lemoyne, Sieur d'Iberville, and consisted of French soldiers and several scores of dejected men who had been kidnapped from French city streets and bundled aboard ship and then told they were to be pioneers in the New World. They were joined by a party of Canadian fur trappers who had been sent down the Mississippi to help form a French colony. D'Iberville put the men to work building Fort Maurepas; the settlement was called Biloxi after the Biloxi Indians who were native to the area.

Here, in a muddy, fever-stricken subtropical jungle, the first settlement of Louisiana was made. The three purposes of this settlement were to serve as the base of a future attack upon Mexico; to act as a depot for ores and furs to be gathered in the interior; to keep the English out of the Mississippi and, so, out of the lands west of the Appalachian Mountains. So far it would seem that the French government was at last acting upon the recommendations of the farsighted Champlain, Frontenac, Talon, and La Salle. There was not only to be a fort, but a colony. Since a colony implied permanence, and families, and a microcosm of France itself, women were sent out. The satirical and thoroughly depraved duc d'Orléans, the younger brother of Louis XIV, took a particular delight in attending to this detail. He filled a ship with whores and sent them to Biloxi to be the future mothers of Louisiana.

The long failure of the French in Louisiana began immediately. The primary reason for failure stemmed from the fact that, with the possible exception of D'Iberville, no one wanted to be there. The four hundred Huguenots who had fled to Carolina heard of the planting of this colony and, still thinking of themselves as Frenchmen, petitioned the king to allow them to join their countrymen in Louisiana. Their presence in Biloxi might have made all the difference, but Louis' cold answer was that he had not expelled heretics from France in order that they should establish a republic in America. So it was only a company of sullen soldiers, harum-scarum Canadian trappers, kidnapped men, and unfortunate whores who found themselves marooned in an unhealthful country, governed by martial law. No food was sent them; the colonists were supposed to raise their own. Any profits earned through the accumulation of furs and ores were not to be kept by the trappers and miners, but were to go to the Crown. Supplies could be purchased only from the Crown, and at fixed prices. No one was allowed to leave the colony. In all, Biloxi more closely resembled a penal colony than any other kind. It was in any case quite different from a Spanish settlement of conquerors, mestizos, and slaves, and different again from a colony of English yeomen who to a great extent had chosen to live in America and who largely governed themselves.

For all that the Biloxi settlement was nominally governed by martial law, obedience proved difficult to obtain. The French soldiers, like other European soldiers before them in America, refused to be farmers and expected to be fed. The Canadians did not care to farm, and the kidnapped wights did not know how. Barter for food began with the Biloxi Indians. Next, when the duc d'Orléans' whores appeared, they were so generally repulsive that even the soldiers protested. For their part, the Canadians wanted nothing to do with them; they were used to Indian girls and found them far more attractive than Frenchwomen. Then, almost no one was in the slightest degree interested in establishing a colony. They wanted to get out of it as rapidly as possible. But on the way out, they wished to find gold and pearls. The inevitable rumors of El Dorado spread, and they all dreamed of acquiring riches in the New World to spend in the Old. The only riches actually found were the coins certain entrepreneurs from La Rochelle were able to get away from the soldiers. These were men who had the foresight to accompany the expedition as purveyors of wine and spirits. They set barrels of brandy up on sawhorses in huts and sold it a dram at a time from the barrel. These establishments were the first of Louisiana's subsequently famous barrelhouses. Since it appeared that none of the Frenchmen were either willing to work or capable of it, and that the colony would

surely starve if it could not feed itself, attempts were made to enslave the local Indians. It then appeared that work was as foreign
to the Indians as it was to the French, and it was proposed to engage in barter for slaves with settlements in the French Caribbean islands: Biloxi would send three Indians to the West Indies
in return for two black slaves. But the order came back from Versailles forbidding such commerce on the ground that the French
in the West Indies would send only their worst and most incorri-
gible blacks to their countrymen in Louisiana. The French government advised the Biloxi colonists that if they wanted black
slaves, they should procure their own from Guinea; how they
were to do this was left unexplained. The infant colony, a squalid
settlement of huts and tents pitched in such a bog that alligators
slithered through the encampment, began slowly to starve, and
then a pestilence erupted. To complicate the misfortunes of this
soggy community, the last of the great wars of Louis XIV took
place in Europe at this time, which meant that Biloxi received
even less attention from France than it might have had.

In Europe, it was known as the War of the Spanish Succession, in America, as Queen Anne's War. It involved almost all
the states and kingdoms of the Western world, and it lasted for
eleven years. Although all of its major events occurred in Europe,
the results of the war were crucial to American history. The
proximate cause of what was tantamount to the first of the modern world wars was the death of Charles II of Spain in 1700. His
death had long been expected, for Charles suffered from hereditary syphilis, dropsy, and epilepsy. His death had also long been
feared, for he was childless, and his will left Spain, New Spain,
the Netherlands, possessions in the Mediterranean and Italy, and
all else of the Spanish empire, to his great-nephew, the duc d'An-
jou, who was the grandson of Louis XIV.

The will provided, however, that if France did not accept
this imperial legacy, then all would go to the Archduke Charles of

Austria, Charles II's Hapsburg relative, who was also heir presumptive to the Holy Roman Empire.

In either case, it was very clear to all European nations that the legacy would give an overwhelming power to whoever accepted it. This thought was repulsive even to Louis XIV, who for a time prior to Charles II's death proposed to England and Holland that the Spanish empire be divided between France and Austria in such a way that neither should be more powerful than any league that could be formed against them. There were limits, it seemed, to Louis' ambitions, and the English and the Dutch quite agreed with this good sense.

Unfortunately, the Archduke Charles had no such qualms, nor did his father, the Holy Roman Emperor. Because the Hapsburgs meant to accept the Spanish empire if France refused it, Louis XIV was more or less forced to take it, and when Charles II died, he did.

At this point, Holland, England, and the Holy Roman Emperor formed a Grand Alliance whose threefold purpose was to obtain the Spanish Netherlands for Holland, obtain Milan and other Italian possessions for the Holy Roman Empire, and keep French trading ships out of New Spain, whose mines were still producing treasure. For a while, it seemed that Louis XIV might be as reasonable about making concessions as he had been with respect to his earlier proposal. But then the deposed English king, James II, who had been living in exile at St. Germain, fell mortally ill. The English Parliament had meanwhile decided that, on the death of William of Orange, the kingdom should pass to his wife's sister Anne, and go thereafter to the House of Hanover, and not revert to a Stuart or any other Catholic. Now, to everyone's astonishment, Louis XIV went to St. Germain and told the dying James II that he recognized James's son as the Prince of Wales, and would recognize him as James III, king of England, upon the father's death. Louis' action can be explained only with respect to his profound belief that kings were anointed of God and that only they, not Parliaments or lesser mortals, had the divine right to choose their successors. He was perhaps thinking not so much about the English throne as about the French, and the succession of his own Bourbon line. The English, however, saw in this only one more papal plot against themselves—and so prepared for war.

For the next decade, France fought alone against the Grand Alliance, whose members now included Denmark and Savoy as well as the three original members. Spain was of no help to France because she was not only weak, but also because the Spaniards themselves did not wish to see the French and Spanish crowns joined. The fighting began in Italy, spread through Europe, and erupted in America. While the grand battles were fought abroad, the squalid horrors of Indian warfare were visited upon the New England frontier and were repaid in kind by raids into Acadia. The forces of regular French and British troops in America were never large, and their warfare was inconclusive. The English made two feeble thrusts in the direction of Quebec; an English fleet was to sail up the St. Lawrence, but it never did. The French attacked into New York via Lake Champlain, but without particular effect. Yet this desultory warfare, meaningless in terms of military accomplishment, had a decisive effect that neither the French nor the British governments appreciated, although they both had warnings of it. As early as 1710, an astute and anonymous French officer wrote a report to Paris, which he called a *Memoire sur la Nouvelle Angleterre*, and which is preserved in the Archives de la Marine:

"There is an antipathy between the English of Europe and those of America who will not endure troops from England even to guard their forts," he wrote. He added that, if the French colonies should fall, then the English would control the continent from Newfoundland to Florida, and "Old England will not imagine that these various provinces will then unite, shake off the yoke of the English monarchy, and erect themselves into a democracy."

A year later, a colonel King of the royal artillery had this complaint to file with the Home Office:

"You'll find in my Journal what Difficultyes we mett with through the Misfortune that the Coloneys were not inform'd of our Coming two Months sooner, and through the Interestedness, ill Nature, and Sowerness of these People, whose Government, Doctrine, and Manners, whose Hypocracy and canting, are insupportable . . . 'tis easy to determine the Respect and Obedience her Majesty may reasonably expect from them."

The antipathy arose from the fact that the English colonists, who had now been in America for ninety years, long enough to have produced a third generation, were no longer so much English as they were American. To the extent they were English, they resembled the Englishmen of almost a century ago; they impressed the modern Englishmen as being old-fashioned and cranky. To the extent that they were new people, Americans, they were outspoken. They gratuitously advised the English army as to how to fight a war in the forest. They had been too long used to directing their own affairs to take kindly to abrupt orders from anyone else. Unlike Englishmen at home, the Americans all bore arms and were quite capable of violence. Further, under the harsh conditions of frontier life, they had become pragmatic egalitarians for whom the exquisitely patterned manners of eighteenth-century Europe had neither charm nor meaning. The English army officers saw the Americans as a clutter of backwoods bumpkins; they were contemptuous of them and rude to them. For their part, the Americans resented English insolence, and thought the English stupid for despising their perfectly sound advice. The Americans thought of themselves as loyal Englishmen, but they could hardly love the strange new Englishmen who called them "colonials" in such a way as to imply they were a particularly low order of animal life. The antipathy was mutual and it grew as the number of English troops increased.

This situation was potentially perilous to both France and England, yet neither nation saw it for what it was. Two prescient officers did, but not their governments. But it would have been difficult for eighteenth-century Europeans to have grasped the fact that a new kind of people was evolving in a savage land thousands of miles away, or that Europeans could evolve into another kind of people, given other conditions of life, or that, if this could occur, the new people could be dangerous to the interests of their mother country. In any case, the French did not take immediate advantage of the situation to try to make allies of the Americans and widen the growing breach between New England and Old England—not till nearly a century had passed when it would be too late to save New France. Nor did the English try to cultivate the friendship of their American kinsmen or establish a special relationship with them that would have assured a continuing American allegiance to the Crown. Instead, they acted in such a way as to inform the Americans of their difference.

The eleven-year-long war ended in defeat for the Sun King, who, nearing the end of his life, with his last years saddened by the deaths of several of his children as well as by the ruin of nearly all his hopes of military glory, at last assented to the Treaty of Utrecht. This was a series of linked treaties that, like the war, principally concerned European affairs, but vitally affected American ones. The important provisions, so far as North America was concerned, spelled out a pattern of future disasters. The provisions were these:

England won recognition of the Five Nations of the Iroquois as British subjects. Perhaps the French would never have agreed to this had they known that the Iroquois had made a treaty with the English, ceding all their lands to the English Crown, and identifying their land, by right of conquest, as running from New

York to Illinois and including areas around the Great Lakes. They claimed to have conquered the Huron and Illinois tribes, or in any case to be the overlords of those people. Thus, when France recognized the Iroquois as British subjects and when the English had made their treaty with the Iroquois, the result was that England had provided herself with a cause of war against the French, to be brought out at any time England decided to make good her claim to Iroquois lands in New France.

Next, according to the Treaty of Utrecht, France was allowed to keep Cape Breton Island, which commanded the entrance to the Gulf of St. Lawrence. The island could be used just as well as a base from which to attack New England as it could be used to defend French Canada, and here the French built the strongest, most modern fortification in North America, and called it Louisbourg. The English, however, obtained Newfoundland, the Hudson's Bay Territory, and Acadia from France. No boundary lines were drawn so as to mark these lands off from Canada, and the western boundaries of the English colonies were left undefined. The architects of Utrecht seemed to know that any attempt to draw boundaries would mean resumption of the war, and no one wanted to resume the war at this time, particularly not for the sake of vague, snowy forests thousands of miles away on the other side of the world. At the same time, they probably knew that to fail to draw boundaries would mean a resumption of the war at some future day.

So there was peace in Europe, but in North America the war never stopped, and the Acadian peasants were still caught in the middle of it. They were now British subjects, according to the treaty, but their Jesuit priests told them they owed allegiance first to the Church and next to the king of France. The priests meanwhile encouraged and sometimes led their Indian converts on raids across Acadia and into that part of the Massachusetts colony that now is Maine, and from Quebec, the governor of New France supplied matériel for guerrilla operations while maintaining the polite fiction that France was at peace with England and was in no way responsible for the depredations committed by a few savage tribes.

During the War of the Spanish Succession, the French managed to give fitful support to their woebegone colony at Biloxi. The fur traders began also to move freely in the interior of the continent, north and west to the Dakotas, west and south to New Mexico, onto the Great Plains. Since their venturing into what the French called Louisiana was also a venturing into a region the Spanish still called Florida, the Spanish government protested. But the Spanish objections were brushed aside because Spain was in no position to fight over the matter; because the French promised Spain to convert the Indians and keep heretics out of the new lands; and finally because the French claimed the interior of the continent by right of discovery. But the French did little other than file a claim to the heart of North America. By 1712, the total population of the Biloxi colony, including troops, government officials, and priests, was only 380, divided into little stockaded settlements at Biloxi, Mobile, Ship Island, and Dauphin Island. Antoine de la Mothe Cadillac, sent by Versailles to be the new governor of Louisiana, reported back that "I have seen the garden on Dauphin Island, which had been described to me as a terrestrial paradise. I saw there three seedling pear trees, three seedling apple trees, a little plum tree about three feet high, with seven bad plums on it, a vine some thirty feet long, with nine bunches of grapes, some of them withered or rotten and some partly ripe, about forty plants of French melons, and a few pumpkins. This is M. d'Artaguette's terrestrial paradise, M. de Remonville's Pomona, and M. de Manderville's Fortunate Islands. Their stories are mere fables." He added that the soil would produce neither grains nor vegetables. To this, the royal intendant, M. d'Artaguette, added that there were only ten or twelve families who tried to cultivate the soil, and that all the inhabitants were naturally lazy. "It is necessary to send out girls and laboring men," he reported to the court. Then, still pursuing the dream that had first sent Europeans venturing to the New World, he wrote, "I am convinced that we shall easily discover mines when persons are sent us who understand that business." La Mothe Cadillac dismissed the intendant's optimism as puerile. "In my opinion," he wrote, "this country is not worth a straw. The inhabitants are eager to be taken out of it. The soldiers are always grumbling, and with reason." A priest, the Curé De la Vente, added his report: the inhabitants "are nearly all drunkards, blasphemers, and enemies of everything good."

Reading these reports, Louis XIV came to a decision. His heirs were dying, he was losing the war, money was draining away, and so was his life. The Biloxi colony produced nothing, and maintaining it was an endless expense. So he leased out not only the Biloxi colony but the whole, huge territory from the Gulf of Mexico to the headwaters of the Mississippi River, from the Allegheny Mountains to the Rockies, to a merchant named Antoine Crozat. The lease was for a period of fifteen years, during which Crozat was to receive a monopoly of all the trade, wholesale, retail, foreign, and domestic, of all this territory, plus all that its mines could produce—except for a one-fourth share, which was to be the king's. Crozat could also send one ship a year to Guinea for black slaves. The king would pay the governor, his officers, and the troops for the first nine years. After that, Crozat would have to pay them. The merchant was also to transport each year, and maintain at his own expense, a specified number of colonists. The laws of the land would be royal edicts, sent from Versailles, and the governor was to rule by martial law.

Like many a merchant before or since, Crozat tried to keep expenses low to maximize his profits. As a result, he recruited his male colonists from the gutters and his females from hospitals and houses of correction—the latter, in the words of a contemporary, being "so ugly that inhabitants are in no hurry to take them." Little or no attempt was made to explore and develop the potentially rich interior of Crozat's leasehold; the colony clung to the soggy Gulf Coast and did a miserable little trade for cash in furs, birds, and maize with a Spanish settlement at Pensacola. Some of the colonists proposed to earn a living by fishing but wanted the king to provide their fishing tackle. The colonists were not in any case allowed to work for themselves, only for Crozat, with the rather natural result that they did almost no work at all. When they asked permission at least to trade with one another at a retail level, Governor La Mothe Cadillac spurned the suggestion as seditious and swore he would hang anyone of them who did. So harsh was his martial law that the colonists were forbidden to hold meetings without his permission. The little trade with the Spanish ceased when the authorities in Madrid learned of it and ordered it stopped; there remained only an unprofitable barter between the colonists and their Indian neighbors; no mines were found; no one believed in the future of the colony. For Crozat, as it had been for Louis XIV, the venture was an expensive fiasco, and five years after he had bought the lease to a potential empire, Crozat gave his charter back to the Crown.

Louis XIV had meanwhile died, full of years and sorrows, leaving behind him a memory of vainglorious grandeur and a unified but nearly bankrupt kingdom in the charge of the duc d'Orléans, who acted as regent for the young Louis XV. It amused Orléans to sell Crozat's leasehold to one John Law, a Scot resident in Paris, who was one of the great flimflam artists of all time. Together, they envisioned a scheme to rescue France from financial disaster by selling shares in Louisiana. They formed the Mississippi Company, also called the Western Company, in 1717, endowing it with enormous powers and privileges. These included the right to collect the royal taxes; a monopoly of the French slave trade, the tobacco trade, and the profits of the royal mint. Notes of the royal bank, and all certificates of public debt, were to be accepted at par for company shares. The ingenious John Law not only issued prospectuses stating there was gold in

Louisiana, but he also had ingots displayed in the shop windows of Paris. These ingots were alleged to have come from the newly discovered land of El Dorado, and they were just as false as the claims made for them. But, besides gold, Law's prospectuses said, the land was one of milk and honey; illustrations showed men and women dressed in silks and jewels, with slaves attending them. Fruit rained down from the trees; crops sprang up out of the ground without cultivation; everyone rode in carriages; the climate of Louisiana was always that of May in Paris. So Law's propaganda said, and so said the regent, and there for all to see were those gold bricks in the vitrines, and from the moment the shares went on sale, the Mississippi Bubble began to swell. Perhaps the bourgeoisie are always the most gullible of purchasers of get-rich-quick schemes; in any event otherwise sensible people literally fought in the streets to buy Mississippi Company shares —which, after all, were the same as shares in the royal bank itself. The prices of the shares bounded to incredible heights, and from these to utterly insane ones. When the money started to flood in, colonists were dispatched to found the city of New Orleans, which would be the splendid capital of Louisiana. "The government," said the duc de Saint-Simon, "wished to establish effective settlements in these vast countries, after the example of the English, and therefore, in order to people them, vagabonds and beggars, male and female, including many women of the town, were seized for the purpose both in Paris and throughout France." This was not precisely a close following of the English example, but Saint-Simon thought it close enough, remarking that in this way we purge France and populate Louisiana. But to preserve the True Faith in Louisiana, only Catholic derelicts and whores would be sent there; Jewish and Protestant ones were not allowed.

In the canebrakes of a malarial country, the familiar lesson was taught again: a viable colony simply cannot be created if its human ingredients are shiftless good-for-nothings, and particularly if these unfortunates are to be ruled by martial law in accordance with edicts promulgated by masters who are thousands of miles away, know nothing of the country and its peculiar problems, and have not the slightest interest in hearing whatever the colonists might try to tell them. One sensible step was taken, however. When it at last appeared that whores were still running a poor second to Indian girls as the popular choice of the French colonists, virtuous orphan girls were sent out to Louisiana under the auspices and protection of the Ursuline nuns. The French government provided them with little trunks, containing a kind of government-issue trousseau; the girls were therefore known as *filles à la cassette*. To send these virgins out to the kind of prospective bridegrooms who awaited them might not seem altogether in the best interests of the girls, but then they might have fared worse in France. They were married off under the eyes of the nuns, and today a remarkable biological fact may be noted: none of the people of French descent in New Orleans today can trace his or her ancestry back to the whores, but all can trace their descent from the *filles à la cassette*. Apart from sending out a more acceptable kind of woman, the French government did little else than put unreasonable restrictions on its colonists. No one could leave the colony without permission; no one entered it except upon government order. No foreign ships could call there; all had to buy everything from the Mississippi Company, none could sell anything except to the company; in either case the company made a two-hundred-percent profit. Spanish currency, the principal means of exchange, was discounted at eighty percent; freedom of assembly, speech, and action were all expressly forbidden. Parkman said, "the settlers, looking always to France to supply their needs and protect them against their own improvidence, were in the habit of butchering for food the livestock sent them for propagation. The remedy came in the shape of a royal edict forbidding any colonist to kill, without permission of the authorities, any cow, sheep, or lamb belonging to himself, on pain of a fine of 300 livres; or to kill any horse, cow or bull belonging to another, on pain of death."

Of course the Louisiana colony produced nothing for the company, but then, this was not the point of the exercise. The whole scheme was a stock swindle, and when the shares stood at their dizziest height and when just before the shareholders would learn they would never realize a penny on their investments, John Law skipped off to Brussels with his gains and let the Mississippi Bubble burst behind him. The failure of the company in 1720 brought down with it the royal bank which was the company's chief creditor, and the resignation of Orléans as regent. From the founding of the Biloxi colony till Crozat took it over, it had cost France 150,000 livres a year; Crozat, the king, and the Mississippi Company had put another eight million livres into Louisiana with nothing whatever to show for their money. The company had shipped overseas some 7,020 colonists to join the 380 souls of the Biloxi settlement, and yet when the Bubble burst, the population had dwindled, by natural death, disease, starvation, and by escape, to 5,420. There were, in addition, 600 black slaves. By contrast, the New England colonies were becoming profitable to England and prosperous in their own right, and their populations were naturally and rapidly increasing. Louisiana brought nothing but bankruptcy to France.

It was nevertheless the policy of France to maintain its Louisiana settlements after the Bubble burst. The reasons were the military ones envisioned by Frontenac and La Salle. More colonists were sent out from France, and, more wisely, the French government also planted a group of Germans along the Mississippi River. These hardy souls gardened, worked as hard as any proverbial Germans, and began to prosper. The expense, however, continued to outrun any returns, even though the colony did begin to amount to something. Trade between the colony and France was permitted; the colonists were allowed to buy goods at rates lower than those of the earlier two-hundred-percent profit.

Plantations began to take form along the Mississippi, but then came Indian wars with the Chickasaws and the Natchez tribes, and to the normal expenses of operating an unprofitable colony, the expenses of war were added. Meanwhile, despite continued immigration, the white population declined instead of increasing, and so little food was raised that, for three months in one year, the colonists' staple food was the seeds of reeds and wild grasses. The black population, however, increased as the white one declined; the slaves promised soon to outnumber the whites. There were two thousand of them in Louisiana shortly after the Bubble collapsed, and the brutality which the French accorded them had made the slaves dangerous. Some of them conspired to lead their brothers to a massacre of all the whites. Fortunately for the French, the conspiracy was discovered only just in time and the conspirators were executed.

From this point, the fortunes of France in America ran steadily downhill while those of England burgeoned. The transatlantic empire named for the glorious Sun King never took form, essentially because no serious efforts were made to create it. The machine-like government of Louis XIV was powerful enough to have directed the energies of the French into any path the Grand Monarch desired. But the king and his ministers were never as concerned as the English were with the creation of overseas empires. Louis sought to enlarge his borders and to make his kingdom the dominant land power in Europe. All during his reign, the English sought to control the seas, to expand their colonies at the expense of Spain and France, and meanwhile to join any alliance that had as its purpose preventing any nation from becoming a preponderant power on the continent.

Insofar as popular will counted for something at the time, these different policies reflected a difference between the French and English peoples. Perhaps this difference was in part genetic: the English were seafaring and the French were not. However this may be, there were certainly those differences in traditions, history, government, and religion that tended to make the ordinary Englishman much more competent and willing than the ordinary Frenchman to undertake the creation of a new civilization in a wilderness. The number of English who came to America was out of all proportion to the number of French who came, and whereas most of the English came voluntarily, most of the French did not. The two peoples, moreover, entertained very different expectations of the New World. The English expected to create a community of overseas Englishmen, and the French expected to return to France. The Englishmen who read the glowing recruiting posters in London might not have believed them, but great numbers of them signed on for passage to America; the bourgeoisie who excitedly read John Law's posters in Paris might not have believed those reports of ladies and gentlemen in silks, riding in carriages in a perpetual May sunshine, but they bought John Law's shares in the hope of becoming wealthy enough to be able to dress in silks and ride in carriages in Paris. Then, when the Mississippi Company failed, they fixed the blame not so much on John Law as upon America.

Three wars finished the business. In 1739, the War of Jenkins' Ear found the Spanish alleging that the English were illegally enlarging on trading rights they had wrung from Spain at the time of Utrecht. France entered this war on the side of Spain. Five years later, the war became more general; Europe knew it as the War of the Austrian Succession, in which France sided with Prussia to defeat Austria, with England allying itself with Austria to preserve the balance of power in Europe. For America, these wars meant an intensification of the always-smoldering guerrilla warfare on the frontier borders, with the English colonists forming militias to work along with British units, and with one operation mounted by Massachusetts militiamen. It was a curious escapade; indeed, militarily speaking, it was a lugubrious one. But however farcical it may have been, the astounding result was that the colonial militia captured Louisbourg, the most potent French fortress in America. To the furious amazement of the colonists, England gave Louisbourg back to the French when peace was made in 1748 at Aix-la-Chapelle, in return for the French surrender of Madras to the English in India. The third and last war, which Europe knew as the Seven Years' War, but which for America was a ten-year-long continuation and ultimate end of the French and Indian Wars, began in part as a result of a collision between English settlers and Frenchmen in the Ohio River valley. It otherwise represented a much-belated effort on the part of France to emulate the English and build a great colonial empire based on sea power. The result was the utter ruin of such hopes. The French were everywhere defeated: at sea, in America, in India. France was brought in the end to the Treaty of Paris in 1763, where the victorious English stripped her of Acadia, Canada, islands in the Caribbean, her possessions in India, and all of Louisiana lying east of the Mississippi. France was permitted to retain New Orleans, but the British received trading rights there and free navigation of the Mississippi River. In the same treaty, France's ally, Spain, had to cede to England the two Floridas, which included territories in what are now the states of Louisiana, Alabama, and Florida, and all other Spanish possessions east of the Mississippi; in return, England gave Cuba back to Spain. All of North America east of the Mississippi was now English. All that was left of New France was that part of Louisiana lying west of the Mississippi to the Rocky Mountains, and north from the Gulf of Mexico to Canada. Geographically speaking, this was still an enormous territory, still the seat of a potential empire, but France was in no position to hold it, or exploit it. All her long adventures in North America had been a constant drain on French resources, never a source of profit. A few hours after France signed the Treaty of Paris with the English, she signed a secret treaty with Spain. She ceded to Spain all her holdings west of the Mississippi, including the settlement at New Orleans. France wanted to rid herself of a white elephant and, at the same time, to give it to

Spain before the English changed their minds and took it for themselves. The Spanish were persuaded to believe they had thereby acquired a kind of buffer zone between the English colonies and their still-valuable lands in Mexico.

In surrendering all their pretensions to North America, the French abandoned their overseas countrymen to whatever mercies the English and Spanish might show them. The Acadians received none. The Massachusetts colonists regarded Acadia as the source of too much bloodshed; the Acadians were judged to be traitors for having preserved a loyalty to the French Crown and the Roman Church during the time they had legally been British subjects. They were turned out of their homes, and their possessions were given to Protestant Scots immigrants, who renamed the province Nova Scotia. The Acadians were cast adrift, with nothing more than the clothes on their backs, to wander into what exile they could find. Eventually, several hundred of them joined their countrymen in the Mississippi settlements, only to find they were almost as unwelcome there as they were in the English colonies. They moved into the watery jungle of the bayou country, becoming—and still today largely remaining— the faintly despised and, as often romanticized, Cajuns, a primitive people supporting themselves by hunting and fishing. Their name appears to be a corruption of "Acadians."

With more generosity than foresight, the English did not similarly dispossess the habitants of Quebec. They were allowed to remain and to retain their religion. But there was now Nova Scotia to the east, and Highland troops were quartered among them, and a Protestant Scots-Irish settlement was planted west of them in what is now the province of Ontario. The status of the French Canadians became what it largely remains today: quite similar to that of the American black man, who is acknowledged to have civil rights equivalent to those of the whites but who in fact is not permitted to enjoy them.

In the Mississippi settlements, the French simply could not

believe that their king had given them to the Spanish. The French troops protested their loyalty to the French Crown, only to be told their duty now was to be loyal soldiers of Spain. The colonists were not to be repatriated. A Spanish governor named Antonio de Ulloa, a naval officer, scholar, and man of infinite tact, arrived in 1766. Appreciating the hostility of the colonists, De Ulloa wisely refrained from making a public demonstration of his credentials, but sought to rule through the French governor, Philippe Aubry, who agreed to collaborate with him. He could do no more till Spanish troops were sent to him. The colonists meanwhile refused to obey either their own governor or the Spanish one and sent a desperate cry to Paris.

"What harm have we done in shaking off a foreign yoke which was made still more heavy and crushing by the hand which imposed it?" they asked in a letter to Louis XV. "What offense have we committed in claiming back our laws, our country, our sovereign, and in consecrating to him our everlasting love?"

Louis replied that they had committed the crime of disobedience and that they should accept Spanish rule forthwith. Instead, the colonists opted for independence. They asked the English, who had now taken possession of formerly Spanish Pensacola, to send them men and arms. The English refused, but the French colonists forced De Ulloa to leave New Orleans, and for the space of several months, a community of Europeans in America was independent of Europe.

News of this revolt brought dissension in the Spanish court. One of the king's counselors advocated giving Louisiana back to the French, pointing out that the French had never got anything out of it but expensive headaches. The majority of the council eventually said no, arguing that while the French at New Orleans detested the Spanish, and much as the colony was an economic rathole, it was vitally important to have the Mississippi River as a border with the English. Since between the Mississippi and New Mexico there was nothing but a vast empty space on the map, any power (particularly the English) might establish itself there at any time. If the Spanish gave the western part of Louisiana back to France, and then the English took it away from the French, the English would shortly be at the gates of Mexico. It was best to have this buffer zone; and once this argument was carried, Spain sent out a general officer, Alejandro O'Reilly, with thirty-six hundred soldiers.

O'Reilly invited the ringleaders of the rebellious French to a reception and a dinner, so that they could, in a civilized manner, discuss matters. When his dinner guests had assembled, O'Reilly had five of them taken out and hanged and sent the rest to rot in the dungeons at Havana. The Conquistadors, it would seem, had returned. All that was left of France in North America were a few thousand exiles living as best they could among their enemies, both Indian and European; a scattering of place-names given to lakes, rivers, settlements, and territories in honor of Frenchmen more visionary than their kings, and two names, Louisiana and New Orleans, given in honor of the two Bourbons who, more than anyone else, were responsible for the ruin of New France.

PART TWO

The Pursuit

of

Property

12

It Was All
Quite Shocking

THE American Revolution was neither wholly American nor revolutionary. Rather, it represented the transatlantic evolution of European ideas whose origins were as old as Europe itself. Nor was the War of Independence a purely American one; in the beginning, it was not even a war for independence. The war was the proximate cause, and became a part, of another general European war for trade and colonies. This time it was England that was the preponderating power, standing alone against France, Holland, Spain, Sweden, Denmark, Portugal, Russia, Prussia, and Turkey, in addition to fighting her rebellious colonials. The military evolutions that really mattered did not take place in America, but rather in India, Africa, the West Indies, and on the high seas. The Americans did not win the war: the British eventually stopped fighting it, to enter a general agreement among the warring powers. Contrary to fond belief, the United States of America was not born in Philadelphia in 1776, with the umbilical cord subsequently snipped by the French at Yorktown. The Declaration of Independence was merely an announcement of pregnancy. The live, but still somewhat premature birth of the new nation took place in 1783, during a secret meeting in Vienna, between agents for the thirteen colonies and those of the British Home Office—behind the backs of America's principal allies, France and Spain, who still had designs of their own upon North America. In sum, America was conceived and delivered in Europe. The infant nation's first real step toward independence, or weaning, was taken when America bought nominal possession of the keys to her continent from Napoleon. This step, the purchase of Louisiana, was also taken in Europe; the purchase itself was a European idea. But by this time, the child of Europe was no longer precisely European, although it resembled its European parents and was still greatly dependent upon them.

"Almost immediately after the peace of 1763," says the French historian Henri Doniol, France "sought in the tendency of the English colonies to revolt against their mother country the occasion by which we could avenge ourselves on England and tear up the Treaty of Paris."

Agents provocateurs were accordingly sent out from France to America to foment all the mischief they could between the English colonists and Great Britain. The duc de Choiseul, who was in charge of this operation, said he did not think he would live to see the day, but that he was sure France would find an opportunity to reestablish herself in North America.

The tendency of the colonists to revolt had arrived with the *Mayflower*. It was inherent in their religion. The tendency had grown all during the French and Indian Wars, nourished by that mutual antipathy between the Americans and the British that prescient observers had noted. But the tendency to revolt merely remained a tendency until the French power in America had been destroyed. With their common enemy vanquished, the Americans and the British were left alone to consider one another.

By 1763, the English colonies were no longer a few scattered settlements of huts and cabins clinging fearfully to a wild seacoast. Harvard was more than a century old; Philadelphia was a city of brick and stone, second only to London in English population, and, being young and vigorously growing, Philadelphia was much more exciting than London in certain respects. The total population of the colonies was in the neighborhood of two million, and in addition to those of English stock, it included Welshmen, Scots, Irishmen, Germans, Dutchmen, Swedes, and French Huguenots. All lived under English law and spoke the English language, but the colonies lacked a sense of common purpose. Instead of political cohesion, there were mutual animosities.

One root cause of the animosities and of the antipathy to Great Britain lay in the mercantile theory responsible for the planting of colonies in the New World. From Tudor times on, the plan was that colonies would produce foodstuffs and raw material for export to Britain, and import from Britain manufactured goods in exchange. This trade would be wholly carried in British ships, manned by Britons, and all port duties and customs fees would accrue to the Crown. In turn, the Crown would provide the armed force necessary to safeguard both the shipping and the colonies. Theoretically, everyone would profit: the colonists, the merchants, the manufacturers, the state. The theory was given the force of law by Navigation Acts, passed in Parliament, spelling out the rules and prescribing penalties for their violation. The theory worked in fact; the colonies became Britain's largest market, and both they and the mother country profited and prospered under this arrangement.

But unfortunately for both the theory and its practice, the ocean was wide. A colonist wanted what he needed the instant he needed it, not whenever a shipper might be able to send it to him. British law might forbid the colonists to smelt iron, but since they needed ironware, they found bog iron and set up their own forges no matter what the law had to say. British law required sugar planters to send their cane to Britain to be refined, but the colo-

nists soon discovered that the French in the Caribbean were re-
fining their sugar on the islands, which were closer to the colonies
than Britain was, and that they could buy sugar there for less
money than they had to pay for sugar refined in Britain. It also
occurred to them that the North American forests were Britain's
prime source of marine lumber, and that they could use this as
well as shipwrights in England could. What with one thing and
another, and given the ad hoc quality of colonial life, plus a religion that was inherently defiant of authority, it was not long in
the colonial experience before a thriving and entirely illegal trade
was being conducted between the British colonies, primarily by
the northern ones, and the French and Spanish islands in the Caribbean. The smugglers, which is what the New England merchants were, developed a triangular trade based on molasses, rum,
and slaves. They bought molasses in the Caribbean, made rum of
it in New England, traded the rum for slaves in Africa, and sold
the slaves in the Caribbean for molasses.

Up till the Treaty of Paris was signed, virtually none of the
colonists so much as imagined political independence from Great
Britain. Even during the Revolution, a majority of colonists opposed such a notion. But practically from the founding of the first
colony, almost all of them could certainly imagine self-government, and they could also imagine their right to protest against
any rules or laws which, passed by Parliament or proclaimed by
royal governors, they found objectionable. For that matter, they
were only too likely to flout such laws as they made for themselves. Throughout the entire colonial period, including all the
years of the French and Indian Wars, they engaged in illegal
manufacture, in a widespread commerce carried out in their own
ships, and ignored port and customs officials and such laws as did
not appeal to them. They also kept up a brisk trade with the
enemy in wartime and then demanded that the regular British
forces defend them. During the Seven Years' War, which ended

with the Treaty of Paris, the colonies were asked to send delegates to a congress held in Albany, New York, to consider matters relative to their common defense. Acting on a British suggestion, one of the delegates, Benjamin Franklin of Pennsylvania, proposed the "Albany Plan of Union." This envisioned a concerted action by the thirteen colonies, with contributions of money, matériel, and militiamen prorated according to the different resources of the several colonies. The delegates agreed, but the colonial legislatures subsequently rejected the plan their representatives adopted. In the event, only three colonies agreed to furnish their quotas of militia, and everywhere the smuggling and tax-dodging continued, and trade with the enemy went on as usual. Far from being willing to share some of the cost of their own defense, the Americans bitterly opposed the suggestion that any of the burden should in any way fall upon themselves.

From one point of view, the Americans were well within their rights in demanding that the home government protect them. That was part of the mercantile theory. It was also their right, as British subjects, to expect the protection of the Crown against the king's enemies. But from another point of view, it is also the duty of the subject to help defend the king from his enemies. British subjects in Britain paid the duties and taxes that supported the military power of Britain; why should the British subjects in America enjoy a tax-exempt status in this regard? Particularly when this power was used in their behalf? Perhaps more to the point, what right had they to claim special protection under the mercantile theory, when they connived at all of *their* responsibilities according to the same theory? The colonials insisted they should pay only such taxes as they levied upon themselves, through their own legislatures, for purely local purposes. No one else in the British empire made the same claim. It seemed to a majority of members of Parliament that the Americans were trying to make too much of a good thing; that they were saying "What's yours is mine, and what's mine is my own." Parliament began to consider legislation to put an end to the privileged status of the Americans.

Parliament and the American colonies were now embarked upon a collision course, with the Americans alleging that if they enjoyed a special status, it was right that they should, because their circumstances were unique. Both were impelled along their converging courses by social forces beyond their control, and of which they were probably unaware, for the eighteenth century was so bursting with startling ideas, inventions, and social theories that a thought became action, and action, a fact, before anyone had time to grasp all the implications of what had occurred. Thomas Newcomen's steam engine, for example, was pumping water out of British coal pits in 1702, but it is more than doubtful if anyone seeing this immediately recognized that the Industrial Revolution was at hand. It is even less likely that anyone then foresaw the creation of enormous urban proletariats. But steam had been harnessed, and machines of all sorts were appearing in an age of invention, and what could be plainly seen was a sudden and great increase in the population of Britain, as work and goods became more plentiful. Parliament's response to the growth of British population and to the problems created by the drift of Britons from the country to the cities was to acquire colonies to accommodate the overflow. Today, with a bit more experience of an industrial society and its resultant population explosion, we might say this response was somewhat naïve, but it did represent an honest effort to solve a problem whose terms were then obscure.

The position of Parliament in the latter half of the eighteenth century was quite different from what it had ever been. The days of absolute princes who ruled by divine right were dead and buried in Britain. The Hanoverian line had been called to the throne, with the clear understanding that the king had no power that Parliament was bound to respect. In Tudor and Stuart times, colonies had been planted in America by royal charter, and it was to the king that the colonists applied at need. A quarrel between colonists and the Crown would be one between the people and their king. But Parliament was now the supreme government in what was well on its way to becoming the British empire. Thirty-one British possessions around the world were now governed by a Cabinet that was in turn responsible to Parliament. If the American colonists had a quarrel with the government in Britain, it was not a quarrel between a people and their king, but between one group of British people and another. The point was appreciated by the Parliamentarian Edmund Burke and by Thomas Jefferson and Benjamin Franklin in America. Together they proposed that an American Parliament be elected to govern the colonies; they envisioned an arrangement very similar to today's British Commonwealth. Here was an answer to almost every difficulty; unfortunately, the eighteenth century was not the time to imagine a commonwealth of coequal dominions. The British Parliament was then trying to give uniform order to an empire, not to break it up into component parts. And the colonies were no more ready to act together for their commonweal than when they had refused to accept the Albany Plan of Union after the recently ended war.

Religious, social, economic, and political differences separated the colonies. The Anglican Virginia planter, with his pretensions to gentility based on a landed estate, was likely to be scornful of the Puritan New Englander who drove sharp bargains in manacled slaves while quoting Scripture to his own purposes and braying his nasal hymns. The New England sea captain, with his pretensions to being a hard, but honest and God-fearing trader, was equally contemptuous of the Virginia aristocrat who philosophized over glasses of Madeira about the rights of man while slaves produced the wealth he spent on cockfights. And no one had the slightest use for the Philadelphia Quakers, whose humility was a form of arrogance and whose pacifist doctrines led them righteously to refuse to vote money for the powder and shot necessary to protect the German farmers outside the city from being hacked to pieces by Indian war parties. Nor, within any single colony, did the English, Scots, Irish, and Welsh get along with one another any better than they had in the British Isles; the Germans, Dutch, Swedes, and French Huguenots among them kept to their own communities. Nor were the interests of the farmers identical with those of the city merchants and workmen; both were different from those of the mariners, and all were different from those of the frontiersman who in hindsight may be seen as more of a pariah than a visionary pioneer. At no time was America ever the social melting pot that some early twentieth-century optimists thought it was. There were too many lumps of self-interest that simply would not melt. What social mobility there was, was vertical, not horizontal. But politically, if not socially, something did begin to melt in the pot. Their unique geographic position led the colonists to appreciate the peril inherent in their isolation, to think of themselves as Americans, and, simultaneously, to see in their isolation a unique opportunity to put into practice certain revolutionary political theories based on scientific discoveries made in Europe during the sixteenth and seventeenth centuries.

The development of a political structure in which diverse if not inimical populations could agree to coexist to some common purpose took slow form throughout the entire colonial experience, without any of the colonists being particularly aware of it until all suddenly seemed "self-evident," as Thomas Jefferson put it. But what was not so evident was that it all began in the earliest moments of voyaging to the New World, when Copernicus made the sun stand still, turned the earth into a minor planet, and thereby destroyed the foundations of medieval faith in the Church of Rome. It was in the next century, the seventeenth, that Galileo confirmed the heliocentric theory (although the Inquisition forced him to deny it), and that Newton, Bacon, and Descartes followed closely in, dealing one blow after another to the now-tottering structure of the True Faith. Briefly, these men broke away from the medieval logic that sought to fit all things into God's plan. They instead discovered that a rigorous examination of the particular could, by inductive reasoning, enable a man to form a valid generalization. And in their practice of what we now call scientific method, they (and particularly Descartes) discovered that all in the universe obeyed mathematical laws. Mathematics could itself be used to express thoughts, and as a means of forming valid extrapolations into the realms of what could not as yet be directly seen or experienced. It also became apparent that the simplest answers were the correct ones; that the properties of all things, living and inanimate, obeyed what the scientists came to regard as natural laws. These discoveries were torture for men like Galileo and Descartes, who wished to live within the Holy Faith, but it appeared quite evident that God the Father, seated upon His throne in heaven, was, if He existed, probably just as much a prisoner of mathematical laws as anything else in all His Creation. As a consequence, miracles and divine intercession were simply out of the question. The concept of God as the compassionate Father and suffering Jesus began to give way to a concept of God as a mathematical, mechanical genius who, having created all things, had no further part to play: the universe ticked perpetually along, emotionless, neither good nor bad, but simply existing, obedient to its natural laws. It was possible to worship God as the Great Engineer, but not as a diety who had any personal interest in the worshiper.

So much was implicit in the scientific discoveries of the time, although the seventeenth century was hardly the one in which to make the point so plain. But it did occur to men, and to the Englishman John Locke in particular, to employ the new scientific method in an effort to discover the natural laws that governed human behavior. Locke took the view that if all things in nature obeyed natural laws, then those laws must be right, and good for those things—else they would not continue to exist. If this was true of nature, he thought, then it must also be true of men: there must be some natural law that distinguished what was right and good for men from what was wrong and bad. He presumed that man could not invent what was right for him any more than a stone could. What was right for him had already been decreed by natural law. Man's problem was to find out what that law was. Locke presumed man could do this by employing reason. He also presumed that all men were rational, be they Red Indians, Pomeranians, or even Irish. He further supposed that the natural laws governing human responses would equally apply to all men at all times everywhere, and not just to Englishmen in the seventeenth century. Locke also took the view that a man's mind is a *tabula rasa* at the moment of his birth, and therefore whatever he comes to think as an adult will be determined solely by his experience of his environment, including the opinions of the people he finds in it. He begins life neither good nor evil, any more than a pearl in an oyster is good or evil, but if he grows up to believe falsely and act wrongly, this can only be the result of his environment and education. Therefore, if man could only discover the natural laws that applied to him, and use them to clean up the environment and correct the education, why then human behavior would become perfect. And since all men everywhere would obey the same natural law that applied to men, then world brotherhood, mutual progress, and world government would not only be possible but inevitable if that natural law was obeyed.

Having said this much, Locke then supposed that men, as isolated individuals, could not by their own efforts in a state of nature obtain for themselves what was absolutely necessary to their existence. He conceived this to be life, liberty, and property. He maintained men had a natural right to life, liberty, and property —and by property, he meant real property, land; land enough to produce the necessities of their lives. He conceived of liberty as meaning each man's freedom to act without compulsion by another man. He by no means envisioned anarchy, but the volun-

[handwritten margin note: LITERALLY, A "BLANK TABLET"— A CLEAN SLATE]

tary assumption of such responsible tasks as each man was capable of undertaking for the good of all. So, Locke concluded, men must rationally agree to establish a government for the common good, a contract between the governed and the governors, the purpose of which would be to discover and enforce that natural law which would be good for all men at all times everywhere. The governed must be willing to listen to reason and obey its dictates; so must the governors. If the government were to break its contract, such as by unreasonably denying a man his life, liberty, or property, then it would be the duty of the governed to rebel and overthrow the government, precisely as it would be the government's duty to arrest the unreasonable criminal.

The Lockean view, like those of his scientific contemporaries, was triumphantly optimistic in its assertion that reason was the key to power and to the secrets of the universe. God was not all-powerful; it would seem that man had powers, too. The way was open now to a belief not just in salvation, but in the perfectibility of man—which could be achieved by the rational perfection of his social institutions.

The works of the scientists and of Locke in the seventeenth century were not widely known in their time. But in the eighteenth century, they found their public advocates. These included three prolific writers—Montesquieu, who argued that the best government would be one whose powers were both separated and balanced; the sardonic Voltaire, who believed that intellectual freedom was the *sine qua non* of any viable society; and the paranoid Rousseau, who believed that feelings were more to be trusted than thoughts. During this century, the number of magazines and newspapers explosively multiplied, and so did the number of men of letters. Literary salons and a secular intellectual community appeared in Europe—particularly in France and England. It was a community that with gathering excitement began to discuss the implications of Locke and the scientists, and its members included men of action and affairs. It was from this community that word spread out to the more general literate public, the more broadly based consumers of the books, magazines, and newspapers that interpreted and explained the new thought. One result was that the age of faith began to give way to an increasing skepticism in Europe. This went so far that the Catholic Church found it expedient to suppress the Jesuit Order. But the particularly important result, both for America and the world, was that the writings of Locke, Montesquieu, and Rousseau were read and reread by the future authors of the Declaration of Independence and the Constitution of the United States. These men began to talk in terms of "natural law," "unalienable rights," the "equality of man" at birth, and of "the pursuit of life, liberty and property." Lawyers began to hunt for "natural law" as avidly as any scientists and politicians. They sought to establish evidential facts by scientific method. From Montesquieu they seized upon the idea of the separation and balance of powers of government, conceiving of the three coequal powers of the legislative, executive, and judicial branches. They considered Rousseau's notion (a twisting of one of Locke's presumptions) that man is not only born with an unsullied mind, but that man is innately good, but subsequently corrupted by civilization. They also fell upon Rousseau's notion that a government should be a social contract, freely arrived at, in which the ultimate sovereignty resides in the whole population; that the purpose of this government is to mitigate the corruption caused by secular institutions.

The fact that there is a great deal of logically unsupportable hypothesizing in Locke, and a great deal more in Rousseau, is not nearly so impressive as the fact that much of this wishful thought is still believed today, and that it still governs the view that most Americans take of themselves, and of the world at large. This is because nowhere in the world did Locke's thought have more immediate appeal and bite than in colonial America. The frontier was then wide open: an infinity of land and (almost by definition) an infinity of possibilities were close at hand. Next, the conditions of life in colonial America not only invited, but demanded invention and experiment. An American pragmatism had begun to develop from the first colonial days, and this turn of thought was far from any theology, including the Puritan, but was a very close cousin of scientific method. Then again, Locke's argument, and Rousseau's, as to the purpose of a government, and to the nature of a government as being a freely determined, rational, and reciprocal contract, had a particular appeal to those colonists who not only had a considerable experience of self-government, but who also wished to give the color of thought to their desire to do as they pleased. In short, they found the new thought a wonderful rationalization. They could construe their smuggling and tax-dodging and furtive trading with the king's enemies to be somehow an obedience to "natural laws"; they could argue that the conduct of their affairs from Westminster was neither wise, rational, natural, or responsive to their innate right to life, liberty, and property.

It was not until after the Treaty of Paris in 1763 that all of these matters—the new thought, the sense of difference the colonists felt between themselves and the British at home, the first implications of the dawning industrial age, and the growing awareness of common political purposes among otherwise mutually antipathetic colonies—began to find a focus in America. The British Parliament quite unwittingly provided that focal point.

The British government, understanding that the lands west to the Mississippi, newly won from the French, could not be exploited by colonists unless they were made safe from Indians and defended against any future French or Spanish designs, dispatched several thousand British troops to garrison the northwestern frontiers. At the same time, the government sought to rationalize its revenues, and in 1764 Parliament passed the Sugar Act which called for the uniform collection of port duties throughout all British possessions. To the unpleasant surprise of Parliament, the American colonies objected—even though the

Sugar Act, also known as the Revenue Act of 1764, actually reduced the customs duties levied in America. Many Parliamentarians were understandably puzzled as to why the Americans, alone of all other British populations elsewhere in the world, should find it so objectionable to have duties levied on their trade, particularly when the effect of the act was to reduce them insofar as the Americans were concerned. Then, Parliament decreed that paper money, issued by the American colonies, could not be regarded as legal tender. From the central government's point of view, trade would simply be chaotic if everyone were free to print his own money; of course, there had to be only one coin of the realm, based on some commonly accepted standard. The British standard was the Carolingian pound sterling. It was difficult to understand what, if anything, the various bits of colonial paper were based upon. But what Parliament did not fully understand was that there was very little silver or any other coin available in the colonies, and that the bits of paper the colonials were using were in the nature of letters of credit based, eventually, on the sale of goods in British markets. In seeking to stop the issuance of what it thought was paper money, Parliament was actually destroying a system of credit; the tragedy was that neither Parliament nor the colonial merchants entirely grasped one another's point of view. Insofar as Parliament was concerned, the colonial howls of outraged protest were entirely uncalled for and quite shocking.

In 1765, Parliament passed the Stamp Act. There was no particular thought that the American colonies might find this objectionable; the act merely imposed stamps on legal documents, and proposed a schedule of taxes that were quite common throughout other European nations, and that no one in Britain found in any way exceptional. But Parliament was shortly deafened by the shrieks of editors, lawyers, and merchants in colonial America. In some bafflement, Parliament repealed the Stamp Act the following year, and in a mood that can only be described as one of goodwill, looked about for some sort of tax that these difficult people would find acceptable. The result, in 1767, was the Townshend Duties which taxed paper, paint, lead, and tea imported into the colonies. The transatlantic uproar was again immediate. Parliament obligingly repealed all the duties except the one on tea; this was a niggling sum, kept on merely as a token that, in yielding to the colonial objections in most regards, Parliament was nonetheless asserting its sovereign right to levy taxes on all subjects of the British empire.

Following repeal of the Stamp Act, and remission of all but one of the Townshend Duties, the angry noises of the Americans subsided, and a genuinely puzzled Parliament—and one certainly willing to compromise—sought to understand what the fuss was all about. Representatives of the colonies explained that it was not the amount of any particular tax their countrymen objected to, it was the principle of the thing. They took the view that, since they were not represented in Parliament, Parliament had no right to tax them. Here was a thought that flowed straight from the theories of Locke and Rousseau with regard to government being a social contract. A somewhat mystified government replied that Parliament did represent the colonies quite as much as it represented the home counties, Great Britain, and every other British population anywhere in the world. To be sure, the colonies sent no elected representatives to the House of Commons, but neither, for that matter, did many communities in Great Britain. Yet all were represented in the sense that the members of the House acted together as a sovereign body charged with the well-being of the entire empire. The American response to this was that if any community in Great Britain was not represented in Parliament, it ought to be—and this was a point with which a considerable number of Englishmen also agreed. Serious men of goodwill on both sides of the ocean began to search for a means of ensuring an equitable representation in Commons for every British community at home and abroad. Unfortunately, this noble thought was quite impractical. The British empire was already so diverse as to be unwieldy, and it would have been far better to have thought in terms of a commonwealth of self-governing dominions.

It is one thing to sit in London and look at a map of the world, find it splashed with British red, and think in terms of uniform rule throughout an empire, governed from the ancient and hallowed seat of power by the Thames. It is another thing to be a mud-spattered farmer, trying to burn stumps out of a wet bottomland, reliant on your own efforts and those of your immediate neighbors to wring some sort of living from the earth, and to imagine that you have anything in common with townsfolk thousands of miles away who ride in gilded carriages and say they've decided how much you'll pay for your tea when you don't have any silver to buy it with and they won't take goods in barter, and they won't let you come and talk to them about it. Then they want to send some soldiers out to western Pennsylvania somewhere, and you've never seen a soldier in your life, especially when you surely would have liked to have seen some of them most, such as last fall when everybody around your place had to get together to shoot the feathers off those damned red devils, and then those people who have nothing to do but ride in their carriages say you have to pay for the soldiers they sent to wherever it is out in Pennsylvania. It's all enough to make you think that if one of those government people set foot on your land, you'd have him off the place one way or another, and maybe feet first.

So you might think if you were that kind of farmer, and if this was the way matters were put to you, both by your own experience and by what you had heard people say about what a fellow had written about people's natural rights. If someone had come to your farm with a petition to send to the king, you might very well put your X on it, because you would have thought yourself a subject of the Crown, and you would have then believed that if the king only knew what kind of fools he had for ministers, he might do something about it.

Such a point of view, or mood, was never entirely understood in the House of Commons. Its members were instead appalled by the vitriolic language of colonial editors; by accounts of bands of ruffians, known as Sons of Liberty, capering around Liberty Trees before setting off to break windows, curse their betters, throw stones at soldiers, and bawl out slogans that could only be described as treasonous. Parliament's mood remained more puzzled than angry, and meanwhile Parliament hesitated to use its sovereign power to put down riots in the colonies by police action. Instead it was Parliament's desire to conciliate and to trust in the fact that most of the two million people in the colonies were law-abiding and faithful British subjects.

But in 1773, an event took place which Parliament could not ignore. The British East India Company had got itself into economic difficulties, and found itself with a huge surplus of Chinese tea on its hands. To help the company, Parliament granted it the right to sell its tea directly to American retail outlets. Thus the American middlemen would be cut out; thus the American consumer would pay a lower price for his tea; thus the consumers might consume a great deal more of it; thus the company could rid itself of its surplus without loss to itself. But the American middlemen in question were the American merchants who, in the colonial scheme of things, were men of wealth, power, and influence, and it was they in Boston who stirred up a mob that, disguised as Indians, boarded tea ships in Boston harbor and threw their cargoes over the side.

If this had been the first of a series of provocations, the reaction of Parliament would doubtless have been different. But for the past decade, affairs in the colonies seemed to have gone steadily downhill, with every conciliatory step by Parliament seeming to provoke a more steadfast intransigence on the part of the colonials, and this latest act was simply insupportable. It was not so much that tea was one of the most valuable cargoes of the age, or that drinking tea was more or less to be equated with being British, but rather that Parliamentary authority had been called into question just once too often. So Parliament ordered the port of Boston closed to shipping and rescinded the charter of the Massachusetts colony.

Shortly thereafter, Parliament delivered itself of the Quebec Act of 1774. Its intentions were entirely humanitarian and, in the context of the time, quite reasonable. The act guaranteed the conquered Canadian French the right to their own laws and religion, and it defined the boundaries of Quebec to be those wherein the majority of Europeans were French. The reaction of the American colonists was as unexpected as it was explosive. What Parliament failed to appreciate was the fact that the British colonists in America had regarded the French ones to have been their mortal enemies for 150 years; that the whole history of the New England colonies had been one of standing up to French-inspired and often enough French-led massacres by Indians of British men, women, and children. The American colonists immediately construed the Quebec Act to be pro-French, and what was worse, pro-Catholic. Furthermore, it seemed to bar colonists of British ancestry from access to the Ohio River valley and the Great Lakes region, and at all times in colonial history, there had been a well-developed hunger for new land. The colonies branded the Quebec Act an intolerable act—along with the Sugar Act, the repudiation of paper currency, the Stamp Act, the Townshend Duties, and the recently imposed closure of the port of Boston and rescinding of the Massachusetts charter. The colonists chose to view the Quebec Act as a final slap in the face, and there were riots in Boston.

Parliament responded to these riots by imposing martial law in Boston. The members of the House of Commons also promised to have treasonous Americans brought to London for trial, under the authority of an ancient law promulgated by Henry VIII. It would seem that the period of conciliation was over. The American colonists promptly responded by establishing Committees of Correspondence among the colonies, in order to share their information and see what mutual steps might be taken to oppose what they considered to be a British tyranny: a Continental Congress was assembled.

It must always be borne in mind that the committees, like the delegates to the colonial Congress, represented the viewpoint of a minority. But revolutions are never made by majorities. They are made by men with axes to grind, but who find insufficient opportunities to sharpen those axes, given the current state of affairs. As is generally the case, the men who made the revolution were, whatever their other qualities, both ruthless and cynical. At this first Congress, a plan for union with Great Britain was proposed, but after it had lost by only one vote, it was then decided to destroy all records that any such plan had been suggested. Instead, the delegates approved a boycott of all British trade, export and import. The Congress sent messages to the king, to the people of the several American colonies, to the people of Quebec, and the people of England. In fact, they sent messages to almost everyone in the world except to the members of either House of Parliament. Yet it was with Parliament, and with no one else, that their quarrel lay. The king of England was oppressing no one except perhaps his court, and then only by reason of his provincial German manners. The oppression, if any, stemmed solely from Parliament. By refusing to petition Parliament, the American Congress meant to deny Parliamentary authority, and this, rather than any alleged tyranny or oppression, was the heart of the matter. But the Congress did not say this. To do so would be to give the show away, to invite discussion and conciliation. It was for this reason that the records relative to the plan for union with Great Britain were destroyed.

Save in the minds of a few radicals, there was then no thought of establishing an independent republic in colonial America. Rather, the delegates to the Continental Congress took the view that they were merely asking for recognition of their rights as Englishmen; for example, to seize a man in Boston and send him to London to be tried for treason was illegally to change his venue and deny him a jury of his peers. But the radicals knew what they were doing, knew how necessary it was to provoke a situation in which a man would be forced to choose between two sides. So it was put about that anyone who did not agree with the boycott of British goods was a traitor to fellow colonists, while if he did agree, then he was a loyal patriot. Nor did matters stop at calling names: if anyone should not observe the boycott, his barn or his house might very well catch fire, or he might have unexpected visitors who carried buckets of roofing tar and bags of chicken feathers. A certain simplicity of thought and a propensity to take direct action were already American characteristics. And so, of course, was a certain genius for avoiding unpleasant regulations, including those agreed upon by the colonists themselves: many a patriot publicly endorsed the boycott while privately contriving to trade with British merchants. There was, meanwhile, open rebellion in Massachusetts, where bands of hotheads acquired supplies of powder and shot, sometimes by theft from government arsenals, and prepared to meet British martial law with military force.

All these activities fascinated the French *agents provocateurs*. Their reports went to a courtier, Caron de Beaumarchais, who laid them before the count de Vergennes, foreign minister for Louis XVI. Vergennes saw opening before him the opportunity for which his predecessor, the duc de Choiseul, had so devoutly prayed. He put his opinion in a paper entitled "Reflections on the present situation of the English colonies, and on the conduct which France ought to hold in regard to them."

He began by supposing that if there should be widespread revolt in the American colonies, it would cost the British a great deal of money and effort to suppress it. But he said Britain could meet this cost, and if Britain was successful, then she would emerge from the struggle even stronger than she now was. On the other hand, if the revolt succeeded and the colonies broke away from Britain, the loss of her colonies would do Britain incalculable damage. French interests would best be served by making the British task as difficult as possible, and all sorts of good things would follow if the revolt should become a successful revolution:

"First, it will diminish the power of England and proportionately raise that of France. Second, it will cause irreparable loss to English trade, while it will considerably extend ours. Third, it presents to us as very probable the recovery of a part of the possessions which the English have taken from us in America, such as the fisheries of Newfoundland and of the Gulf of St. Lawrence . . . we do not speak of Canada."

Then, he went on, the victorious colonies would form a republic, which would mean they would be a very weak and divided nation, which in turn would mean that they would represent no threat to the French Caribbean islands and Spanish possessions in Louisiana and Mexico. On the other hand, he said, if the British stamped out the revolt and took a firmer grip on her American possessions, she would be a greater threat to France in the Caribbean, and Spain in America, then she already was.

Vergennes' thinking ran far ahead of the colonists' thinking at this time, and so did his action. He instructed Beaumarchais to set up a purely fictious concern called Rodrigue Hortalez & Cie., traders in arms and munitions. Hortalez & Cie. would buy these goods with money donated by the royal treasuries of Louis XVI and Charles III of Spain. The company would then make a free gift of its wares to any rebellious Americans who might arrive to ask for them.

All began to work out as the French might wish when, in the spring of 1775, a column of British troops set off from Boston to seize a quantity of illegal munitions from a rebel band. As millions of American schoolchildren subsequently learned,

> By the rude bridge that arched the flood,
> Their flag to April's breeze unfurled,

Here once the embattled farmers stood,
And fired the shot heard round the world.

To be sure, they had no flag, and not all of them were farmers, but they were an armed mob engaged in an illegal activity in open defiance of their government. At the time, and ever since, the Americans portrayed these men as selfless heroes who reluctantly took arms to protect their lives, sacred honor, and the inalienable rights of man from tyrannous aggression. The plain fact, however, was that they were violent men who provoked a long-suffering British government into taking police action to protect itself and the lives and property of the loyal majority of its colonists.

THE AUTHOR IS EXTREMELY LONG ON CONCLUSIONS, AND NON-EXISTENT ON FACTS!

In any case, the fighting at Concord and Lexington enabled the radicals to say that British troops had fired on peace-loving farmers whose only desire was to preserve their lawful rights as British subjects and their natural rights as human beings. They could now state to their fellow colonists: You must either be for us, or against us. If you are for us, you will help us. If you do not help us, you are against us. If you are against us, we will know how to deal with you. The outbreak of fighting also resulted in a second Continental Congress being hurriedly assembled, and the delegates voted to raise an army that should capture Quebec and ask the Canadians to join the other colonies in the common cause, and to send a delegation to Paris to seek French support. At this time most of the delegates, like most of the colonists, still did not envision independence from Great Britain, although it is difficult to understand why they should not. After all, they were not only supporting armed insurrection, but invasion of another British possession, and seeking the support of a foreign power: if they were not successful and did not become independent, the delegates could only expect to be hanged as rebels and traitors on Tower Hill. The point indeed occurred to the radicals among them, and before another year was out, it would be plain to them all.

It Was All Quite Shocking

The major business of the Congress was not so much the conduct of military operations, however, as it was that of convincing themselves, and the general public, that it was right and just not only to revolt against their lawful government, but also to seek help from (of all people) the hitherto-hateful French. As a matter of practical politics, they could not identify Parliament as their enemy, for this would imply that Parliament was the government, and it was precisely Parliament's right to govern them that the colonists protested. Nor could they say the British people were the enemy, for they were British themselves and thought of themselves as such, even though they were aware of the difference between British Americans and British Britons. It was just here they hit upon the happy thought that King George III was their enemy: they were true Britons, one and all, unwillingly driven to taking up arms against a tyrannical king, even as the barons at Runnymede had been driven to dictate to King John; even as the Puritans had been forced to decapitate one tyrannical Stuart, and, later, to depose another. As Dr. Joseph Goebbels was to observe, the larger the lie, the greater the chances it will be believed. *REALLY?! THE ANALOGY SIMPLY DOESN'T LIE !!*

The polemicist and propagandist of the American Revolution was an English immigrant named Thomas Paine, who called the figurehead king "the royal brute of Great Britain," and, picking up odd bits and pieces of Locke, together with sundry catchwords of the day, Paine described the American cause as the cause of all mankind, based on science and natural law. It is, he argued, "repugnant to reason to suppose that this Continent can long remain subject to any external power . . . There is something absurd in supposing a Continent to be perpetually governed by an island. In no instance hath nature made the satellite larger than its primary planet; . . . it is evident that they belong to different systems, England to Europe; America to itself." Today we can say that Paine's pamphlet, *Common Sense*, was at least common enough; that his later work, *The Rights of Man*, was predicated on the debatable assumption (among others) that people are inherently entitled with "rights." But at the time, Paine was simply and forcefully saying something that a great many people could believe because they wanted to believe it; because they had better believe it if they were to excuse the actions they had taken. Paine's role was to translate the theories of the radical intellectuals into a language that the backwoodsman, or the man in the gutter, could understand, and as a translator, he was enormously successful.

Just as Paine was bursting into print, an American agent, Silas Deane of Connecticut, arrived in Paris on behalf of the Continental Congress to open discussions with the French. His cover was that he was a businessman, not a secret agent, but his business was to buy arms. To his pleasant surprise, he was put on to one Beaumarchais, who, it seemed, was the executive officer of Rodrigue Hortalez & Cie., a munitions firm open and ready for business. Deane had no idea that this was a dummy corporation and that Beaumarchais was empowered to make a free gift of its wares to the American rebels. (Immediately deciding that what Deane did not know would never hurt him, Beaumarchais gladly *sold* the goods to Deane, and then deciding that what the kings of France and Spain did not know would not hurt them, either, Beaumarchais pocketed the money himself.) In addition to filling his shopping list, Deane also made an agreement with Vergennes whereby American ships could trade in French ports, and bring into them for sale any British ships that American ships might capture.

At this point, control of the American Revolution began to slip out of the hands of the Americans. What had begun as a colonial riot began to assume the form of still another contest for empire between Great Britain and France, with France, as Doniol put it, seeking to avenge itself and tear up the Treaty of Paris. Yet in 1776, the French were not quite sure it was altogether safe for them to play an overt role. When the Continental Congress issued the Declaration of Independence in that year, the French found two ways of construing this remarkable document. First, that the declaration meant nothing if it could not be made good by armed force; second, that if it could be made good, Spain would be horrified. The Spanish king and his court found all mention of republics singularly repellent and were fearful that if colonists in North America could revolt and set up a republic, Spanish subjects in New Spain might follow their example. Since France would need all the help she could get from Spain in the event of another war with Great Britain, the French policy in 1776 was to give the American rebels all the powder and shot she could, to wait to see what sort of chance of success the Americans might have, and to try to persuade Spain to see opportunities for herself in Great Britain's troubles, before France would recognize the new nation and openly enter the war on the American side. Meanwhile, ninety percent of the rebels' arms and explosives were made in France.

From a military standpoint, the American chances were extremely poor. The British sea power was overwhelming; the British could land armies anywhere they wished on the American coast at any time they pleased. Britain could bring more munitions into America than the rebels could ever make for themselves or hope to smuggle in from France. Well-trained British armies, the veterans of continental wars, were at once more numerous and more lethal than a rabble of untrained, underarmed, ill-supplied, scantly organized and poorly led farmers, woodsmen, and townsmen. It thus appeared the rebels had no chance at all in a conventional warfare of marches, countermarches, and pitched battles. Nor would they seem to have much of a chance in guerrilla operations. The rules of guerrilla warfare were then exactly what they have always been, and remain today. To be successful, the *guerilleros* must have the logistical and military support of a friendly foreign nation at least as powerful as the nation with whom they are at war. They must also have the unqualified support of the local population and constant and accurate intelligence reports on the enemy's strength and intentions. Further, they must never fight except when they have the advantages of terrain, surprise, superior numbers, and safe escape routes to a secure re-assembly point. Finally, they must have faith in their cause and some reason to believe they will win. If any of these conditions is lacking, the guerrillas will lose—and most of these conditions were denied the Americans. Their most grievous lack was that of unqualified support by the local populace, and this they sought to remedy by terror.

In looking back on the Revolution, if any tyranny is to be imputed to either side, it was that tyranny which a highly organ-ized minority of radicals always seeks to impose upon a disorgan-ized majority. In revolutionary situations, the radicals at least have a program, whereas the majority has none; this indeed is often the sufficient precondition of the revolt. In a worsening situation, the rebels will take any means to dragoon a populace into servility if they cannot win its enthusiastic cooperation. In the American Revolution, there were indeed times that tried men's souls, as Paine put it, but the souls most sorely tried were not always those of the rebels. Many organizations of militia were formed by loyal colonists to protect their communities from revolutionary terror, and to cooperate with the regular British forces. And tens of thousands of hapless citizens fled overseas, back to England, to the Caribbean islands, to Australia. More than sixty thousand escaped to what is now the Canadian province of Ontario, where their de-scendants today call themselves United Empire Loyalists with as fierce a pride as the descendants of the rebels call themselves the Sons and Daughters of the American Revolution.

Insofar as the purely military situation was concerned, chaos prevailed upon both sides. George Washington, one of the wealthier men in America and an otherwise imposing figure, lent his prestige and reputation for incorruptibility to the rebel cause, but students of military history rather sadly agree that he was not

the most competent general officer history has ever known and
that he made at least his share of serious blunders. For their part,
the British failed to follow up every one of their many victories. It
was as if the British commanders felt there was no particular reason to act with speed and violence, that they had only to wait till
a weak and half-starved rebel force saw the futility of it all and
surrendered. This might indeed have happened. By the fall of
1777, the American position seemed fairly hopeless, and the British government, tiring of the waste and expense and wishing to
resume trade with its largest single trading partner, considered a
plan to give the American colonies home rule. Had the plan been
offered in time, the Americans would very probably have accepted it. This possibility thoroughly alarmed Vergennes, who,
when he heard of it, sought to persuade his colleagues in the
French government to recognize the Americans as a sovereign
nation, form an alliance, and enter the war. Much has been written of Benjamin Franklin's brilliant embassy to Paris, but neither
his cogent arguments nor those of Vergennes might have prevailed had not the Battle of Saratoga ended as it did. In October
of 1777, an American army successfully ambushed and defeated a
British army pushing through the New York forests. The Americans were able to make their victory good because a second British army, which was to have taken the Americans in the rear,
failed to arrive on the scene. To speak of a failure of British coor-
dination is not to denigrate the American victory, however; Saratoga was one of history's decisive battles because it put an end to a
series of British victories and gave the Americans a new spirit to
carry on, while at the same time it enabled Vergennes to carry
his point in Paris. After Saratoga, a British offer of home rule
would not have been acceptable to the colonies, and after Saratoga, the French government could be persuaded to believe that
the Americans could free themselves from Britain, provided that
France joined the war.

Early in 1778, France recognized the American government

and signed two treaties with the new nation. One was a most-favored-nation trading agreement; the other was a military alliance. Then, French diplomats sought to find additional allies in what promised to become another general European war. The Dutch were persuaded to recognize the American nation and to go to war with Britain. Spain refused to recognize the new republic because of her hatred of republics and her fear that the idea of revolt would spread to her territories in New Spain, but she was persuaded to believe that a British supremacy in North America would be potentially more dangerous to her American possessions than a weak American nation would be. Moreover, Spain wanted Gibraltar back, and the two Floridas. Spain therefore declared war on Britain in 1779, and a Spanish force, setting out from New Orleans, successfully invaded and regained possession of the Floridas.

At this point, the rebel forces in America became the least of Britain's problems. Britain was now engaged in a commercial and naval war with France, Spain, and Holland, and the principal engagements took place in European and West Indian waters. When in the course of this warfare, the British sought to proclaim blockades and to search and seize vessels suspected of carrying contraband, Russia, Sweden, Denmark, Prussia, Portugal, and Turkey proclaimed an alliance of "armed neutrality"—meaning that while they intended to remain neutral, they would go to war with Britain if the British navy did not leave their ships alone. In effect, Britain found herself alone with all Europe against her. This situation was far more dangerous to the island kingdom than the loss of her American colonies would be; after all, the colonies needed British trade quite as much as Britain needed the colonial trade, and therefore matters could be patched up with the Americans, and, at a later time, perhaps the rebellious colonies could once again be reconciled. While this thought forced itself upon the British government, French fleets and armies appeared off the American coast. The French landed an army of six thousand men on Rhode Island; like the Spanish centuries earlier, the British fleet enjoyed naval superiority, but it could not be everywhere at once in superior force. From this point on, the determining military factor in America was the presence of French military and naval forces on the coast: a British army operating against a rebel army inland might be taken in the rear by a French one landing on the coast, or its lines of communication might be snipped by a French fleet. This occurred in 1781, when a British general, Lord Cornwallis, sat down to regroup and await reinforcements at the Chesapeake Bay town of Yorktown, Virginia, only to be attacked from inland by a French army, acting together with American troops, while a French fleet entered the bay, blockaded Yorktown, and so caught Cornwallis between two fires.

The loss of one British army at Saratoga and of another at Yorktown was not fatal to British military power in America, but these actions, together with the invasion of the Floridas by the Spanish, indicated the expensive difficulty of waging war on several fronts, with several enemies, at the end of a long and perilous supply line. There was a question as to whether it was really worth the trouble, particularly when considering the threat from the Dutch, Spanish, and French in Europe, and the fact of Britain's diplomatic isolation.

The British began to explore avenues that might lead to peace. The result was that, in 1783, the warring nations sent delegates to a congress in Vienna. The American representatives found themselves shunted aside; their status was that of an "American Commission" attached to, and under the control of French delegates representing the French foreign ministry. It became shortly apparent to the Americans that the French intended to use the independence of the Americans as a bargaining counter in a European trading game. Depending on how they envisioned their own advantage, the French might repudiate their recognition of the tiny nation, and declare their treaties with it null and void, if the British would give the French something in return.

Among other things, it seemed the French wanted to reacquire fishing rights off the northeast American coast. They also wanted the new nation, if it was to be recognized as such, to be confined between the Allegheny Mountains and the Atlantic coast.

The Americans also learned that the Spanish had ambitions of their own. They intended to keep the Floridas, now that they had them back again, claiming these lands by right of conquest and denying that they had ever been a part of the rebellious colonies. Their seizure of the Floridas had nothing to do with the American Revolution, the Spanish said. But more than this, the Spanish wanted to claim all the land east of the Mississippi River and west of the Alleghenies north to what is now Michigan. This, together with lands France had ceded to Spain west of the Mississippi, would have given Spain the entire center of the American continent—the vast tract that La Salle had called Louisiana, and to which the Spanish had once laid claim in the days of the Conquistadors. Further, Spain wanted Gibraltar and the island of Minorca back from Britain.

France took a somewhat dim view of her hungry ally's desires. The French indicated they would be willing to let the British keep all the territory north of the Ohio River in order to keep the Americans cooped up behind the Alleghenies, and to put a limit to Spanish ambitions. They also suggested declaring the territory now embraced by the states of Tennessee, Kentucky, Mississippi, and part of Alabama an Indian territory—but under Spanish protection.

When the American delegates realized that their European allies intended not only to draw the map of North America to suit themselves, and determine the fishing rights, but also to affirm or repudiate the independence of the republic at their pleasure, the Americans began a private discussion of their own with the British. They found a ready welcome. The British, of course, had never recognized the thirteen colonies' claim to be an independent nation. Therefore, they had never transferred responsibility for American affairs to the British Foreign Office. Instead, colonial affairs had remained assigned to the Home Office.

Now that being the case, the British in effect told the Americans, we can keep all this in the family. We can allege there never was a war for independence, but that there was instead a certain amount of civil disorder within the British community, and that putting this to rights is strictly a matter for the British community to sort out; it is no business of anyone else. So we, too, can use the matter of independence as a trading card when it comes to making treaties; actually, as far as Britain is concerned, you can have it—we decided on that at Yorktown. You can certainly make a better deal with us, through the Home Office, than you shall ever make with all those bloody foreigners.

Benjamin Franklin, who was one of the American commissioners, wanted the British to cede Canada to the Americans, as well as to pay reparations for damage done to American property during the war, and to grant American ships the same trading rights as British ships enjoyed. The British thought this was going a bit far, and after weeks of private bargaining kept secret from the French, the British agreed to recognize her American colonies as a sovereign nation, and to convey to them all the British possessions in North America (with the exception of Canada), from the Atlantic to the Mississippi. This was not only much more than the Americans could have got from the Spanish and the French, but also more than the Continental Congress had envisioned; at that time, Congress would have accepted the Alleghenies as the western boundary of the nation.

Between them, the Americans and the British presented the Congress of Vienna with a *fait accompli;* in the course of a general agreement, Great Britain gave Minorca back to Spain, recognized Spanish claims to the two Floridas, but kept Gibraltar. The French got nothing out of North America for their considerable efforts, except the satisfaction of having weakened the British empire by detaching its largest single trading party from it, and acquiring favorable trading rights with the Americans for themselves. To some extent, the Treaty of Paris had been ripped, if not shredded. The next steps could be taken at a future time.

13

America's
Oldest Profession

For its first six years, the American republic was hardly a united nation. The thirteen former British colonies viewed themselves as thirteen separate, sovereign states, loosely allied in what they called a confederation. Some were barely on speaking terms with others. There was no President or any other executive officer of this confederation, no central authority to regulate commerce among the states or with foreign nations, no central judiciary, no legislative body to formulate national laws, no foreign ministry, no army and no navy. Any state could withdraw from the confederation at any time it pleased, and the whole rickety structure promised to collapse at any moment.

Worse, the confederation existed at the whims of Britain, France, and Spain, all of whom still entertained ambitions in North America. The new nation was not a year old when, in 1784, Spain closed the Mississippi River to American navigation. Spain told the Americans they could not claim to inherit shipping privileges on the Mississippi from Britain, for while it was true that Britain had wrung such rights from Spain and France in

1763, they had ended when Spain and Britain went to war in 1779. Moreover, the Spanish refused to recognize American claims to land, ceded to them by Britain, that extended from the Appalachian Mountains to the east bank of the Mississippi: Spain briefly said the British never had those lands to grant. Further, Spain claimed sovereignty over the Cherokee, Creek, Chickasaw, and Choctaw Indians in these western lands south of the Ohio River, incorporating them into an "Indian state." Nor would the Spanish discuss ownership of the Floridas with the Americans, and they flatly forbade the Americans to trade in Mexico or anywhere else in New Spain. The Spanish point of view was at least clear. To the north, the British in Canada were intriguing with Vermont to have that state leave the confederacy and join Canada instead. The British also continued to maintain garrisons in forts north of the Ohio River and west of the Allegheny Mountains, instead of quitting them as the Treaty of 1783 provided. They furthermore retained their alliance with the Indians in the northwestern region between the Ohio and the Great Lakes, and the Indians promised to exterminate American settlers who arrived in their lands.

The position of the confederation was therefore one of internal impotence and external threat. The land La Salle had called Louisiana, lying on the infant nation's western flank, was filled with enemies. Yet the Americans contemplated chasing all these people, Spanish, British, and Indians, out of the western lands given them in the Treaty of 1783. To a foreign observer at the time, such an ambition might have seemed preposterous. He might also have thought it preposterous that some of the leaders of the confederation should have thought of invading Mexico, in the conviction that it was America's manifest destiny to take possession of the entire North American continent.

The conviction was there, however, and the reasons for it were a curious mixture of the historical, the practical, and the mystical. The best way to explain this is to step back to the first moments of the colonial experience.

It was hunger for land, rather than a desire to secure religious or political freedom, that had led most of the colonists to leave England—even if this meant their having to go out to the New World as indentured servants. And, from the moment the first Englishman stepped ashore in America, west was the only possible direction for him to take. Never exploring far afield, never casting about for El Dorado, never concerned for bringing a True Faith to the savages, the arriving English slowly and steadily chopped their way west into the forests, claiming and clearing and farming the land. It was true that there were other ways of making a living in the world; business, shipping, and manufacture were three of them; but the possession of arable land was the surest path to personal independence, if not also to wealth, power, and position. So a simple desire to own land and prosper on it was the proximate cause of the wholesale English migration to America, with the example of Virginia always in glittering view.

Here, on the long, slow slope leading from the sea to the Appalachian Mountains, was a well-watered, fertile region of broad plains, blessed with the most bearable of America's outrageous climates. And here in Tudor times, the first, most valuable cash crop had been developed. Tobacco made Virginians rich—particularly those Virginians with the widest fields and the most slaves. In Virginia, any man willing to work like a dog could look forward to living like a king, or at least like a baron, upon his own estate.

It was otherwise in New England. The sea shelf was narrow; a jumble of hills and mountains soon rose behind it. The growing season was short, the northern forest soil thin and marginally productive, and the climate was ridiculous. Until the Revolution, the New Englander's way north and west had been blocked by French and Indian enemies; afterward, the way was still blocked by the British who, contrary to the Treaty of 1783, remained in control of it. For most of this period, New Englanders gave quite as much attention to the sea, manufacture, and commerce as they did to trying to wrench a living from an unpromising land. To a considerable extent, geography and the climate determined their responses: if for the winter months they could not work outdoors, their thought turned to what could be done indoors. There was also in their religion that which tended to form them into egalitarian communities. Even had they not had to huddle together in self-defense against Indian raids, they were disposed to be Calvinist townsmen rather than Anglican country gentlemen. As the population increased, as a result of both propagation and immigration, they pushed inland to New Hampshire and Vermont, where they disgustedly discovered they had exchanged one rock pile for a worse and colder one, and they gave increasing attention to manufacture, commerce, and the sea. The boy who ran away from the farm to go to sea was a typical New Englander. But so was the boy who dreamed of finding the end of the hills and broad river bottoms in the west.

The Middle Atlantic colonies were neither so bleak as New England nor so opulent as Virginia, but the land was fruitful, and water paths led far into it from well-protected deepwater harbors. Here a more balanced economy of commerce and agriculture was developed, but here, as elsewhere, the promised land lay in the west.

In every colony, the first people to push west into the forests included land prospectors. In the earliest colonial times, entrepreneurs set up land companies to claim, subdivide, and sell tracts in the wilderness. The surveyor's chain was as necessary a tool as the ax; the real-estate salesman was contemporaneous with the log cabin; speculation in land was America's oldest profession. The pattern was everywhere the same: first the hunters, frontiersmen, and the speculators; next the bands of determined men and women who had the hope, courage, and ability to make a new life for themselves on land they typically bought sight unseen; then the third wave of merchants, lawyers, physicians, and politicians: civilization's auxiliaries.

By the time the colonies were given their independence by Britain, this westering movement had been under way for nearly two hundred years. It had at all times been characterized not only by a desire for land, but also by the liveliest curiosity. It is one thing to live in a civilization a thousand years old, where all is known and familiar, but quite another to enter a land where the unknown begins at the end of town; wherein all the plants, birds, animals, and people are strange, and no one knows what he might find over the brow of the next hill. A quality of intellectual excitement was therefore a part of the colonial experience. From the first days, the Americans were concerned for what was new. For reasons of survival, then for reason of sheer excitement, the colonists were their own experimental botanists, naturalists, and agronomists. They were, of course, their own artisans and inventors. They were new people in a New World—free, if not compelled to experiment; to find out how things worked; to contrive; to find ways to produce a better crop of strange fruits and grains on a strange land; to examine every possibility of novelty. This quite naturally made the Americans a particularly receptive audience for the scientific discoveries made in Europe, and for the social theories of Locke and Rousseau.

In addition to a historical land-hunger, inevitable westward movement, and a practical openness to experiment, a quality of mysticism fed the Americans' belief in their destiny. The New England Puritans had originally believed that America was God's country and that He had led them to it; the devout in all the colonies saw the hand of God in their deliverance from British rule. Founding Fathers like Benjamin Franklin and Thomas Jefferson privately doubted that God had anything to do with the victory, but they believed that natural law had. Ordinary folk, in the jubilation of independence, erroneously believed that they had won the Revolution all by themselves, and believing this, imagined that Americans were invincible. So, land-hungry, pragmatic, and self-confident, the Americans looked west and saw nothing but opportunity out there. If there were Indians and Spaniards in the way, that was too bad for the Indians and the Spaniards. After the Revolution, the Americans began pouring west over the mountains by the thousands and then by the tens of thousands. And they took the Revolution with them.

When anyone says "the Spanish wanted this," and "the Americans wanted that," it must never be supposed that all Spaniards wanted the one and that all Americans wanted the other. But nations do want things. And nations are guided by governments. The governments are always composed of an absurdly small number of people, and within this miniscule group, a few individuals, or even one individual, can exert a decisive influence. But no government, particularly not a republican one, can long lead in any direction the people will not go. To the extent that a people can be guided along a particular path, it can be said that a national will exists.

In this context, if you are the leader of a nation, it does not really matter what you tell the people. What matters is whether you can persuade them to believe it. If you are going to ask a man to leave his Virginia fireside to freeze at Valley Forge, you must give him a good reason why he should. If you truthfully tell him this is just your opinion, based on your book learning, or that this will help a Boston merchant make more money, the Virginian might decide to stay home and listen to his tobacco grow. But if you falsely convince him he will lose his life, liberty, and property if he doesn't get himself off to Valley Forge, and that in addition he will be fighting for the just cause of all humanity, he will very likely take the musket down from over the mantelpiece and push off for Pennsylvania.

But no matter what the ostensible reason for persuading a man to go to war, the ostensible reason becomes the real reason for the war once the shooting starts. And when the war is won, the veteran is going to insist that the ostensible reason for fighting it must now remain operative: that life must take the form he fought to give it. It is for this reason, more than any other, that wars are dangerous. The American Revolution was particularly dangerous to America and the world because the ostensible reason for fighting it was to proclaim and protect the rights of man. Since these were seen to be natural and universal, the American Revolution was implicitly designed for export.

The Revolutionary veterans began to export it without waiting for their government's approval. Within nine years after the war ended, there were no less than two hundred thousand Americans—one-tenth of the national population—settled in the eastern Mississippi valley lands claimed by Spain. In view of this wholesale migration, it could safely be said the Americans did want something; that there was a national will; and that here was a case of a people leading its government.

To the Spanish, the newcomers were violent, armed revolutionary republicans. Worse, they were heretics who belonged to a race long inimical and dangerous to the Spanish one. The Spanish government, nervously fearing that these unpleasant people would soon pose a threat to New Orleans, increased their military force in the Mississippi valley. Settlers in Kentucky were meanwhile approached by Spanish agents. If the settlers would acknowledge Spanish sovereignty in the land, the agents said, then Spain would grant the Kentuckians a privilege no one else enjoyed. They could float their lumber, whiskey, furs, and crops down the Mississippi for trade at favorable rates for Spanish goods at New Orleans.

The danger in the wholesale western migration had not escaped the American government's attention, or rather, the attention of the thirteen American governments. There was a distinct danger, for the idea had already occurred to some of the pioneers that the settlers might set up a republic of their own on territory promised to the American government by the Treaty of 1783. This notion was scarcely more tolerable than the thought of the Spanish claiming the pioneers' allegiance. Therefore, in 1787, while the western tide was running strongly, the confederation passed the Northwest Ordinance, an act providing that new states would be formed in the western lands north of the Ohio River.

To be sure, it specifically applied to the Northwest Territory, but the general principle could be applied elsewhere. When sufficiently populous, a region could become a state and join the confederation, and the new states would have all the privileges and responsibilities that all the original ones possessed, although slavery would not be permitted. The ordinance was not arrived at without difficulty, but when it was adopted, the way was legally clear for a rational development of the west. The older states with western frontiers, such as Virginia, were precluded from simply extending their own boundaries to the Mississippi, as they might well have done. Thus the danger of jealous competition between the older states was removed. So was the danger that settlers in the west might find themselves in the position of a colonial population, ruled by a remote government on the Atlantic seaboard. And so was the danger that pioneers, venturing into the unknown west, might claim a right to the lands they settled and there establish an independent republic.

The dangers were removed, that is, providing that the confederation could actually back up its own ordinance. There was reason to believe it could not, but the ordinance was at least reflective of a national policy, insofar as the tenuously allied American states could be said to have one.

It was first and last a policy with respect to acquiring new land—specifically, the eastern portion of La Salle's Louisiana.

This policy had five major objectives. The first was to persuade the British to surrender the forts they still held north of the Ohio River and turn the northwest lands over to the Americans as the Treaty of 1783 had stipulated. Next, it was to push the Spaniards west over the Mississippi, where, according to the American reading of the treaty, they belonged. Third, it was to force the Spanish to open the Mississippi to free navigation. Fourth, it was to develop the western lands in an orderly manner, as specified in the ordinance. Finally, it was to win, by force if necessary, permission from the Spaniards to trade with Mexico and with other possessions of New Spain.

The Americans also had a policy with regard to the Indians in these lands. Even Thomas Jefferson, who professed a great admiration for the noble red man, wanted to deport every last one of them west of the Mississippi. There was no place for the Indian in the American scheme of things.

But the pursuit of these or any other policies could not be undertaken by anything so weak and vague as the confederation. Worse, the confederation was unable to exert any effective control over the scores of thousands of Americans who were taking lands for themselves in the west. Some of these self-reliant and self-confident people, very much afire with Revolutionary ardor, were entertaining ideas of capturing New Orleans, invading Mexico, liberating the people there from Spanish rule, and so extending the blessings of republican liberty to a people tyrannously denied their natural human rights. The soberest of the leaders of the confederation were well aware that the military power of the United States was nonexistent, and that its political powers were nearly so. This thought, among others, led Congress, in the same year the Northwest Ordinance was passed, to call a Constitutional Convention. The purpose was to find a way to form a more perfect union, so as to secure the blessings of liberty, provide for the common defense, and promote the general welfare. In other words, it was to weld thirteen separate republican states into a single military power that could control and protect its property.

The delegates succeeded in producing a powerful legal instrument to this end, but two years after the Constitution was adopted, a popular concern to protect the gains of the Revolution demanded that the other shoe be dropped: a Bill of Rights was tacked on. Once this was done, the Revolution was now legally ready for export, because the ostensible reason for going to Valley Forge was built into the law of the land. Any future American war would, *ipso facto,* be a war in defense of the rights of man. In defending them, the Americans would always be on the side of humanity. The Revolutionary Americans, caught up in the mystique of their own ardent rhetoric, believed this at the time, and many Americans have believed it ever since: what is good for Americans is good for everyone in the world; the world must be made safe for republican democracy whether the world likes it or not. So the Constitution, as amended, was a document that first created a military power, and then in the names of God, natural law, and human rights gave the people of the United States a sacred and legal command to use it. It is not, therefore, a historical accident that in its subsequent 193-year history, the United States of America has probably engaged in more wars with more different people in more parts of the world than any other nation in the long story of man on earth.

CAN THIS POSSIBLY BE TRUE?!!

At the time the Constitution was adopted, however, the new nation was in no position to go to war with anyone. The American states might now be a single nation, but the United States was still the least of nations. The Constitution was a patchwork of compromises which, if a tribute to the Americans' ability to compromise, was nevertheless a testimony to their differences of opinion. The Constitution did provide for a regular military establishment, but it was kept insignificant out of a republican fear of central authority taking the form of a police state. Out of the same fear, the Constitution provided that each citizen had the right to bear arms. Two million armed people is a large enough number to represent a considerable military force, but only if their energies can be coordinated to a common end, and in the United States, this was physically impossible. The population was first of all scattered, unconnected by any road network. Where roads rather than tracks or trails existed, they were either dusty, muddy, or icy horrors. More important, the prevailing American mood was each state for itself. It was difficult in the first decade of independence for a man to think of himself as a United States citizen when all his life he had thought of himself as a Virginian or as a Pennsylvanian. Within any state, or within a single city, differences in the modes of life contributed to differences of interest and opinion. Much as anyone might believe that all men were created equal, it was obvious they did not remain so. A republican rhetoric that demanded a fulsome lip service to the equality of man only complicated the practical relationships of inequal men, and it pointed up the social, political, and economic differences of interest among them. And the states themselves had different economic interests that led to political differences. And so there was no real unity, and thus no single will or means to use what military power might be said to exist in the infant nation. Worse still, the existence of military power, and the ability to use it, depends on the existence of money. And the United States had virtually none. A trace of gold was found in Rock Creek, near the site of the future capital city, but for all practical purposes, the only specie in the United States was foreign. It consisted of Dutch, British, Spanish, and French coin, which could only be gained in exchange for American goods sold in foreign markets. So, to risk war with any European power would be to reduce rather than to increase the United States means of waging war.

All of these points entirely escaped the attention of those self-reliant souls who, naïvely supposing they had won the Revolution, argued that a volunteer militia of American riflemen could shoot anybody out of the western woods. Given a virtually penniless and unarmed nation whose populace was at once scattered, diverse, in disagreement, and existing only at the sufferance of foreign powers, the position of the United States was precarious enough without the addition of such feckless ardor. The facts were clear enough to the responsible men in the American government.

On the other hand, if the American people could be said to have a single national objective, it was to cross the mountains and spill into the fertile, empty lands that stretched west to the Mississippi River. A government that failed to lead the people in this direction would be voted out of office, whereas one that did might lead a terribly weak nation into a collision with one or more well-armed European powers, possibly including France. The French alliance was not dependable. The French government had grown noticeably cooler to the Americans from the moment it had lost control of the American Commission at Vienna in 1783—and since France and Spain had been closely allied in a Bourbon family compact for the past several decades, the United States could hardly count on French support in event of a Spanish-American war in the Mississippi valley.

The situation in the west meanwhile grew more ominous. In the year the Confederacy was passing the Northwest Ordinance and convening to arrive upon a Constitution, the Spanish ambassador was plotting with sundry Congressmen, including those from Kentucky, Tennessee, and North Carolina. One prominent American was a very willing conspirator. He was a sot and a schemer named James Wilkinson. During the Revolution he had been a general in the Continental army. His military career was distinguished by his having engaged in a cabal to depose George Washington as commander in chief, by the quantities of spirits he consumed, and by the wholesale swindles he perpetrated in his capacity as clothier general. Caught in his peculations, he was fired from his post, but managed to retain his rank as a general officer—probably because of the influence of the prominent Biddle family of Philadelphia, one of whose daughters he married. For all his slippery swinishness, Wilkinson had an ability to manipulate people; he was not without plausibility and influence. He went to Kentucky after the Revolution to trade and to speculate in land sales, and in 1787 he led a flotilla of traders down the Mississippi to New Orleans. Perhaps what the rustic traders on the flatboats did not know was that Wilkinson had an appointment with the Spanish governor at New Orleans. In the governor's palace, Wilkinson took a secret oath of allegiance to the king of Spain and, according to Spanish records, thereby became Spanish Secret Agent No. 13. His duty was to keep the Spanish informed as to American intentions in the Mississippi valley and to intrigue with his countrymen to set up an independent state in Kentucky and lead it into a dependent alliance with Spain. In return for becoming a Spanish secret agent, Wilkinson received special trading privileges for himself in New Orleans, Spanish pay, and a pension. When he returned to Lexington, Kentucky, a suspicion gathered that Wilkinson might be a Spanish spy; it was formed, however, on no better evidence than Wilkinson's advocacy of a Spanish alliance and the arrival at his door of Spanish mules bearing sacks of gold. No one was able to prove anything against Wilkinson, but no one doubted that there was a Spanish Conspiracy and that he was deeply involved in it.

The ominous feature of the Spanish Conspiracy was the fact that Spain was meddling in the internal affairs of the United States, seeking to subvert American citizens from their national allegiance, and to detach America's western lands from the nation's territory. Any or all of these actions were a quite sufficient cause of war and, given the revolutionary character of the American people, particularly likely to cause it. But two matters helped to delay a collision. Wilkinson's efforts to persuade the Kentuckians to stay out of the Union were unsuccessful, and Spain decided to take some of the heat out of the simmering situation. In 1788, the king of Spain decreed that Americans could float their lumber and produce down the Mississippi, providing they paid a fifteen-percent import duty, and on paying a further six-percent export tax, they could ship their goods out of New Orleans to any port in France or Spain, or to any French or Spanish port in the Caribbean. For Wilkinson and his friends, however, there would be a special, lower rate. Of course this arrangement was still unsatisfactory, for it implied a Spanish right that the United States could not accept, and it further discriminated between American citizens in general and Wilkinson's Americans, the friends of Spain. The temperature did, however, fall as a result of what everyone agreed to call a Spanish concession, but the danger always remained that a navy of Kentucky keelboats might at any time come floating down the Mississippi, loaded with riflemen in coonskin hats and deerskin suits, full of whiskey and the desire to see how fast a Spanish customs agent could run. It was part of Wilkinson's duty to keep his Spanish masters informed of any such intentions on the part of his enthusiastic American countrymen.

While it is interesting to wonder which way Wilkinson would have flopped if Spain and America had gone to war, he was spared such a choice. In 1790, Europe's attention was riveted on what was taking place in France. It was no time for Spain to press upon America. And Britain presently became quite willing to see the American point of view with respect to the northwestern lands in the Mississippi basin.

It was not that Spain or Britain feared the United States. It was rather that the French Revolution was much more important to Europe than a squabble over a transatlantic wilderness. One effect of the French Revolution was to give the still-weak American nation a foreign policy that could be reduced to a formula: Europe's distress equals America's opportunity. It was a policy America would follow for many years to come, because for all her own Revolutionary rhetoric, she was powerless to create opportunities of her own. It was no time for American bellicosity. The times instead called for a policy of resolute timidity, as for example, that of a hopeful jackal at a feast of quarreling lions. While it is always arguable whether the times create the man or the man creates his times, it can certainly be said that Thomas Jefferson was a man of resolute timidity, and that he took his part on the American stage at the very moment a man of his peculiar quality was most urgently required.

14

The Man
Who Changed
His Clothes

In 1784, when lords and ladies played at being shepherds and milkmaids at Versailles, France led the world in manners, fashion, gastronomy, the fine arts, and in scientific and philosophical speculation. She was also the most populous, largest, wealthiest, and most civilized of European nations. It was to this fortunate land that Thomas Jefferson was sent as the American ambassador.

In that year, Jefferson was forty-one years old. The French saw in him another of those incredible Americans, a kind of latter-day Renaissance man who, like his predecessor, the aged Benjamin Franklin, was a wit, writer, man of action, the creator of a nation, and a philosopher whose mind was large enough to assimilate all the accumulated knowledge of man. He was a naturalist, botanist, geographer, musician, inventor, architect, political theorist, and, best of all, a man of the world who was in love with France.

He took for his quarters the Hotel de Langeac off the Champs-Élysées, once the home of a mistress of Louis XV. He extensively altered it, hired a maître d'hôtel, acquired one of the best wine cellars of France, maintained one of the best kitchens in Paris, powdered his sandy hair, dressed his tall, lean frame in a red silk suit with ruffles, took to wearing large, jeweled rings, adopted the red-heeled shoes of the French nobility, and presided over a kind of perpetual house party of the rich, the gifted, and the fashionable. He was in every way formidable.

What the French might not have known was that Jefferson, unlike Franklin, was not always tough, wise, and prudent. He was a romantic revolutionary. He could write fiercely at his escritoire in the Hotel de Langeac that "the tree of liberty must be refreshed from time to time with the blood of patriots and tyrants. It is its natural manure." But when in a position of command only three years earlier, as governor of Virginia during the Revolution, he made a complete botch of Virginia's defense, finally scampering in panic from a British force that swept through the state. A proposal to try him for mismanagement and cowardice was only narrowly averted. His appointment to Paris was not wholly a reward for his Revolutionary services; it was also a means of providing him with a graceful escape from political embarrassment.

He was, however, the most important single catalyst of the Revolution. Never an orator, never a politician on a stump, he found his role in talking to influential men in small rooms, helping to guide their thought and then sum it up in a way acceptable to them all. It was he who discreetly changed Locke's phrase about "life, liberty, and property" to "life, liberty, and *happiness*" when clamorous radicals could not agree as to what was meant by property. He was also the philosopher of the Revolution. But he was the kind of philosopher who can love mankind in general while loathing his neighbor in particular. He was privately troubled to think that he could write the Declaration of Independence while keeping slaves. Still, he managed to console himself with the notion that freeing slaves would be like abandoning children. He felt pity for his slaves. He promised himself to do something to alleviate their condition the moment their efforts should get him out of debt.

Jefferson was first and last a Virginian, a member of the landed gentry of America's oldest, wealthiest, and largest of colonies. Like aristocrats elsewhere, the Virginia gentlemen had neither reason nor inclination to enter manufacture or commerce, but rather faintly despised those who did. Jefferson carried his distaste so far as to include cities and artisans. He hugely enjoyed the musical instruments, mirrors, and furniture that only cities full of merchants and artisans could produce, but he regarded the people who made and sold these good things as "the panders of vice, and the instruments by which the liberties of a country are generally overturned." He wanted none of them in his America. Let all the cities and their squalid populations remain in Europe, he argued. Let America be a land of well-educated, intelligent farmers—by which he meant squires like himself. Borrowing here from Locke and there from Rousseau, Jefferson's view was that natural law ordained that all human virtue flowed from husbandry, whereas all vice and corruption flowed from any deviation from it—such as by living in a city, divorced from nature. Jefferson's noble farmer was a sort of aristocratic, agrarian version of Rousseau's noble savage.

He came to Paris with two daughters and their young personal slaves; with a sense of failure and shame for his unlucky role as Virginia's inept governor; with a sense of personal emptiness, for he was newly a widower; and with a further sense of unease because he was far in debt. He was an experimental agronomist, but somehow his experiments kept going wrong: his Virginia plantations kept losing money. Nevertheless, he played the pianoforte; collected books, statues, paintings, and wines; danced and entertained the brilliant international set he called his charming coterie; and elaborated the already expensive amenities of the Hotel de Langeac. In sum, he enjoyed every comfort the panders of vice could supply him on credit—while brilliantly arguing the case of the noble agrarian and pointing out the wickedness of the city.

Some of his American visitors, Patrick Henry among them, disgustedly said that Jefferson was becoming more French than the French, but Jefferson's coterie saw only the perfect example of the new man of the new age. He discussed painting with artists, architecture with architects, music with musicians, natural science with the natural scientists, and speculated with geographers as to the Northwest Passage to China. He enthralled the French with his descriptions of America and its Indian populations; in his telling, America became a sort of super Eden whose fruits were fresher, whose animals were larger, whose savages were more noble, whose climate was more wonderful, than those of any land on earth. It was the land of opportunity and mystery, particularly in the west—and even more particularly, there were opportunities and mysteries awaiting discovery in the unexplored regions of unknown extent lying west of the Mississippi. Jefferson gathered and traded what information he could with the French geographers who told him what they had heard of the adventures of French trappers who had penetrated the northern plains to the verge of the Rocky Mountains. But it was Jefferson, the gentlemanly revolutionary republican, not Jefferson, the amateur scientist, who most particularly fascinated his French friends. These included the Marquis de Lafayette, that good friend of the American Revolution, and French intellectuals who were concerned for the condition of France.

What Jefferson seems not to have appreciated, as he enjoyed his French apple, was the existence of the worm. The recent cost of troops, ships, and military aid sent to America, added to the still-outstanding obligations incurred during the wars of Louis XIV, was more than the French government could bear. No less than half the government's revenue was devoted to servicing the national debt—not to repaying it but simply to paying the interest on it. The French national debt was by no means the highest in Europe, and considering the amount of money available in France, it should have been discharged. The problem was, the government could not or would not collect sufficient taxes to pay it. Those who had the money were those who paid the least tax— or none at all. It will be recalled that Louis XIV had prudently (or so it seemed at the time) refused to tax the wealthy for fear they would seek a share in his government: this policy was now seen as quite mistaken. France was outwardly prosperous, but its government was going bankrupt. Meanwhile, prices were rising much faster than wages were increasing: inflation was well begun. Perhaps it was impossible for Jefferson, the gentlemanly philosopher, to understand this. He seemed forever unable to understand money; his own financial affairs were always a mess. His view of the urban poor seems to have been that tangles about money were the kinds of things in which city people find themselves involved. It is possible that Jefferson saw in his French friends' concern for France only a humanitarian desire to bring the blessings of republican liberty to the oppressed subjects of royal tyranny. That, in any case, is what they chiefly discussed, rather than tax reform, and the importance of Jefferson's embassy to the French was his contribution as the apostle of revolution.

During his years as ambassador, while the economic affairs of the French government grew worse and then impossible, and while the number of the French urban poor increased as inflation grew, and the countryside and cities became increasingly infested with beggars and bands of brigands, Jefferson and the radical intellectuals eagerly discussed the constitutions the American states had adopted and the one produced by the Constitutional Convention. The implication of the American Revolution was not lost on them: as students of the new thought, they understood that the rights of man were universal ones; that freedom of inquiry, freedom of the press, of religion, of assembly, were natural rights; that all men must have equality before the law; that government was a social contract. These notions may originally have been European ones, but it was the Americans who had put them into practice, and now America was the object of intellectual attention. The Americans had freed themselves, and it seemed they were proving quite competent to manage their affairs in a most enlightened manner, just as theory suggested. What Americans could do, everyone else could, and indeed, must do for themselves. And here, in Paris, was one of the most distinguished Americans of them all, one who could answer their questions and advise them as to a course of action. In this context, the words in the United States Constitution, "we the people," were profoundly significant to the French. One lasting accomplishment of Louis XIV was that his unification of France had given the French a sense of national identity, and this, plus the new thought, made it easy for Jefferson's French friends to think in terms of "we, the people of France."

Of course they were not the people of France, any more than the delegates to the American Constitutional Convention were the people of the United States. Jefferson's French friends were merely some of the more intelligent and most privileged of a small number of Frenchmen who were indulging themselves in a romantic notion that was potentially explosive. What made the notion so dangerous was that the people of France, unlike those of the United States, comprised a stratified society, so that revolution in France did not imply a people turning away from something remote, as it had in the United States. It implied overturning something at hand.

This point was soon to impress itself upon the French members of Jefferson's coterie, but Jefferson never understood it. His experience of revolution had been almost idyllic—except, of course, for the time he cut and ran. But the American Revolution was a temperate affair. There were no lords, prelates, royal court, urban proletarians, or peasants in Jefferson's colonial America. There was no established church that owned most of the land and paid no taxes. The structure of colonial America was not a feudal one, and quarrels between king and nobility and church and state had been settled in England more than a century before the American Revolution. Most important, there was no tremendous difference between one man and another in America, and no class hatred, as there was in France. American society was reasonably mobile and fluid, and the open frontier implied opportunity for anyone to better his lot if he could. French society was at once static and stifled, and there was no open frontier. To speak of the natural right of every man to equality of opportunity to acquire property in France was to imply the wholesale revision of French society through class warfare. So when Jefferson spoke of revolution to the charming people about his table, he had in mind the revolution of literate intelligent Virginians of goodwill, learned in lessons of ancient Greece and Rome, acting together as free equals in the Garden of Eden to establish a model republic based on reason and science. He did not envision a Parisian mob ululating through the cobblestone streets carrying dripping human heads on poles. There was never that measure of fury and hatred in the American Revolution; the terror visited upon the American loyalists was, by comparison, innocuous.

Jefferson did see the poor in Paris trying to warm themselves in winter by huddling about little fires flickering in gutters. He wrote about this. He must have had knowledge of peasants arming themselves against the bands of brigands pillaging the countryside, and of peasants burning the manor houses in which the records of their manorial fees and dues were kept. He could not have helped knowing, during the years of his embassy, that something was going progressively wrong with his beloved France, but knowing this and appreciating this are two different things. In the year 1789 a crop failure and general famine were added to the manifold miseries already caused by a ruinous inflation and a concurrent diminution of foreign trade (particularly with America), and then in summer there was a sudden panic in Paris.

Somehow the rumor began, and was wildly believed, that criminal gangs were marching on the city. And other rumors said that royal troops had been assembled at Versailles for use against the people of Paris.

On July 14, a crowd of Parisians gathered before the dilapidated medieval fort called the Bastille, scheduled for destruction so that the space it occupied could be used as a public park; until then, it was used to house a few prisoners, some of them political ones. Voices in the crowd called for the governor of the Bastille; they wanted him to remove the cannon from the embrasures of the old fort, and to give them arms to defend themselves against the arrival of the brigands. It seems that the governor did not entirely understand what the voices were shouting, nor did the crowd entirely understand what the governor was replying. The crowd became a mob; a cannon was fired, then another. Ninety-eight Parisians were killed before the mob forced its way into the Bastille, where it murdered six of the soldiers after the governor surrendered. Then the governor's head was hacked off and stuck on a pole; the mob caught the mayor of Paris and decapitated him, too, and the heads were carried through the city streets. News of these events appalled the shepherds and milkmaids at Versailles, but in the crisis, Louis XVI dithered. He did not send his troops into the city. Instead, he allowed the people of Paris to form a "National Guard" under the leadership of Lafayette. Lafayette chose a tricolor flag to be the ensign of this command, its center white, the color of the Bourbons, bordered by red and blue, the colors of Paris.

National Guards were formed in other French cities, also to defend the townspeople from the presumed arrival of brigands, and in August a National Assembly, meeting in Paris, published a document called the Declaration of the Rights of Man and Citizen. It declared feudalism abolished. It proclaimed that men "are born and remain free and equal in rights." Birth was to be no obstacle to employment or social position. All would enjoy their natural rights to freedom of liberty, property, security, speech, press, due process of law, religion, and their natural right to resist oppression. There would be no taxation except those taxes to which all the people consented. Henceforth, the sovereign power of France would repose in the people of France: in short, all power to the people.

The declaration electrified the French, and, published throughout Europe, it gave various restive populations in Germany, Austria, and Italy much to consider. Jefferson was wholly delighted with what he saw as a "beautiful" revolution. The ability to find beauty in howls and bloody murder is given to few rational men, and they are almost never the ones with the knives. But philosophical revolutionaries seem to possess a curious serenity with regard to the shedding of other people's blood. In any case, Jefferson was able to look beyond a few screams and a bit of mess on the cobblestones to see humanity victorious and a new republic rising in the future. And he called it beautiful.

He also wisely left Paris. He was merely leaving France for a holiday in Virginia, and to straighten out his financial affairs, he said. He promised to return shortly to his wonderful Paris. But he was careful to take home with him, for this brief vacation, all his wines and everything else he possessed, except the Hotel de Langeac itself. One part of his baggage traveled with him, his two daughters, and their two slaves. It was enough to require his chartering a vessel of 230 tons, solely for his party. The rest of his goods and chattels were to follow on another ship the following year, and this second lot was so enormous that it was suspected of being the worldly goods of an absconding aristocrat, not that of a simple republican man of the people. The homeward voyage was placid. Jefferson was spared the seasickness he always dreaded. If anyone suffered discomfort, it would have been one of the slaves, a sixteen-year-old octoroon named Sally Hemmings, who was pregnant. The father, according to Jefferson's slaves, was their master.

The Man Who Changed His Clothes

Once returned to his Virginia palace, Monticello, high above his ten thousand mortgaged acres, and returned, too (if we are to believe his daughter), to the ecstasy of his two hundred slaves who wept for sheer happiness at the sight of him and kissed the ground beneath him, Jefferson found waiting for him a message from President Washington. He was invited to join Washington's Cabinet as Secretary of State. During the years since Jefferson's time, that office has been whatever its holder is able to make of it, depending upon his intelligence and will as compared with that of the President, but in 1789 Jefferson had no high opinion of it. He envisioned the duties of the secretary to be more consular than diplomatic; that the simple foreign policy of a free republic should be a willingness to trade with all, while forming alliances with none.

It was, however, a position in government at the President's ear. Jefferson's last government position in America had been a fiasco, but this one would not be administrative, merely advisory.

The extent to which Jefferson was ambitious for power is debatable. His enemies saw him as a hypocritical schemer, always pretending he would rather be in Paris or on his Virginia estate than in public office, but covertly reaching for the keys to the government. A more charitable view is that Jefferson was one of those people who feel they always have to tell other people what to do—not because they desire power, but simply because they believe that what they think is right. Still, reading Washington's message, Jefferson was undecided. One part of him really did want to return to Paris where he had spent five of the happiest years of his life. His coming home, bag and baggage, indicated he did not *intend* to return, certainly not at any early time, but when he said he *wished* to return, there is no reason to disbelieve him. It was also his real and urgent desire to stay at Monticello to do what he could to pay his debts, even if this meant his having to sell some of his joyful blacks. As matters stood, he was not solvent: he was master of his estate only at the forbearance of his

English creditors. While he thought of saying no to the President's request, his friend and Virginia colleague, James Madison, told him to say yes.

Madison, a small, didactic man, was described by an enemy as "a schoolteacher dressed for a funeral," but however unfortunate Madison's appearance, he was a profound student of politics and he had a genius for sniffing out where political power was, and for getting himself to it. It was important to Madison that Virginia's interests should always be protected, if not paramount in the United States; therefore it was important for Virginians to take part in the government. And, it seemed, those interests could be jeopardized if the direction of the nation were taken over by political henchmen of the merchants and financiers of New York and New England. What Madison had to say was new to Jefferson, who, while he was in Paris, feared he was becoming something of an expatriate. "I know," he said in a letter from Paris, "only the Americans of 1784. They tell me this is to be much a stranger to those of 1789." Now, back in America, Jefferson was finding this true. Even in Jefferson's time America was in such volatile pursuit of the new that its only state was one of constant change. Because he wished to reestablish touch with his countrymen, because he was concerned for the direction of the nation he had helped to create, because Washington wanted him, because he wanted to be of service to Virginia, and because Madison told him to, Jefferson decided to say yes.

It was in fact a different America to which Jefferson returned—and a different Jefferson who returned to it. Arrived in New York City, which was then the capital, he found a kind of carnival in progress. If a spirit of selfless resolve had ever really characterized the Revolution—that, say, of determined farmers in shirt sleeves and frontiersmen in buckskins, volunteering to fight for human decency and freedom from oppression—that spirit was absent from New York. Former loyalists who had remained in the city during the Revolution were robbed of their businesses and their property; those who had been city officials were thrown out of their offices (no matter what their talents as compared with the talents of those who replaced them); those who had been lawyers were summarily disbarred from their profession. The selfless patriots who had led the good fight for the rights of man were each busily helping themselves to all they could seize from those whose fault it had been to choose the side of law and order. Worse, the cleverest among them were helping themselves at the expense of their gullible neighbors and erstwhile comrades: there was a frenzied speculation in the paper debts of the former colonies and later confederation, and an even more frenzied speculation in land—particularly in the west.

Of course such activities had been a part of the entire Revolutionary experience. One remembers the ladies arriving in carriages at Valley Forge; the barrels of Madeira; the candlelight; the army bandsmen providing the music for the dances; the fun and flirtation at Washington's headquarters while, at a little distance from this revelry, the soldiers starved and shivered in their huts. One remembers Washington and his generals and the statesmen buying up, for derisive sums, the land warrants given the soldiery in lieu of pay; the padded bills of the merchants; the black market; the swindles of Clothier General Wilkinson to whom nothing happened other than a change being made in his military duties. Throughout the Revolution, and for that matter throughout the entire colonial experience, the rule had been that position meant advantage. So much could be said of any human society, but in America after the Revolution, the rules of society were significantly different from those in civilized lands elsewhere.

Here was a society caught up in a republican dream of human equality. Yet, like any other society, it was necessary for this one to establish hierarchies in order that it might function. Someone had to make the policies and tell other people what to do, and see that they did it. In the course of mundane affairs, such as those of running a business, someone had to give commands to those who might theoretically be his human equals, but who, for the purposes of getting the business done, had to be his subordinates—if they were not also in business, as well as in fact, his human inferiors. Concepts of public ownership of the means of production were virtually nonexistent in the eighteenth century: the rule then was that the man who owned the business was the one who gave the commands and determined the wages of those he commanded. In the more complex business of running a town, a state, and the nation, it was necessary to establish hierarchies of legislative, executive, and judicial power. Theoretically, any member of the society had a free and equal opportunity to be elected by his peers to a position of power—and to hold it so long as he continued to merit the confidence of his electorate. In practice, it was only quite unusual men who sought to gain public office, and their reasons for seeking it were not always altruistic ones. Nor, in practice, did any particular electorate send its chosen representative to a state or national legislature for altruistic reasons. As in any other society, position was advantage, and once a man achieved a coveted position, he meant to take advantage of it. In republican America, this generally meant he intended to make money out of it.

The point is more complex than banal. In any society, a man has power over others only to the extent that people are willing to believe that he has power over them. They are customarily talked into believing this. In European societies then and now, there were and are all sorts of hierarchies of power and position that have nothing whatsoever to do with making money or having money but that do relate to traditions, inherited responsibilities, and the practice of the arts of civilization. But such European hierarchies were absent from colonial America, except in emergent forms in the nearly two-century-old cities of Boston and Philadelphia, and in the squirearchy of Virginia. In colonial America, in a raw and largely egalitarian society that had neither a hereditary aristocracy nor a civilization with established traditions, the sound of money was the loudest voice of all in the virtual absence of any others. A general preoccupation with economic self-interest had grown at once and directly out of the primitive conditions of colonial life. The emphasis was on immediate growth and change: the possession of money could speed the progression from log cabin to a brick mansion. So there was a concern for money, whetted by the fact that money was scarce and difficult to earn. And people who had less money listened to a man who had more of it, or who promised to get them more of it for themselves. A popular respect for money lent respect to its possessor and enabled him to achieve a position of power. Light as British control over the colonial economy had been, it was nevertheless felt to be so restrictive as to be the sufficient cause for revolt. In short, money talked the colonists into treason, and after the Revolution, money fairly shouted in America. Its voice was loudest in New York, which had never been anything more than a commercial city and which, as the capital of the United States in 1789, drew to it those leaders of republican democracy who saw gold in the bills they intended to pass.

The spectacle of moneymakers in the temple of Liberty was quite revolting to Squire Jefferson, a product of the nearest approach America had so far been able to make toward a hereditary aristocracy whose entrance into public affairs derived from a disinterested sense of responsibility. But then, aristocrats, and particularly philosophical ones, almost never concern themselves about money, except perhaps to be suspicious of the motives of the mercenary. Jefferson's immediate suspicions, fed by no little personal envy, centered on the glittering figure of a genuine military hero of the Revolution, Alexander Hamilton, secretary of the treasury.

Hamilton was preparing a report urging passage of an Assumption Act, by means of which the Federal government would assume the outstanding obligations of the former colonies and subsequent confederation. Beyond this, he envisioned establishment of a national bank. His twofold purpose was to put the nation's economy on a rational footing and to give the wealthy a vested interest in maintaining the union of the states. The language of the Constitution was open to the implication that a state had the right to withdraw from the union. But Hamilton, who saw in union the only possible protection the little nation might have, was eager to find ways to make it powerful and bind it together no matter what the Constitution might have to say about the rights of states to secede—and so he envisioned a golden chain.

He also told his moneyed friends about his plans and confided them to certain Congressmen. When Jefferson arrived in New York to take up his new duties, Hamilton's report had not yet been published, but insiders were literally racing to buy up colonial and confederation debts at a discount. For years, a few wealthy men had engaged in such speculations, but now those who knew the treasury secretary's mind were sending agents by fast horses and fast ships to buy up the paper from country people and revolutionary veterans who had no idea the Federal government might redeem it. From Virginia, Madison wrote to Jefferson about the fast-moving and fast-talking businessmen busy among the ignorant.

If Jefferson entertained suspicions of Hamilton, the businessman, he also was suspicious of Hamilton, the politician, and of Hamilton, the friend of Great Britain. Jefferson had been in France while the Constitutional Convention met, but he had followed its work and devoutly believed that the Federal government possessed only such rights as those specifically given it by the Constitution. This belief, which in time was to be called "strict constructionist," proceeded from the fear that the Federal government might, unless rigidly checked, encroach upon the rights of states to govern themselves and protect their own interests. It was the notable fear of Virginians, who felt a jealous pride in their state's historical preeminence among the former colonies; they still referred to Virginia not as "my state" but as "my country." Since Hamilton publicly championed the creation of a strong Federal authority, Jefferson was therefore suspicious of his politics. And since Hamilton was not only friendly but intimate with a Major George Beckwith, a British officer acting as a business agent representing certain British affairs in America, Jefferson suspected Hamilton of using his Cabinet position to keep the British government informed, through Beckwith, of all that took place in the highest councils of the United States government. In fact, it was not an unreasonable suspicion, for although Jefferson did not know this and Hamilton may not have known it, Beckwith was actually a British intelligence agent.

· Jefferson's suspicions grew as he took his place in the capital city's society. He wrote in his memoirs that what he heard at dinner tables filled him with "wonder and mortification." He gathered that Hamilton belonged to a group of powerful financiers who desired first to create a strong central government at the expense of the states, and then convert it into a monarchy patterned on the British one, and finally to bind this kingdom to that of Great Britain. "A preference of kingly over republican government was evidently the favorite sentiment" of these people, Jefferson wrote. He convinced himself they already formed a "court" about President Washington and entertained dark schemes to make him King George I of America. Washington somewhat testily told Jefferson there were not ten sensible men in North America who imagined any such thing, but Jefferson continued to believe it. Meanwhile, Jefferson found it impossible to agree with the talk at the dinner tables.

"An apostate I could not be," he wrote, "nor yet a hypocrite; and I found myself for the most part, the advocate of the republican side of the question, unless among the guests there chanced to be some member of that party from the legislative houses."

As in prerevolutionary days, Jefferson maintained a discreet silence whenever anyone else championed a point of view with which he agreed, although he was not afraid to speak out if he found himself a lonely minority. But he found himself in a somewhat anomalous position. If the country had changed its mood in the five years he had been in Paris, Jefferson himself had undergone a kind of sea change that variously delighted and disgusted his former colleagues of the Revolution. Seeing him remodel the New York mansion he had rented and setting his tables with French food and wines and donning for social occasions his French courtier's costumes complete to the red-heeled shoes, there were those who thought Jefferson added a fine new glitter to the capital's society. But there were those who shook their republican heads at Jefferson's expensive elegance. They thought it was un-American and therefore bad. Their friend "had been long enough abroad to catch the tone of European folly," one of them complained.

Now while it is true that clothing cannot make the man, it is also true that the way a man dresses and acts indicates who he thinks he is and how he expects others to regard him; it is his advertisement of himself. Jefferson's problem was that his French fashions were admired by those with whom he disagreed politically, whereas they disgusted those with whom he did agree. There have been statesmen in the world to whom this would not have been a problem, but Jefferson was not one of them. He felt he could not dress like one man and vote like another; it was as if he could not act a part without the proper stage setting and costume. There was never a doubt in the philosopher's mind as to which part he should play, and this led the actor in Jefferson presently to affect plain fare, threadbare cloth coats, old carpet slippers, and egalitarian manners rather than elegant ones. This metamorphosis, from butterfly to caterpillar, began soon after Jefferson blundered into political error.

For all Jefferson's suspicions of Hamilton, the relationship of the two Cabinet officers was correct, if not cordial toward one another on the day in April, 1790, when Hamilton took Jefferson aside to moan into his private ear that the union was in danger of breaking apart. Hamilton needed votes in Congress for his proposed Assumption Act, and he despaired of getting them. It appeared that a majority could not agree that the Federal government should assume the outstanding debts of the several states. Some states had no debts, and their representatives saw no reason why the people in those states should be asked to share the cost of liquidating the debts of others. There was such a feeling about this, Hamilton said, that some states might secede from the union. He appealed to Jefferson's patriotism. Could Jefferson use his influence with Virginia's Congressmen to ensure Virginia's votes for assumption? Hamilton admitted that the Assumption Act was anathema to the Southern states, but if Jefferson could get him Virginia's votes, then he, Hamilton, would do something for Jefferson and Virginia: Hamilton would deliver the votes that would first put the nation's capital in Philadelphia for ten years and thereafter place it permanently on the Potomac in Virginia. This, he argued, would relieve Southern fears that the national capital would be located in the North and so represent Northern commercial and financial interests at the expense of Southern agricultural ones. Jefferson hedged. He would not give his support, but he would give a private dinner party for the Virginia Congressmen, to whom Hamilton could make his proposition. What Jefferson did not know at the time was that Hamilton had privately promised the permanent capital to Pennsylvania in return for the Pennsylvania delegation's votes.

The bargain was struck, and, in the event, Hamilton doublecrossed Pennsylvania rather than Virginia. For a moment, Jefferson was delighted to think he had been instrumental in obtaining the nation's capital for his state, but only until he felt the heat of the lava pouring from that veteran volcano, Patrick Henry. Haranguing the Virginia legislature, Henry obtained from them a Protest and Remonstrance that branded the Assumption Act a scheme to "erect and concentrate and perpetuate a large monied interest in opposition to the landed interests." It would put "agriculture at the feet of commerce." More important, Henry argued, the Assumption Act was unconstitutional because it gave the Federal government a power not granted by the Constitution, and thus represented a "change in the present form of Federal Government, fatal to the existence of American liberty."

The resolution of the Virginia legislature went no further than to express a disagreement: Virginia did not choose to disobey the act or secede from the union. But it did make Jefferson feel himself a fool, because on reading Patrick Henry's fulminations, Jefferson had the awful feeling that the old patriot was entirely right. Why, Jefferson wondered, had he not seen this for himself? He, too, believed in strict construction of the Constitution. He, too, could now see the scheme in all its naked dishonesty. He later wrote that Hamilton had tricked him, leaving him "to hold the candle," and he sought to excuse himself by saying he was still such a stranger to America, after all those years in Paris, that he had not known what he was doing.

But from them on, Jefferson swore never to deviate from the path of strict construction. He built his subsequent political career upon it. And he saw the part he had to play. Perhaps because he had been so long away from America, he could in one way view the American political scene more clearly than those who were immersed in it—particularly in the light of what had just happened to him. He saw something that, oddly enough, no one else seems to have observed at the time. He saw that factions were forming in the United States, and that political parties were emerging. This was something the Founding Fathers had not envisioned when they wrote and agreed upon the Constitution. But it was clear enough to Jefferson that, on one side, there was a Federalist party, led by Hamilton.

This party, he felt, had made a virtual prisoner of Washington (who in retrospect appears to have been the Hindenburg or Eisenhower of his day, a father figure too honorable to be clever) and was hiding behind his prestige to effect its nefarious scheme of converting the United States into a monarchy for the specific benefit of the Northern financiers. Hamilton, Jefferson somewhat wildly wrote, "was not only a monarchist, but for a monarchy bottomed on corruption." Jefferson saw the Federalists as aristocrats who were the enemies of natural law and the rights of man. They interpreted the Constitution to mean the Federal government could seize any rights not specifically denied it, in order to destroy liberty. They were hand in glove with the financiers of Great Britain, and their opposition to slavery was not humanitarian, but just a hypocritical way of seeking to undermine the economy, and hence the power, of the agricultural Southern states.

On the other side, in Jefferson's view, there ought to be the "anti-Federalist" party, which would stand for strict construction and the rights of states in order to safeguard the rights of man. As he saw them, the anti-Federalists were those who feared the creation of a national bank as another Federalist plot to destroy these rights; they were the true revolutionaries, whereas the Federalists represented the forces of reaction. As revolutionaries, the republicans were therefore the enemies of monarchical Great Britain and the friends of revolutionary France. If they believed in slavery, it was because—well, of course nobody could really believe in slavery; the South was at heart republican and of course someday slavery would be abolished, but not right now. It was not the time to raise that question: the times now demanded opposition to the antirevolutionary Federalists. The anti-Federalists should form a party.

Such was the Jeffersonian view, modified by his realization that while the political division generally followed geography, there were both Federalists and anti-Federalists in all the states. In 1791, he and Madison made a tour of the Northern ones. Jefferson and his pedantic little friend explained it was just a holiday pursued for reasons of health and their mutual interest in botany and in the life cycles of insects and animals. They were two amateur naturalists enjoying a blessed relief from what Jefferson called the detestable duties of public life. Few people believed that explanation then, or since—preferring to believe that the two Virginians were really embarked on a fishing expedition. They were sounding the Northern political waters and fishing for the future support of Northern anti-Federalists—and for that of such Northern gentlemen as might have personal if not political reasons for opposing Hamilton and his faction.

While, dressed now in plain clothes instead of French silks, Jefferson set about building the foundations of what would shortly become known as the Republican party, he also had to consider his duties as secretary of state, particularly with respect to the relationship between the United States and France.

Here, it appeared that if Jefferson had been too long away from the United States, he had also been too long away from France to appreciate what was taking place there. Perhaps because he was a romantic revolutionary, he could not believe the bloodcurdling stories told by the escaping noblemen. What had begun as Jefferson's beautiful revolution, as a kind of humanitarian and tax reform movement mounted by the bourgeoisie and peasant landowners against the feudal privileges of the nobility, was becoming something ugly and inchoate. For generations, the kings of France, like the Tudors in England, had reason to fear the power of the nobility, and Louis XIV had the good sense to enlist the support of the bourgeoisie as one means of enhancing the power of the throne. But Louis XVI had chosen to side with his nobility, with the result that he was promptly made a prisoner by the Revolutionary government. The possibility of reform was lost, and a progressive warfare of class against class was now begun. The escaping nobility were seeking the military support of other European princes and noblemen to invade France, rescue Louis XVI, and destroy the Revolution. The situation was a delicate one for the United States, which by the Treaty of 1778 had both commercial agreements and a military alliance with France.

[handwritten marginal note: LITERALLY, "To HITCH UP" SOMETHING ONLY PARTLY IN OPERATION]

The question was whether the Treaty of 1778, made by the confederation with the kingdom of France, applied in 1791 between the United States and the revolutionary government of France. If so, and if the escaping French aristocrats persuaded the kingdoms of Europe to make war upon the French revolutionary government, then it seemed as if the infant American republic would find itself at war with these kingdoms—if it were to honor its commitments to France.

The implication was clear enough not only to Washington's Cabinet members, but also to the informed section of the American public. President Washington, Hamilton, and the Federalists wanted no part of the French Revolution and nothing to do with any wars in which the French might become involved. Jefferson and his anti-Federalists discounted the grisly reports from France and ardently supported the French Revolution, seeing it as the continuation in Europe of the American Revolution. They saw in France the first true friend of the United States, and more than this, a sister republic enlisted in the cause of the rights of man. Not only national honor but duty to universal humanity must call the United States to the side of the French revolutionaries. There nonetheless remained a practical question as to just how far the virtually unarmed United States should go in answer to the call.

In England, a similar division of opinion appeared, which shortly had its effect in America. Edmund Burke, the Parliamentarian who had sympathized with the complaints of the colonists in America against the English Parliament, entirely disagreed with the English radicals who sympathized with the French Revolution. He saw the emergent class warfare in France as needlessly destructive fanaticism, and he shrewdly predicted in his *Reflections on the Revolution in France* that the Revolution would disintegrate first into anarchy and then into dictatorship. His essay was soon answered by Thomas Paine, who had returned to England after the American Revolution to urge his kind of common sense upon the English. Paine replied to Burke by writing

The Rights of Man, a document so stridently subversive of the British monarchy that Paine had to skip to France to avoid being hanged for treason. Insofar as the United States was concerned, the most important fact about *The Rights of Man* was that Jefferson endorsed it.

In a letter to its American printer, Jefferson said he was "extremely pleased to find that it will be reprinted here, and that something is at length to be publicly said against the political heresies which have sprung up amongst us. . . . no doubt our citizens will rally a second time round the standard of Common Sense."

Having said this much, Jefferson professed surprise when the printer published Paine's work with Jefferson's endorsement on the flyleaf.

"I certainly never made a secret of my being anti-monarchial and anti-aristocratical," he assured President Washington, "but I am sincerely mortified to be thus brought forward on the public stage, where to remain, to advance, or to retire, will be equally against my love of silence and quiet, and my abhorrence of dispute."

If Washington actually believed this, no one else did. *The Rights of Man*, with Jefferson's endorsement on it, was read everywhere in the United States from north to south, from the sea to the mountains. And, both Federalists and anti-Federalists passionately believed that, in view of the entire context of Paine's publication as an answer to Burke, Jefferson's endorsement meant that the peaceable farmer of Monticello was putting himself at the head of what we may now call the Republican party, and that he was simultaneously stating his position as the enemy of the British government and as the American champion of the French Revolution.

It was an age of political pamphleteering in which statesmen like John Adams, Madison, Hamilton, and Jefferson hired literary hatchet men to attack one another, and when the statesmen themselves wrote position papers under classical noms de plume. Their use of cat's-paws and pseudonyms enabled them to pretend to one another they were not the authors of the lies, slander, libel, and innuendo they slopped on one another's heads in print. It was necessary for them to maintain this pretense in order to meet and do the work of government. But Hamilton knew it was really Jefferson who was depicting him as an aristocratical monarchist with a hand in the public till. And Jefferson knew it was Hamilton who was ridiculing the Virginian's sudden change of costume, charging that beneath that affected "garb of Quaker simplicity," Jefferson remained a sensual, epicurean voluptuary, secretly aristocratic, and, like Caesar, only pretending not to grasp at the power in the state. Nor was the real authorship of these printed screeds unknown to the literate public. In an age lacking any other form of mass entertainment and information, the papers were all closely read and violently argued. Their unfortunate effect was to distort and divide. Whatever was purposed was suspected of being something other than it seemed. A perfectly sound plan to establish a national bank became a scheme to create a kingdom. A rational proposal to recognize the de facto government of France was seen as a Jacobin plot. On the one hand, a Federalist was an enemy of the people; on the other, a Republican was the enemy of civilization and property.

Jefferson stepped warily along through this potentially lethal political labyrinth, privately bold and publicly meek, the cautious leader of an opposition party. Hamilton careered boldly through it all, the leader of the party in power, toward his appointment on a dueling ground. There was meanwhile a nation to govern—one whose destiny lay clearly in the west. Here, between the Appalachians and the Mississippi, were two hundred thousand American settlers whose political opinions could be decisive. Both Federalist and Republican politicians saw votes in the west. Both saw opportunities to speculate in western lands. But both feared that the balance of political power might shift from the East Coast to these broad western lands with the swift growth of population there. It was a possibility that occurred to western politicians as well. Sectionalism had been a part of American politics since colonial days, and now the settlement of the west was adding a third section to the old ones of north and south. It was one more complication to an already sufficiently complex political scene, particularly in view of the character of the westerners.

Too many of them were the runaways, dropouts, and rejects of society. The frontier was always open to absconding swindlers, murderers, fugitive slaves, bankrupts, brigands, and failures. Lawless men did not venture into the west so much as they were expelled into it—together with thousands of men and women who had been hounded out of their home communities because they had either opposed, or had failed to join, the Revolution. It could certainly be said that the westward-rolling chariot of American civilization was preceded by misfits. Yet the majority of the settlers seem to have been simple, hopeful souls, determined to find a better land and make a better life for themselves upon it. Whether this implied relative failure in their original homes, or greed, or adventure, it in any case demanded that the settlers possess courage, physical hardihood, and a certain ability at armed and hand-to-hand combat. Pioneer men and women had to be able to protect themselves and their cattle from criminals, Indians, and, often enough, their neighbors. The leading men in western settlements might not always be the wealthiest or most intelligent, but they all had a well-developed reputation for readiness to fight with any man or beast. When the politicians of the long-established eastern communities gazed thoughtfully over the mountains into the Mississippi valley, they saw wild men there.

The political problem, therefore, posed both to Federalists and Republicans in the eastern states was how to win the allegiance of the wild westerners and so maintain a measure of control over them. No doubt the westerners would give their allegiance to those politicians who got them what they wanted. The sympathy of the westerners was, in general, Republican—but it might not remain so. What the westerners wanted was the use of the Mississippi River as a highway to market. Few of them had any use for the Spanish. Most of them had brought with them to the Mississippi valley a general xenophobia inherited from their English forebears, together with a specific loathing of Spaniards, and of Catholics, derived from the days of the Inquisition, Armada, and religious war. Those who had ventured down the winding river to New Orleans saw nothing in that squalid, fever-stricken town to change their minds about Spaniards or, for that matter, about Frenchmen. Some of the westerners were willing to negotiate with the Spanish authorities for trading rights on the Mississippi. Others were willing to shoot the Spanish off the river. Still others not only dreamed but planned to cross the river and push on into whatever lands might lie between it and the Pacific Ocean, accomplishing the conquest of Mexico *en passant*. Nor was the latter dream exclusively a western one. There were some New England Federalists who entertained it, and within the Republican party its exponent was that brave and brilliant hero of the Revolution, Aaron Burr.

If Thomas Jefferson ever meant what he said about finding public duties detestable, he could have had the western complication in mind. As a Republican politician, he needed the political support of the westerners. If he were too cautious, as secretary of state, in dealing with Spain, he might find the westerners giving their political allegiance to Burr, who in that case might very well supplant him as leader of the Republican party. But if he were too bold or not sufficiently careful, the United States could become involved in a disastrous war with Spain.

He was meanwhile aware of the Spanish Conspiracy, although not, apparently, of the extent of General James Wilkinson's involvement in it. In 1792, Wilkinson managed to slither back into the regular army as a brigadier general with special responsibility for western affairs. As Secret Agent No. 13, he continued to draw his pay from Spain; as a brigadier general in the United States army, he was paid by the United States. It says something for Wilkinson that he managed to do nothing in either of his capacities to merit any of the money. Yet Wilkinson's new army appointment was potentially dangerous; the Spanish Conspiracy was very much alive, and it was still another complicating factor in Jefferson's hydra-headed problem.

For all the time he spent in purely political warfare with Hamilton and the Federalists, Jefferson looked steadily west. He had looked west all his life. As a boy, Jefferson had been fascinated by the fact that he and his countrymen lived on the edge of an enormous continent, almost all of which still awaited exploration. No one knew what kinds of terrain, animals, or people might live out there. There were rumors of Welsh-speaking white Indian tribes, presumably the descendants of a legendary Welsh prince who may have led his people west over the seas. The notion that there might be new Mexicos and Perus awaiting discovery was never too far from men's minds, and men still dreamed of the fabulous Northwest Passage to Cathay. The romanticist, the geographer, and the natural scientist in Jefferson had always looked west into the unknown, although neither the boy nor the man ever ventured, physically, in that dangerous direction.

Jefferson also looked west in his simple capacity as a Virginia planter. He and his neighbors had been progressively destroying their estates by planting them in tobacco year after year, and until further discoveries were made in the science of agriculture, their best and quickest route to solvency was to acquire new lands where, as farmers said, the earth was still strong. No small part of Jefferson's yearning for the west was his personal desire to acquire profitable land for himself.

The philosopher of revolution gazed west as well. Jefferson's desire was to see the entire Western Hemisphere united into a single agrarian republic. It was a vision that certainly implied war, both civil and foreign, but it was Jefferson's dream nonetheless.

But in his more realistic moments as a politician and as a Cabinet minister, Jefferson had to nibble his way west. It was in both capacities that he wrote that "natural law" held that those who live on the upper reaches of any river have a natural right of access to the sea. It was a statement of position intended for western and Spanish consumption. To the westerners, it meant that Jefferson was going to help them gain trading privileges on the Mississippi; to the Spanish, it meant that the United States was going to do nothing at this time.

Jefferson's caution extended to secret matters as well as public ones. Early in 1792 he gave his entire attention to an eighteen-year-old Virginia neighbor, Meriwether Lewis, when the boy asked Jefferson to put him at the head of an expedition to penetrate whatever mysteries might lie west of the Mississippi. The purpose of this expedition was not simply to satisfy scientific curiosity, but rather to satisfy military curiosity. Young Lewis would report on Spanish and Indian strength in those parts. Jefferson told Lewis the time was not yet ripe, although perhaps he felt the boy was not yet ripe enough, for in January of the following year, Jefferson evidently felt either that the times were more propitious, or that a more plausible instrument had come to his hand. In his capacity as vice-president of the American Philosophical Society, Jefferson proposed that the society send a visiting French botanist, André Michaux, to examine whatever vegetation might be found growing along the Missouri River to the Pacific Ocean. Funds were privately raised for what was ostensibly a scientific exploration led by an eminent scientist. Jefferson told Michaux to take pains not to be captured either by the Spanish, who were presumed to be in strength south of the Missouri, nor by the British, who were presumed to be north of it. But before the expedition could be mounted, a political gale from France blew all the plans away—and Jefferson into retirement.

15

A Plot
That Sickened

O<small>N</small> April 8, 1793, one Edmond Genet stepped ashore at Charleston, South Carolina. He was a handsome, young, blond French linguist and career diplomat, newly appointed as the French ambassador to the American republic. He was also a not-so-secret agent of world revolution, sent to America by a radical splinter party that had momentarily taken over what had begun in 1789 as Jefferson's "beautiful revolution." Genet's specific instructions called for him to pry Canada away from Great Britain, and Florida and Louisiana away from Spain, and to "emancipate" all other Spanish possessions in North and South America. He was to do this with or without the aid of the United States, although he was certainly to try to solicit American support, promising the Americans that in event of common victory, France would not object to the United States acquisition of the two Floridas. Meanwhile, the French were reportedly contemplating the dispatch of a fleet including forty-five ships of the line and a force to be commanded by a Venezuelan revolutionary named Francisco Miranda. This expedition was to attack New Orleans, and, after accomplishing "the deliverance of our ancient brothers of Louisiana from the tyrannical yoke of Spain," it was to go on to free Mexico and otherwise establish republics in Central and South America. Moreover, Genet was to fit out and license American warships as French privateers to raid British commerce, since France was then at war with Britain.

As secretary of state, Thomas Jefferson had received reports as to Genet's mission and as to French intentions to attack New Orleans and Mexico, and he had been further advised by the French government that the United States ambassador to France, Gouverneur Morris, was unacceptable to them and must be replaced.

The situation would seem clear enough to anyone today. To assist Genet in any of his objectives, or France in any other, would immediately involve the United States in war with Great Britain and Spain. Since this invited nothing but disaster for the United States, Jefferson's plain duty, and that of the United States government, was to pack Genet back to France straightaway— and accept the risk of alienating France. But the path of duty was by no means plainly seen in the spring of 1793. It was partly obscured by emotion and made much darker yet by what then seemed to be practical political considerations. The major problem was that the French Revolution not only had all of Europe by the ears, but had radically increased the bitterness and distance between Federalists and Republicans in the United States.

Since 1789, the French Revolution had been following the morbid course Edmund Burke predicted for it. A first step toward chaos was taken in 1790, when the revolutionary government, the Constituent Assembly, confiscated the property of the Catholic Church, dissolved the monastic orders, divorced the Church from Rome, nationalized it, and decreed that henceforth all parish priests and bishops would be elected. They were to be elected by the French people, including not only French Catholics, but all other emancipated citizens—including Protestants, Jews, and atheists. Churchmen would be given government salaries. (The Constituent Assembly did not simply abolish the Church, because it felt that, without religion, the poor might lose their respect for, and sense of obedience to, the rich.)

· The immediate result of this reform was that the pope angrily denounced the act, and all the rest of the Revolution as well. The longer-range result was to make it appear in France and throughout all Europe that no man could be at once a republican and a Catholic. To a considerable extent, the choice was seen as one between being a republican and being a Christian. The issue was not confined to France, because the French Revolution, like the American one, was implicitly designed for export, inasmuch as its principles with respect to the natural rights of man were announced as universal, applicable to all men everywhere. From Sweden to Italy, from Russia to Spain, and upon the European island of Great Britain, the proponents of republican revolution had appeared. But as civil disorder and bloody repression took place in France as a consequence of nationalization of the Church, and as the French bourgeoisie began to lose control of the Revolution, the position of foreign sympathizers became less comfortable. To the kings, princes, and ruling bourgeois oligarchies of Europe, their native republicans were seen as pro-French, and now, by a process of extension, as anti-Christian hooligans. The same view was held by Hamilton and the Federalists in America, who, as republican bourgeoisie, were horrified by the stories that escaping French aristocrats told of mob rule in France. Jefferson and his radical Republicans continued, however, to believe in the French Revolution and to view anyone who disagreed with them as being the enemies of outraged humanity and the allies of monarchical tyranny.

For a while, European nations agreed with the British that what happened inside France was none of their business, but when the French government abolished the feudal rights of German princes in Alsace, and those princes appealed to the Holy

Roman Emperor, the situation was remarkably altered. The Holy Roman Emperor, Leopold II, met with the king of Prussia at Pillnitz in Saxony, and in the Declaration of Pillnitz Leopold announced to the world that he would lead an army into France to restore order if all the other nations of Europe would join this crusade. It cost him nothing to say this because it was quite certain that not all of them would, but the declaration had a result Leopold did not expect. It enabled a faction of the French revolutionary government, first called the Jacobins and later the Girondists, to take over control of the Revolution. Like the Americans who believed the world must be made safe for democracy, the Girondists took Leopold at his word, and held that the world must be made safe for the French Revolution. So they promised support to revolutionaries everywhere. They called for "a crusade of universal liberty." They would send French armies throughout Europe to help local revolutionaries overthrow their governments and establish a federation of republics—a kind of United States of Europe. And in the spring of 1792, the Girondist-controlled Constituent Assembly declared war on the Holy Roman Empire. But before the war could be fairly joined, control of the French Revolution passed out of the hands of the middle-class Girondists and into those of much more radical Jacobins who were the champions of the working classes—the peasants, artisans, and wage earners. A commune was set up in Paris; a Parisian mob swept into the Tuileries, massacred Louis XVI's Swiss guard, and slammed the king into prison. Soldiers who said they would not fight abroad till they had first cleansed France slaughtered in Paris more than one thousand people they alleged to be counterrevolutionaries. A wretched period of senseless fears, blood and anarchy was now begun. A National Convention was created in Paris, proclaimed universal suffrage and a universal military draft, and envisioned universal education. Calling for an international revolution, the convention ordered all French generals to confiscate the property of anyone who opposed them in countries they conquered, and they sent one French revolutionary army into Belgium and another into the Rhineland. Then the convention dragged Louis XVI out of prison in December 1792 put him on trial for treason, and a few weeks later, chopped off his head.

As the new year began, the British had military staff conferences with the Dutch. The two governments then announced that the French could do whatever they pleased to themselves as far as Great Britain and Holland were concerned, but they would have to get out of Belgium. The two nations next opened staff conferences with the Prussians and the Austrians. The French reply in February 1793 was to declare war on all four powers, and to send armies into Nice and Savoy, as well as continuing operations in Belgium and the German Rhineland.

However chaotic the French government was, the French revolutionary armies were far from weak. The work of Louis XIV had lived after him so far as the French army was concerned. To the general soundness of the basic military structure, the Revolution added the important reform of promotion solely on merit; thus in 1793 a twenty-four-year-old artillery captain of genius, Napolione Buonaparte, who was not French but a Corsican-Italian, was promoted to brigadier general for his work in expelling a British force from Toulon. The revolutionary armies enjoyed the high morale that derives from revolutionary ardor, but more important, they had behind them the resources of what was still the largest, most numerous, and technically furthest-advanced nation in Europe—no matter what its political structure might be. Beyond this, there was at first no serious opposition. The British and Dutch had no great land forces on the Continent, while the Prussians and the Austrians were too suspicious of one another to act in concert against the French. Yet all the revolutionary armies did not win all of the battles all of the time, and in the spring of 1793, while Ambassador Genet was arriving in America, allied armies succeeded in clearing Belgium and prepared to invade France.

A Plot That Sickened

At this point, there was panic, and worse, in Paris. There was an allied army on the doorstep, and radical, working-class revolutionaries in France were now denouncing the comparatively moderate Girondists as counterrevolutionary enemies of the people. France began to slip into civil war. To repress what they called the counterrevolution, the radical element appointed a Committee of Public Safety in Paris, and the committee in turn established what history has called the Reign of Terror. What the world chiefly remembers is the slaughter of Marie Antoinette, and that of men, women, and children whose misfortune it was to have been of noble birth. It is more to the point to recall that nearly three-quarters of the more than forty thousand victims were workers and peasants whose crime it was to have retained their faith in the Roman Catholic Church and to have refused conscription into the revolutionary armies. The radicals of the Committee of Public Safety, acting through the convention, proclaimed Christianity counterrevolutionary. A new calendar was devised to wipe out all reference to Christ and His saints. There was now the Year One of a calendar without Christmas; churches and cathedrals were vandalized, and, in the name of reason, the Gothic statues of the saints were mutilated or destroyed. For the new religion was Reason. A ceremony was held in Notre Dame, in which an actress personified not the Virgin, but the Goddess of Reason.

It was against this background of horror, regicide, and general European war that Citoyen Edmond Genet arrived in Charleston. In the Cabinet, Alexander Hamilton argued that the United States should not receive such an emissary from such a government. Jefferson said of course that the country should, and must. As he saw it, France and the United States were the only two republics in the world; their interests were identical insofar as the rights of man were concerned; each must stand by the other in a world full of predatory monarchies. But with the French now at war with Great Britain, the practical question arose: Was the

United States bound by its old alliance with monarchical France to recognize the French Revolutionary government and join it in war against its enemies? There was disagreement; President Washington was for compromise. Genet should be received, he thought, but not "with too much warmth and cordiality," while with respect to the war, the United States should remain neutral. Jefferson was of two minds about this. He was so suspicious of Hamilton and Washington, imagining a Federalist cabal to convert the United States into a monarchy, that he saw in a policy of neutrality a deep plot to serve the interests of Great Britain. He let this be known, privately, to a newspaper editor in his employ, with the result that the newspaper attacked both neutrality and the character of the President. But publicly, in the Cabinet, Jefferson took the view that much as he loved France and the Revolution, there was merit in neutrality: America could produce in peace while France and Britain spent themselves in war. Accordingly, he consented to the Neutrality Proclamation, which was issued unanimously by the Cabinet.

Genet, meanwhile, did not rush to present his credentials to President Washington. He instead busied himself in Charleston, commissioning the French consul there to fit out American ships as French privateers to raid British shipping, and being lionized by Southern planters who, like Jefferson, were ardently pro-French and who, like Jefferson, had their eyes fixed on the Mississippi River and its valley lands. From them, Genet heard that the eastern seaboard lands were rapidly being farmed out, and that the population was moving west; it seemed to him these men were more than ready to join the French in an adventure into Spanish-held Florida and Louisiana. Genet was made aware of the temper of the United States. He learned of the rift between Federalist and Republican and heard that to be a Federalist was to be pro-British, antirevolutionary, and representative of Northern commercial interests—whereas to be Republican was to be the friend of France, of universal humanity. He was led to believe that the great majority of Americans were Republican, and that if President Washington refused to put the United States in the war firmly on the side of France, Genet himself could appeal to Congress to do so; failing there, he could appeal over the heads of the President and Congress to take his case directly to the people. He was also led to believe he could count upon the formidable support of that well-known friend of France, the brilliant philosopher of revolution, Thomas Jefferson, secretary of state.

Nothing he found on his way to Philadelphia caused Genet to change his mind. His tour took on the aspects of a triumphal procession, with towns turned out to meet him and militia firing salutes. His reception would have been very different had he landed in Boston and proceeded from there. Such a journey would have given him grounds for reflection. In the North, he would have found no great love for the British. A New England merchant might well agree with a Southern planter with respect to kings and republics. More doubtfully, he might even be willing to swallow an alliance with the detested French under certain circumstances. But the hard, crucial fact was that New England's livelihood was predicated on commerce. Virtually all of America's merchant ships were New England ones. And most of those ships sailed to British ports. Just as before the American Revolution, so it was afterward: Britain and America were each other's principal trading partners. Ninety percent of the Southern planter's tobacco was sold in Britain whether he liked it or not. A Southerner might look down his aristocratic nose on commerce if he wished, but his prosperity was based on commerce nevertheless. Moreover, as the Southerner did not, the New Englander had British troops to the north of him and British troops to the west of him. He could sail the seas east of him only at the sufferance of the British royal navy. All rhetoric and sentimentality about sister republics to one side and the royal navy on the other, there was no doubt in the New Englander's mind as to which he should choose. If he could not be neutral, and had to take a side in the European war, he would certainly choose alliance with Great Britain. It was in his vital interest to do so. More broadly, to do so was also in the vital interest of the United States.

But rhetoric and sentimentality could not all be put on one side in America in 1793. The matter was further confused by class interests. There were New Englanders who were poor farmers, poorly paid wage earners. The least prosperous tended to be Republicans who saw their Federalist neighbors as fat and privileged antidemocrats. There were Southern Republicans who professed belief in the rights of man, but who saw no good in what they called the mob; men who would agree with Hamilton that the right to vote should be granted only to men of property. Genet had entered a country many times divided in its opinions —one in which no man might be counted on to be consistent to a set of principles, although he might be depended upon to be quite vehement as to what he thought of any particular issue at any particular time. What Genet might not have appreciated was that no matter how vitriolic the contending articles in the American press, and no matter how violent and sentimental the American arguments, and how wildly public opinion in America could swing, a reasonably sensible consensus could emerge in America at the ultimate point of decision: that remarkable bit of patchwork, the United States Constitution, is an interesting example of this phenomenon. Perhaps Genet, who was only thirty years old, was too young and too full of grandiose revolutionary rhetoric to be astute. In any case, he saw only republican friends of France as far as Philadelphia, where he was met with jubilation in the streets and with adulation in the drawing rooms. He saw people waving the French tricolor, heard them singing the "Ça Ira" and "La Marseillaise" in their Philadelphia accents; saw them dancing around Liberty Poles in their red French Liberty nightcaps, read the attacks upon Washington in the Jeffersonian press, and met with men eager to sell him cannons. In his youthful innocence, he mistook an early American fad for a crusade.

For his part, Jefferson was delighted with Genet's reception in Philadelphia, seeing a political demonstration against the Neutrality Proclamation as a general repudiation of the Federalists. Jefferson's attitudes otherwise exemplified the way in which American opinions could gyrate: the revolutionary in him was heart and soul for France, and for Genet and his mission. But the practical politician in Jefferson told him he ought not make an issue of neutrality and resign from the Cabinet. So he stayed in the Cabinet and signed the proclamation—a decision no doubt also shared by the realist in Jefferson who could see the immense dangers in war at this time. Yet, after wisely endorsing neutrality, Jefferson returned to his romantic frame of mind, endorsing Genet's arming and fitting out of a Philadelphia ship to be a French privateer. He excused this blatant act of war as being nothing of the sort, but rather as an expression of France's decision to give "us in all her possessions all the rights of her native citizens & to receive our vessels as her vessels." From this remarkable bit of logic, he soared on, bitterly opposing the wise government decision to blow the privateer out of the water if she tried to leave Philadelphia harbor, arguing, "I would not gratify the combination of kings with the spectacle of the two only republics on earth destroying each other . . . nor . . . add this country to that combination, turn the scale of contest, and let it be from our hands that the hopes of man received their last stab." Having said out of one side of his mouth that arming a privateer was not an act of war, saying out of the other that it was a decisive one, Jefferson pulled up short, advising his friends that he was trying to do all he could to curb Genet's "impetuosity." Whereupon, romantic fantasy grasping the helm once again, Jefferson sailed away on the opposite tack, encouraging Genet in a scheme far more impetuous than the fitting out of a few commerce raiders.

This was the invasion of the west. It was Genet's idea to make much more sinister use of the botanist, Michaux, than Jefferson had ever intended. Genet told Jefferson, not as the

French ambassador to the United States secretary of state, but just as one revolutionary conspirator to another, that he was going to send Michaux west to foment revolution in Canada and Louisiana. Michaux's status would be that of an official representative of the French government; as such he was to rouse up the French Canadians to form themselves into an army and, with Indian allies, overthrow their British masters. He was to assure them that they would have the support of the American people in this endeavor. Similarly, Michaux would touch off a revolution in Louisiana, with the assistance of an army of Kentuckians and whatever Indians could be persuaded to join the fun. He had, Genet confided to Jefferson, already bought the allegiance of two "generals in Kentucky" with an offer of three thousand pounds sterling, payable after the expedition assembled outside United States territory in Louisiana. He intended to commission Americans to serve as officers in this expedition; when victory was achieved, Louisiana would be established as a separate republic, friendly to France and the United States. Now, Genet asked, would Jefferson please give his written consent to the appointment of M. Michaux as "Consul of France at Kentucky"?

Jefferson explained that he could not do that, because Kentucky was a state, not a seaport. But he did something more: he furnished Michaux with a letter stating that the United States secretary of state knew Michaux to be a man acting with the knowledge of the French ambassador. Jefferson then came somewhat more to his sober senses. He assured Genet that he had no objection whatsoever to the French starting a revolution in Louisiana, but that the United States really could not allow an army of Americans from Kentucky to take part in it. In fact, he said, the United States would have to hang any of its citizens who did, because the United States could not afford to give offense to Spain.

Apart from that, Genet wrote at once to Paris that Jefferson "showed me the ways of acting with success, gave me the addresses of many reliable men, and promised me that he would apply all his influence to the success of our projects."

Jefferson could very well have given such a promise in the heady ambiance of two revolutionaries chatting happily away over a bottle of wine; it is equally possible that Genet, in his enthusiasm, merely thought that Jefferson did. However this may be, Jefferson must surely have had second thoughts upon the morrow, when he could reflect that his earlier reports on the nature of Genet's mission to the United States had now been proved to be true by the young man himself. But how could he possibly assist Genet? The British had just proclaimed a blockade of France, reserving their right to seize any ship, of any flag, that attempted to bring foodstuffs into France. This was a sobering reminder that the Royal Navy ruled the seas; the British could not only seize whatever ships they wished on any pretext at all, but they also could and certainly would send armies into America if the United States had anything to do with insurrections in Canada; already there were British ships standing off the coast to deal with Genet's privateers, and they might stand in to bombard the American ports from which ships sailed. Nor was the idea of a separate republic in Louisiana an altogether welcome one, particularly because a great many Americans, including Jefferson, were looking in that direction themselves. Jefferson must have wondered to what extent he had ever believed in, or even sympathized with Genet's mission, as compared to the extent he had really been using the youthful Frenchman's crowd appeal to further his own political ambitions. The romantic revolutionary and the equally romantic patriot in Jefferson must have had a difficult time living under the same skin, and both would have been dismayed by the politician who lived there, too.

In a way, Genet came to Jefferson's rescue. Scornful of the Neutrality Proclamation, he jibed at its cowardice, thereby imputing perfidy and cowardice to the President as well. He

threatened to take his case to the people, and so heated were public feelings at this time, particularly after the British announcement of their blockade, that many a sober Philadelphian believed
the country was on the verge of a second revolution. Hamilton
and the Federalists thought so: they believed Genet was inspiring
Jefferson and the Republicans to overthrow the United States
government by the same terrible means the radicals had used to
seize control of the government in France. Genet's undiplomatic
activity and his blunt speaking against the government to which
he was the French ambassador gave Jefferson an opportunity to
reconsider his own position. Only two days after he had led
Genet to believe that he would give the Frenchman all possible
support for his incendiary adventures in Canada and Louisiana,
furnishing Genet with that letter of endorsement for Michaux's
use, Jefferson privately unburdened himself to his close colleague,
James Madison. "Never in my opinion was so calamitous an appointment made," he said, "as that of the present Minister of
France here. Hot headed, all imagination, no judgment, passionate, disrespectful and even indecent toward the P. in his written
as well as his verbal communications . . . He renders my position
immensely difficult."

What Jefferson called his position, today's politician would
call his image. Jefferson's position, or image, the thing he had to
sell at the polls, was his appearance as the staunch Republican
friend of France and enemy of kings and aristocrats. His difficulty lay in trying to find a way to act in one fashion while seeming to act in another. For unless he was willing to put party before country, not to mention acting the traitor by using his Cabinet position secretly to subvert United States policy, he simply
could not allow Genet to go on with his plans. Nor could he as a
Cabinet officer, or even as a Virginia gentleman, allow Genet to
insult his country and its President. Perhaps more important to
the politician in Jefferson, he perceived that Genet's activities
were alienating some prominent Republicans; they were carrying

their distaste for Genet in particular into a general disenchantment with the French Revolutionary government. So Genet's
plans would have to be spiked, and Genet himself would have to
go.

To accomplish the first goal, spoiling the plot to seize Louisiana, was apparently more difficult for Jefferson than accomplishment of the second. For it would seem that some of his Republican friends in Kentucky had been allowed to believe he was all
for an adventure into Louisiana, while others impatiently regarded his delicate negotiations with the Spanish government, for
trading rights at New Orleans, as indicating that Jefferson was
really conspiring with Spain rather than negotiating. For a while,
Jefferson seemed not to know what to do, for he allowed Michaux's and Genet's plans to go forward for nearly two months.
But then, when Michaux actually set forth on his mission,
carrying the secretary of state's endorsement, Jefferson at last
wrote another letter, this one to the governor of Kentucky. It
warned him of the plot and ordered him to arrest any persons
conspiring to mount an invasion of Spanish territory.

At the same time, Jefferson decided to repudiate Genet, and
to ask France to recall their troublesome ambassador. In a letter to
Madison, Jefferson mapped out the political strategy. He told
Madison that, in the present circumstances, he had come to believe it "will be true wisdom in the Republican Party" to go along
with the government's decision to remain neutral in the war between France and Great Britain, and meanwhile to dump Genet
overboard with, however, "expressions of strong friendship & adherence to his nation & confidence that he has acted against their
sense. In this we shall keep the people on our side by keeping ourselves in the right."

He meant, of course, "by *seeming* to keep ourselves in the
right," but then Genet unwittingly made this easy. For the
Frenchman took it into his boyish head to deny that he had ever
thought of appealing directly to the American people to come to

the aid of France, and he virtually ordered President Washington to back him up. "I dare therefore," he wrote to Washington, "to expect from your candor and probity an explicit declaration that I have never intimated to you an intention of appealing to the people." Washington did not deign to answer this ingenuous demand. He left the task to Jefferson, who briefly told Genet his embassy was finished. France would be asked to send another ambassador.

It probably did not occur to Jefferson that any American, not even the staunchest Republican, could tolerate any foreigner's giving abrupt, direct orders to the President of the United States. But to his painful surprise, it seemed that some of them could, and worst of all, these people were among his Republican friends. With respect to Genet, Jefferson was damned if he did and damned if he did not; to espouse the fellow was to lose a measure of Republican support, and it now turned out that to repudiate him was to lose a measure of Republican support. Genet's Republican friends were bitter about his dismissal, as was Genet himself, who subsequently wrote Jefferson a long, tiresome letter to the general effect that Jefferson had stabbed him in the back, calling him, *en passant,* a pro-British coward and a liar. Worse things were meanwhile being said about Jefferson in Kentucky, where some said he had been behind a scheme to involve the United States in a war with Spain, while others accused him of betraying it. As a result of the uproar in Kentucky, Jeffersonian Republicans lost votes and their offices.

So Jefferson did not succeed in preserving his position or public image, in his attempts to extricate himself from Genet's embraces. Throughout the Genet affair, Jefferson as secretary of state had never been closely associated with the young Frenchman. The one occasion when they discussed revolutionary operations in Canada and Louisiana had been a private, unofficial meeting. Otherwise Jefferson's official relationship with Genet had been correct, if not almost distant. But through the Republican press, and through his friends, Jefferson had allowed himself to appear as standing behind, if not standing arm in arm with, Genet and, by a process of extension, behind the French government that called for world revolution. This permitted others to think of him as the champion of radical republicanism, although no one could say that Jefferson ever made such a claim for himself, or that he had taken any action to put himself at the head of an opposition party.

If this was his policy, it succeeded only too well. He did become in the public mind the champion of Genet, of France, of revolution, and when Genet's antics were seen to be both dangerous and insulting, Jefferson's prestige and that of the Republican cause suffered accordingly. A worse blow to Jefferson's position was dealt him in Paris, where the Terror condemned and then guillotined the Girondists who had sent Genet to the United States as their ambassador. Genet was no longer an ambassador, nor could he return to France. For Jefferson to appear the friend of France was now for him to appear the champion of a mob that howled for blood and decapitated its own leaders.

It was all too much, but an escape presented itself. Over and again during his public life, Jefferson had reiterated his desire to withdraw to the simple life of a Virginia farmer. President Washington now asked Jefferson if he still intended to resign, and if so, who did Jefferson think should succeed him as secretary of state? Of course, Washington said, he would be sorry to lose him. If Jefferson was surprised and hurt to find Washington taking seriously his professed desire to resign, he also saw the wisdom of retirement. He could withdraw from his exposed position on the political front, as it were, and fall back to a rear area to regroup his demoralized Republican forces. He left Philadelphia for Monticello in January 1794. Two years later he was to return to public life, this time as Vice President of the United States. At the time of his retirement, Jefferson said he preferred growing lettuce to practicing politics. He doubtless did: everything about the

Genet affair had been politically disastrous for him, and the wonder of it is that Jefferson ever allowed himself to become involved in it.

One possible explanation lies in Jefferson's view of himself. He once said it seemed his fate never to "continue for any time with a person whose manners and principles had excited my warm attachment." He had spoken in the context of admiration for a woman, and in that regard, Jefferson's trouble seems to have been that he was ever too cautious a lover. But if so, so in politics: Jefferson's entire public life seemed, in a sense, to consist of warm attachments to principles. If the attachments proved transient, this was because reality opportunely presented itself: love is after all built on a certain amount of illusion. Jefferson was warmly attached to Genet and the French Revolution. Perhaps his disillusionment began when, in the course of his amours, he was at length forced to admit to the nasty fact that the French government had designs upon Louisiana. One can believe in the brotherhood of man, but seldom to the point where one is willing for one's brother to share the bed of one's fiancée.

To put the matter somewhat less fancifully, Jefferson had something in common with the American electorate: Both could give their hearts to a cause, but both had a fortunate ability to come to their senses in the last possible instant before folly could lead to disaster.

In retrospect, the absurd Genet affair had one salutary effect. It inoculated Jefferson against a second experience of the French pox.

16

The Genius
and the Bishop

I would seem that no matter how often or how radically nations change their governments, nations retain their basic interests and will, if necessary, go to war to pursue or protect them. For all Genet's talk about establishing new republics in Canada and Louisiana, the essential meaning of his mission was that the French had not lost sight of former French possessions in North America. In one way or another, they meant to reacquire them for France.

France, then, was apparently not the good friend that Jefferson and the Republicans thought she was. For, unknown to the American government, the French ambassadors who followed Genet were under orders to try to prevent the United States from coming to any agreement with Spain with respect to the navigation of the Mississippi River. Meanwhile, the Directory sought to make a deal of its own with Spain. For three years, in 1795, 1796, and 1797, the Directory tried to get the Spanish government to cede Louisiana back to France. While these negotiations were in progress, France dispatched a secret agent, a General Collot, down the Ohio and Mississippi rivers. Collot floated downstream with a sketchbook, mapping the strategic features of the terrain with a view to future military operations there. He recommended to Paris that it would be advisable for France to seize certain portions of the United States western territories, adjacent to the rivers, in order to safeguard French possession of the Mississippi River valley. Accordingly, French agents were sent among the Indians to urge them to take the warpath against American settlers to prevent extensive American occupation of the lands the French meant to àttack. Nothing in any of this spoke to the rights of man; all of it spoke of the ambitions of France.

Just so, when black slaves revolted in 1794 on the French Caribbean island of Santo Domingo, massacred their masters, and declared a republic (all of this inspired by the example of the French Revolution), the reaction in Paris was not as joyful as an enthusiast of revolution might have hoped. True, the French Revolutionary government was the enemy of the aristocratic planters who had been massacred; yes, it preached world revolution and the establishment of republics everywhere; indeed, it championed the emancipation of slaves. But it did not look with favor upon the loss of a sugar-rich French possession, and it intended to have that island back again.

In that year, France was waging a general war in Europe. She had in the field armies totaling eight hundred thousand men, the largest armed force the world had ever seen; it was the first one in history to be an army of the people, enlisted from the citizenry of a nation and inspired by a single national ideal. But that ideal was only partly new. The new part of it was to carry the message of liberty, equality, and fraternity throughout Europe in order to make the old part come true. The old part was to extend the borders of France from the Pyrenees to the Rhine; from the Channel to the Mediterranean; to establish the position of France as the Great Nation of Europe, and to reconstruct a French colonial empire overseas. Colbert and the Sun King would have approved.

For its part, the British nation had changed the form of its government remarkably from Tudor times, but not its interests and not its essential foreign policy. Its interest was to acquire territory and colonize it and to expand its trade and commerce. Although admitting the independence of its former American colonies, Great Britain had by no means lost its interest in the possibility of winning some, if not all of them back again, and imperial interest in America otherwise invited British attention to the huge empty spaces upon the map of North America—to the regions lying west of Canada to the Pacific and north to the Pole; to whatever lay west and south of Canada from the Great Lakes to Mexico. British policy was to command the oceans of the world in order to pursue British interest, and meanwhile to prevent the emergence of any great nation in Europe. Such a nation would be too dangerous a backdoor neighbor and too formidable a rival for European trade. For this reason, even if the British government had been a band of republican radicals, it would scarcely have shaken hands with the radical republicans of France: national interest could not tolerate the emergence of France or any other country as the great nation of Europe. And for this reason, there was war.

Spain in 1794 was well within the twilight shadows that would steadily darken and from which she has yet to emerge. But she was not then the least of European nations, and so far as her interest was concerned, it was to try to retain those American possessions upon whose wealth her own economy was still predicated. In this regard, Spain with nervous certainty looked upon her possessions in Louisiana. Her nervousness arose from her certainty that the French, the British, and the Americans were looking at them, too. Her policy, however, was limited by her fears: it was to negotiate with everyone and hope for the best.

It was in the interest of the United States to take its way

west across the map of North America, but its policy, shaped by impotence, was to appear to be the possible ally of France, or of Great Britain, or of Spain, in the fervent hope that all of these nations would therefore pay court to the little republic, each of them supposing that if it did not, either of the others would. It was a policy shaped largely by Jefferson, who has enjoyed a reputation as a pacifist. Instead, he was cautiously bellicose, as his involvement in the Genet affair suggests.

As the eighteenth century drew to a close, something very like a human meteor appeared out of the welter of general war and revolution—a man with interests and policies of his own, whose brilliant failure enabled the United States to survive its precarious infancy.

He was conceived and born to a fugitive family of minor Italian nobility on the island of Corsica. The family was in flight from the French at the time of his birth, for they were involved in an unsuccessful attempt to free Corsica from French rule. When some years later a general amnesty was granted the defeated rebels, the boy's father, Count Buonaparte, managed to have his son Napolione entered in a royal French military academy that prepared the sons of noblemen to become commissioned officers in the French army. He was graduated from this school at age fifteen in 1784, the year Jefferson arrived in France to serve as the United States ambassador, and the faculty report had this to say of him:

"Reserved and diligent, he prefers study to any kind of conversation . . . He is taciturn, with a love for solitude; is moody, overbearing, and extremely egotistical. Though he speaks little, his answers are decisive and to the point, and he excels in argument. Much self-love, and overweening ambition."

With equal truth, Napolione's tutors could have remarked there was nothing in any way usual about the boy. He was, for example, unusually short and thin, and unusually poor; his only possessions were his uniform and sword. But far from being a negligible figure among his taller, better fed, and wealthier noble classmates, he passed among them like a disdainful prince. His view of education was that he needed to learn in order to rule. He already demonstrated an almost terrifying power of intellect and an almost horrifying ability to see into the recesses of anyone else's mind and character: at age fifteen, he gave commands. Beyond that, he believed in what he called his star, entirely confident that he had appeared on earth to perform immortal deeds. His reading of the social theories of the day led him to believe that Rousseau was an ass; he did not for a moment believe in fraternity; the thought of men enjoying liberty made him smile. And as for equality, history would have something to say about that. His own social model was that of the hero. He read and reread Plutarch's *Lives* and determined to become a second Alexander. At age fifteen, he was already considering the central strategic importance of Egypt as the seat of another Alexandrine empire.

Measureless opportunities opened before Napolione when the Bastille fell and the French Revolution began. Then a twenty-year-old second lieutenant of artillery, his first act of war was to open fire upon a revolutionary mob that appeared in the streets of his garrison town; his second was to obtain a furlough from his regiment and speed to Corsica to lead a revolt there. He would free his native island from French rule—in order to rule it himself. The discrepancy between the first act and the second is a fair measure of Napolione's amorality; as he once told his schoolboy diary, "Only the sword-belt belongs to France; the edge is my own."

With respect to his adventures in Corsica, he was unsuccessful, emerging from these escapades not as the master of the island but a fugitive from it, and more than this, cashiered from the French army. But he then disappeared into the chaos of the Revolution, a soldier of fortune, moving surely and shrewdly in the chaos to the Jacobin radical left, working his way in the Revolutionary army, despising the French and their Revolution, but using both as a means to power.

On fleeting sight, he might have seemed a scarecrow, an angry little wight in a shabby uniform; a small, coarse-mannered youth of gloomy countenance and misanthropic views. But such a glimpse would have been fleeting indeed. It would vanish in his intensity. His skin might be yellow and sickly, but what compelled attention was the remarkable brilliance of his eyes and then, immediately, the enormous range and power of a completely informed and exceedingly rapid mind. It was then perceived that yellow-skinned or not, and short as he might be, and shabby as were his clothes, he was handsome and well formed almost to the point of beauty, and listening to him, despite his Italian-accented French, men felt themselves oddly moved. There was apparently nothing he did not know. There were apparently no solutions to any problem that were better than those he suggested. He was tireless; his physical courage was beyond question; to be with him was to see thought at once translated into action. He gave men the curious impression that, in meeting him, they were in the presence of history. Perhaps he was able to do this because he was so sure of it himself.

The Revolution was peculiarly useful to him because of its insistence that all men were born with equal natural rights, and that accidents of birth should never debar the poor or foreign born from positions to which merit might otherwise entitle them. However much a genius Napolione surely was, he almost certainly would never have become a brigadier general at age twenty-four in the royal French army. But the Revolutionary army forgave him his Corsican birth and Italian accent and his youth. It gave him command of the artillery, and in 1795 the Directory, which had succeeded the Committee of Public Safety as the revolutionary government, called on the young general to protect it from the terror of a Parisian mob. He dispersed the urban savages with what he contemptuously called a whiff of grapeshot and turned his thoughtful, brilliant eyes upon the frightened lawyers who comprised the Directory. Those gentlemen were more than glad to hear him ask for command of a woebegone French army facing Austrian and Sardinian enemies on the Alpine frontiers of northern Italy. There was that about the young general that made the Directors wish him as far away from Paris as possible.

While the youthful general followed his star toward immortal glory, certain figures and events moved on history's stage during the years 1794–1796, preparing it for the scenes to be enacted when the new century began. All their activity ultimately focused on the Mississippi River valley, where the national interests of Great Britain, France, Spain, and the United States converged. In 1794, while Jefferson grew lettuces in retirement at Monticello and carefully rebuilt his political position, John Jay went to London.

· Jay, who had been one of the least revolutionary of delegates to the Continental Congress, was an ardent Federalist and chief justice of the United States Supreme Court. He was sent by the Federalist administration to London as a special ambassador to arrange a treaty with the British. At the same time, James Monroe, the close Republican colleague of Jefferson and James Madison, and, like them, a Virginian, was sent to Paris as the United States ambassador to France. The Federalist administration did not tell Monroe the nature of Jay's mission. If he had known what it was, he and every other Republican would have exploded. Nor did the administration make the nature of Monroe's mission entirely clear to him. Ostensibly, he was to repair the frayed relationship between the two republics. The Revolutionary government of France had objected to what it believed to be the aristocratic ways, manners, and beliefs of the prior American ambassador, who was a Federalist; more important, they were irritated that the Americans had opted for neutrality in the current war with Great Britain. In Monroe, who was every bit as much a Francophile as his friend Jefferson and just as radical a Republican, the United States had the very man to send to France. But Monroe did not know that his embassy was designed to do more than soothe French feelings: it was to divert French attention from Jay's purposes in London.

The dispatch of both ambassadors was related to the war at sea. The British navy, in seeking to seal France off from foreign trade, was halting American ships, searching them for contraband intended for France, and kidnapping American sailors at pistol point, enlisting them as seamen in its warships. The French point of view, which was shared by more Americans than just a majority of the Republicans, was that the actions of the British navy were acts of war and that the United States should honor its military alliance with France, or at any rate protect the French and American shipping that sailed the Atlantic in accordance with the commercial treaty between the two nations. The United States official point of view was rather different. It was simply that the high seas should be free to unrestricted trade among all nations. This was more a convenient expression of hope than it was a policy: in time of war, no nation really believes in freedom of the seas. Instead, a warring nation seeks to control them. In any case, the United States point of view in 1794 was that Britain ought not have the right to halt American ships bound for France, nor should the French have any right to halt American ships bound for Great Britain, and Jay was to explain this to the British while Monroe explained it to the French.

But there was more to Jay's mission than this. Freedom of the seas was an idle argument, rather than an issue. The more important purposes of Jay's negotiation were disclosed in the treaty which he and the British minister, Baron Grenville, signed in secret. The treaty provided for British evacuation of the northwestern frontier posts they had held since 1783—the forts that blocked America's way west into the Great Lakes and upper Mississippi areas. It provided for unrestricted use of the Mississippi for British and American shipping. It granted American ships trading privileges in Great Britain and in the East Indies. But it severely restricted American trade in the British West Indies, and in effect it acknowledged the British right to halt and search neutral ships and impress their sailors. Jay and the Federalist administration had every right to congratulate themselves. They had got what they wanted from the British in the west and on the great river; they had got additional trading privileges besides, and they could never have got these things had the British not been involved in a war in Europe, at sea, and around the world with Revolutionary France. The Americans had not won freedom of the seas or freedom from impressment from the British, but then, the British would never have bargained away any of the powers of the British navy, for in the end, all imperial interest, as well as the safety of the island kingdom itself, entirely depended upon that navy. So Jay and the Federalist administration had reason to rejoice over what they had won. There were, however, other opinions.

One of them was Spanish. While the Spanish might not have known the details of Jay's treaty, they did sense a detente between Great Britain and the United States, and they correctly feared this had something to do with the Mississippi. Their worst fear was that the United States and Great Britain would form an alliance, and that an Anglo-American army would come floating down the Mississippi to seize Louisiana and New Orleans and then, wheeling right, invade Mexico. (By Mexico, the Spanish did not refer to the current boundaries of that nation, but rather to the entire American southwest, including California.) These fears led the Spanish minister, Manuel de Godoy, duke of Alcudia, to make a separate peace with Revolutionary France in 1795. A more unlikely alliance could hardly be imagined than one between a still-feudal Spain that was still more Catholic than the pope, and a nation of godless regicides bent upon world revolution, but national interests must be served—and the Spanish preferred to ignore the anti-Christian aspects of France and to reconstruct the family compact of the two Latin nations. Having prepared this European position as one defense of its overseas possessions, Spain next sought to conciliate the Americans. Godoy agreed to confirm the United States–Spanish boundary of the two Floridas at 31 degrees north latitude; to declare the exclusive freedom of United States citizens and Spanish subjects to navigate the Mississippi River; to give the Americans a free port at New Orleans for three years; to stop sending Indian war parties on raids against American settlements in the river valley. With the conclusion of this agreement in 1795, the Spanish Conspiracy was momentarily at an end, and Kentucky tempers somewhat subsided. In negotiating with the Americans, the Spanish evidently meant to undercut any British-American cooperation on the Mississippi; to have only the weak republic as a neighbor, not a United States allied with Britain, and to wait for a better day. The three-year limit on free trade at New Orleans indicated the arrangement was temporary. It says something for Spanish nervousness at this time that Godoy was rewarded for his efforts with an honorific title, "the Prince of Peace." Unfortunately for Spanish hopes, the concessions they and the British extended the Americans merely made the United States even more conscious of the Mississippi than it already was, and the point was not lost upon the French ambassador to the United States. When he heard of what the Spanish had done, he immediately wrote to his superiors in the Directory that it would be well for France to get Louisiana back from a jittery Spain in order to put direct French military pressure on United States policy. He, too, feared a British-American detente, and he, too, looked west to the Mississippi.

In France, meanwhile, James Monroe was playing his sentimental role as the lover of France and revolution. He was every bit as ingenuous as Genet, and only seven years older. And just as Genet had found the United States government as cool toward him as the public seemed warm, so it was with Monroe. Baffled when the Directory was loath to treat with him on maritime matters, Monroe did in France what Genet had intended to do in America. He appealed over the heads of the Directory to the National Convention, appearing before that body to give a tearful harangue on ancient friendship, human rights, the brotherhood of republics. He presented the convention with an American flag and a protestation of the undying love of the American people for the French. Of course there was applause; it was a touching scene. Moreover, on Monroe's part the emotion was entirely genuine. His puzzlement grew when it appeared the Directory was, if anything, icier than ever. He did not know the French had got wind of what Jay and the British had agreed upon; when a Frenchman at last apprised him of it, Monroe refused to believe it. He told his French informant this could not be true; that he would query his government and shortly be able to provide official proof to the contrary.

When to his horror he learned that it was true—that the United States had given inimical Britain privileges it refused to extend to friendly France—Monroe felt himself betrayed. Worse, he had been made a fool, and worse than this, he had been made to appear a hypocrite to the French. He had studied law with Jefferson and was the great Virginian's protégé, and if he had ever believed his mentor's fears of the Federalists' desire to make Washington a king, he certainly believed them now. It was only too clear to him that the Federalists were using the French Revolution to betray all revolution, while serving the cause of commercial interests, aristocracy, and monarchy. He now saw Washington not as the gruff and incorruptible father, but as a man too clever by far. And so he asked the French government to conspire with him to bring about his own government's defeat in the forthcoming election of 1796: to help the Republicans unseat Washington and the pro-British Federalists and to elect Thomas Jefferson, the friend of France. Instead the Directory angrily told Monroe to go home. He was no longer welcome in France, nor was any other American. The Directory had had enough of American ambassadors; France would not receive another one. All relationship between France and the United States was at an end, now that the Americans were giving aid to Britain in her war against the French. Henceforth, the Directory told Monroe as it handed him his orders to leave, the French navy would treat American ships exactly as the British had done. In this, they were better than their word, for the French treatment of American ships not only included the impressment, but sometimes the torture, of American sailors.

In the United States, news of Jay's treaty touched off public demonstrations against it, and so exacerbated the animosities of Federalists and Republicans that it was not till May 1796 that the Federalist administration was able to obtain funds from Congress to put the treaty's provisions into effect. By this time, Washington was no longer speaking to Jefferson; their friendship, which had been cool, but correct, was over. John Adams, who with his wife Abigail had been among Jefferson's most intimate friends in the early years of the Revolution, was at least still speaking to the Republican leader, but just barely. The Founding Fathers vilified one another in their pseudonymous pamphlets, and the aging Washington, tired, disgusted, and rather baffled by the whole business, said he would not be a candidate for a third term as President of the United States. His last, impossible advice to the nation was to avoid entanglement in foreign affairs.

At that time, the election laws of the United States provided that the candidate who won the most votes would be President, while the candidate with the next largest number of votes would be Vice President. Under these rules, the bitter campaign of 1796 saw the Federalist John Adams become President, while the man he could scarcely now abide, the Republican Thomas Jefferson, was summoned from retirement to serve as Vice President. On taking office in 1797, Adams, therefore, found himself at the head of a disunited Cabinet, and the leader of a disunited nation which was involved in an undeclared naval war with France. It was a one-sided war, inasmuch as there was no United States navy. It took the form of American merchantmen trying to avoid capture by French warships. To add to Adams' troubles, and as if to demonstrate how confused a political situation could be, the Republicans still favored the cause of revolutionary France, which was making war upon their country, as opposed to the cause of Britain, with whom the United States was at prosperous peace. But there was a further confusion: the Republican Senator from Tennessee, William Blount, was trying to form an alliance of Creek and Cherokee Indians and Great Britain to combine into an Anglo-American-Indian force to take the two Floridas and Louisiana away from Spain, with whom the United States was also at peace. If it seemed grotesque for a Republican Senator to imagine such a scheme, much less wanting British help in it, an equally grotesque suggestion was made by the Spanish governor at New Orleans. He asked Secret Agent No. 13, James Wilkinson, to make himself "the Washington of the West"; to form an army and take Kentucky out of the Union, and establish a separate republic. It was an honor Brigadier General Wilkinson warily declined, pleading impossibility.

While the United States was making its dissident and confused way through a tangle, a way which ever and again led west, away from Europe and yet with Europe pursuing astern and simultaneously lying ahead in the Mississippi valley whither the United States was ultimately bound, a young man with a sword began to emerge as the arbiter of all events.

Arriving in the spring of 1796 in the mountains bordering Lombardy, he paraded before him the thirty thousand dejected souls of his new command.

"Soldiers, you are half starved and half naked!" he shouted in his execrable French, stating nothing but the truth.

"The Government owes you much, but can do nothing for you," he said.

"Your patience, your courage, do you honor, but give you no glory; no advantage.

"I will lead you into the most fertile plains of the world. There you will find flourishing cities, teeming provinces. There you will reap honor, glory, and wealth.

"Soldiers of the Army of Italy, will you be wanting in courage and firmness?"

A remarkable speech: The government cannot feed and clothe you, but I can. You are patient, courageous, and honorable soldiers, but you would rather be glorious and wealthy thieves. Follow the government and starve: follow me and we shall all be rich and famous.

Following this appeal to the instincts of his troops, the boyish commander next issued no less than 123 orders, all of them relating to provision and supply: an army moves upon its stomach. He next gave his army food for thought by promptly relieving lazy commanders and making it clear that in his army, the lowest private would swiftly rise to whatever heights his military ability might carry him. One of his future marshals had been a vagrant; another, a deserter and thief. No matter about that—what counted was energy and ability. A soldier, he mused, does not really serve for the sake of the few coins he receives each year. What a soldier wants is what any man wants: prestige, fame, glory, medals, titles—in order to acquire money, women, and immortality. Napolione Buonaparte's private opinion was that men were dogs: feed them and pat them on the head and they would follow you and lick your hand; starve and kick them and they would run away if they did not bite. To his mind, the revolution and its prattle about human rights was all nonsense. On the other hand, if these Frenchmen wanted to believe it, he would certainly encourage them to do so, for he knew that men were moved by ideals. He entertained one of his own. So as the commander of a revolutionary army of France, he told his men they would appear on the plains of Lombardy as liberators. They would free the Italian people from the aristocrats and princes who oppressed them. Just how they were to loot and free the Italians at the same time was left unsaid: the point was to appeal at once to the thief that lived in every one of these dogs, while simultaneously appealing to their dreams of themselves as selfless heroes, as the altruistic champions of the rights of man.

By the time his army was ready to leave winter quarters, he had by his orders and his example given his troops reason to believe in themselves, and in their young commander. He led them through the mountain passes in the spring for the excellent reason that no one expected an army to attempt those passes at that early season, and he fed his soldiers' confidence by first leading them to careful minor victories over surprised and unprepared garrisons in provincial towns.

Thereafter he revealed his full genius for the art of war, moving from victory to victory, in a matter of a few weeks clearing the army of the king of Sardinia from western Lombardy and the Austrian armies from eastern Lombardy. He captured Milan. And now, as if he had been waiting for victories to confirm his belief in himself, he changed his name. Napolione Buonaparte was too Corsican, and Corsica, too minor. He became Napoleon Bonaparte: that was more French; France was more believable than Corsica. He had plans for himself, and for France. An indication of this was disclosed by his brief dispatch to the Directory in Paris. "I have received your peace treaty with Sardinia," he wrote. "The army has approved it."

Having with these iron words informed the Directory what to expect from him, he drove the point further home by ignoring the commissioner the Directory sent to sign the treaty in the name of France. Napoleon conducted the negotiations, and signed the treaty himself. After this, he opened negotiations with the dukes of Tuscany, treating with them as if they were less than his equals, and meanwhile living in a fashion that more resembled that of a conquering prince than that of a servant of the French republic. In short, he did not hold office; he held court. At the same time, he issued proclamations to his soldiers and to the Italians, designed to preserve the pretense that he was the champion of revolution.

"Soldiers," he wrote, "Milan is yours. . . . We are the friends of all the peoples; but, above all, we are the friends of the offspring of Brutus and Scipio and the other great men who are our models. To re-establish the Capitol, to set up there the statues of the heroes, to awaken the Roman people which for centuries has been paralysed by servitude—that is the fruit of your victories, that will amaze posterity. It is your title to immortal fame that you have given a new visage to the most beautiful land in Europe."

Summoning the Milanese to a reception in the palace he had taken for himself, Napoleon told them he was establishing a Cisalpine Republic.

"You will be free, and in a safer position than the French," he said. "Milan will be the capital of this new republic, which has a population of five million. You shall have five hundred pieces of ordnance, and the friendship of France. From among you, I shall choose fifty men, who shall rule the country in the name of France. Adopt our laws, modifying them to suit your own customs. Be sagacious and united, and all will go well. Such is my will. . . ."

To the Lombards in general, Napoleon proclaimed:

"The French Republic has sworn hatred of the tyrants, brotherhood with the peoples. The principle of the constitution is the principle of the army as well. The despot who has so long kept Lombardy enslaved, has done great injury to France. . . . The victorious army of an insolent monarch was compelled to spread terror among the conquered. But the republican army, while waging war to the death against its enemies, the kings, gives a pledge of friendship to the peoples it has set free. Respect for property, humanity and religion—this is our animating principle. But the Lombards owe us, who are their brothers, a fair return. . . . We need provisions, for France is so far away that we cannot supply our requirements thence. We are entitled to them by the right of conquest; friendship must hasten to offer them to us. We have to requisition twenty million francs from the [Lombard] provinces. They are so rich that this will not be a serious burden."

Respect for religion was far from the policy of the French government of the moment, but Napoleon was addressing himself to Italians. He would gladly appear to be the champion of whatever beliefs anyone held, including the Moslems, if this would help him obtain what he wanted from them. To the Directory in Paris, he first portrayed himself as indispensable, and then in the same dispatch added, "I hope this language will not be ascribed to personal ambition. For my own part, I am unfortunately overburdened with honors, and my health has been so seriously undermined that I may soon have to ask you to appoint my successor. . . . I am continuing the negotiations. Troops! Troops!—if you want to keep Italy. Bonaparte." In fact, his health had never been better, nor his ambitions more personal. He was simply waging propaganda warfare with the Directory, as he was with the enemy and the conquered populations.

He meanwhile destroyed Austrian forces by speed and violence, by outmarching the enemy and massing superior firepower at the critical point on the battlefield. The art of war is very simple. It amounts to no more than, as one American general put it, getting there "firstest with the mostest." But, as Clausewitz observed, to do the simplest things in war is often most difficult. Napoleon's genius as a commander lay in his ability to identify the decisive place and time for action, and manage to arrive at that place and time in superior force. He drove through northern Italy and Styria, and began to move upon Vienna.

When apprised that an insurrection against French occupying forces had broken out in Venice, he paused for the brief moments required to snuff out the independent existence of that ancient republic. "This wretched and cowardly population, unfitted for freedom, without land or water, must, of course, be handed over to those to whom the hinterland is allotted," he wrote to the Directory. "First of all, we shall take the ships, empty the arsenal, carry off the big guns, and close the banks; we shall also keep Corfu and Ancona." Having told the Directory what France was going to do, he next informed the Venetians.

"I shall have no more constitution and no more Senate," he explained. "For Venice, I shall be a second Attila. Make me no more proposals. I will be your lawgiver."

After Venice surrendered to him, Napoleon turned his attention back to Austria, writing now to the archduke. He offered the archduke an opportunity to become "the benefactor of mankind, saviour of Germany." All the archduke had to do, to win this distinction, was sue for peace. Otherwise, Napoleon said, he would regretfully lay waste to the Holy Roman Empire. The Austrians could see the point only too well; they had been beaten everywhere, and the French army was already in their land.

Again it was Napoleon, rather than France, who dictated the terms of the Treaty of Campo Formio in October 1797. In less than two years, and beginning with a small and tatterdemalion force, Napoleon had stripped Sardinia and Austria of their Italian possessions, had made himself the master of all Italy, destroyed the ancient Venetian republic, and utterly defeated the most potent rival France faced on the continent of Europe. In so doing, he put an end to the war that had burned on the continent for the past six years.

As apprehensive and paralyzed as a bird fascinated by a snake, the Directory could only watch and wait as Napoleon reshaped the map. Austria surrendered Belgium, then the Austrian Netherlands, to France—together with all lands to the left of the

Rhine. She also recognized the Cisalpine Republic that Napoleon fashioned out of Lombardy, and agreed to the dismantling of the Venetian republic. In return, as a sort of crumb, Austria received the Dalmatian territories of Venice from Napoleon.

While playing the role of a Roman *imperator,* treating with emperors, dukes, and princes as the first among equals, and acting as the lawgiver to the populations in conquered lands, this fantastic young man simultaneously continued to present himself to Europe as the champion of freedom and human rights. He was, he assured the world, merely the servant of republican revolution. He told the conquered how fortunate they were. "Yours is the first nation in history to win freedom without partisan struggles, without a revolution, and without a blow," he proclaimed to his puppet creation, the Cisalpine Republic. "Let your minds be full of the sense of your own strength, and of the self-respect proper to the free man. . . . To consolidate your liberties, and with the sole end of bringing you happiness, I have completed a task such as hitherto has only been performed by ambition and the will-to-power. . . . In a few days I shall leave you. . . . Your happiness and the glory of your republic will always be matters very dear to my heart."

To the Directory, he wrote, "It is absolutely indispensable to our government that we should speedily overthrow the English monarchy. . . . Let us concentrate our energies upon increasing our navy, so that we may crush England. Then Europe will be at our feet." But as for himself, he assured the Directory, "I should like a rest. I have justified your confidence in me; I have covered myself with more glory than the most fortunate man could wish. . . . Calumny vainly attempts to discredit my intentions. My civic career, like my military career, will be unique and simple."

There was perhaps one man in the French government who completely understood Napoleon's last sentence; we shall meet him in a moment, but first listen to what Napoleon had to say in private to a fellow Italian:

"Do you fancy that I have won my triumphs in Italy that I may help the lawyers of the Directory . . . ? Or can you imagine that I want to stabilise the republic? What a ridiculous notion, a republic with thirty million inhabitants! With our customs! With our failings! France will soon forget these whims. The French need glory and the gratification of their vanity, but they do not understand the elements of freedom. . . . I am the idol of the soldiers. If the Directors, for instance, were to try to withdraw my commission, they would soon see who is master of the army. The people needs a chief, made resplendent by fame and victory; it does not want theories and governments, the phrases and the oratory of the ideologues. Give the masses a toy! They will play with it, and allow themselves to be led—provided always that the leader is adroit enough to hide his true aims! . . . Peace is opposed to my interests. . . . If peace were firmly established, and if I were no longer at the head of the army, I should have to renounce the power and position I have gained . . ."

He was by no means ready to say this much to a Frenchman, but he came very close to it in letters sent to that one man who had a very good idea as to the kind of simple and unique career Napoleon had in mind for himself. That man was Charles Maurice de Talleyrand-Périgord, then serving the Directory as the French government's minister of foreign affairs.

"With Malta and Corfu in our hands," Napoleon had advised him, "we could be masters of the Mediterranean. If we cannot dislodge England from the Cape, we must take Egypt. With twenty-five thousand men and from eight to ten ships of the line, the expedition could be risked. . . . The break-up of the huge Turkish Empire, day by day more imminent, must lead us to think of our trade in the East. . . . If our doings are guided by sound policy, which is nothing else than the calculation of combinations and chances, we shall for a long time to come be the Great Nation and the arbiter of Europe. The scales are in our hands, and, should fate be propitious, within a few years there may be great happenings. Today, these may seem the vague anticipations of a visionary enthusiast; but a cold, pertinacious, and far-sighted man will be able to make them a reality."

There was not a word here about bringing men happiness. Sound national policy simply consisted of weighing your chances of doing whatever you wished to your neighbors. If the chances were favorable, you immediately proceeded. If France was to be the Great Nation, then she needed a cold-blooded and accurate gambler for a master, and it was easy enough for Talleyrand to imagine whom Napoleon was suggesting.

History has been unkind to Talleyrand to the extent that it depicts him as utterly amoral. It is quite true that he was a defrocked, excommunicated priest, an epicurean, a gambler for high stakes, the pursuer of other men's wives, a stockjobber, possibly the salesman of his nation's secrets, certainly a man with his hand ever out to receive a bribe, and a traitor to his emperor. But these little faults were not seen as such at the time, except possibly by puritans. It is more to the point, historically speaking, to consider that Talleyrand was always moved, throughout his long and eventful life, by a patriotic concern for the national interests of France. In that context, he betrayed no one.

This man, who touched upon American history at a critical time, was a son of one of the oldest, noblest, and most honorable of French families. He would have followed the family's military tradition had he not been lamed as a child. It was therefore determined that he would be a priest, the boy's objections notwithstanding, for it was an aristocratic belief that the sons of the nobility had no option except to choose to serve as priests or soldiers; as lords spiritual or as lords temporal. But since Talleyrand felt no call to serve God, and resented the situation in which he found himself, it is at least understandable, if not excusable, that he failed to fill his priestly office. He was a young man of trenchant intelligence, enormous presence; of great wit, charm, and sensual appetite. He soon established a reputation for cynicism and licentiousness in the cynical and licentious society that Paris knew in the time of Madame du Barry and Louis XVI. But apart from playing cards for tremendous stakes, investing his winnings in dubious stock transactions, and seducing fashionable women, he brought his mind to bear on politics. He joined those liberal intellectuals who, before the Revolution, were advocating tax reform. When the king made him a bishop, out of consideration for Talleyrand's family rather than for his faith, Talleyrand surprised those who knew him only by profligate reputation. He used his office to work hard and well for clerical reform. In the earliest days of the Revolution, he favored the liberal cause because he felt the French government should be remodeled along the lines of the English one. But when the Bastille was stormed, he begged the Count d'Artois, the king's brother, to urge the king to use force to stop the riot in the streets: Talleyrand did not want bloody republican revolution; he wanted the creation of a constitutional monarchy. When the Bourbons failed to follow his advice, Talleyrand did not, however, follow his fellow aristocrats into exile abroad to help them plan the reconquest of France. He joined the Revolution instead, to work for France within it, and it was he, as a bishop, who introduced the motion that the state should seize all Church possessions and nationalize the clergy. There were Catholics, the pope among them, who felt Talleyrand betrayed the Church: he was subsequently excommunicated, but by that time he had resigned his holy office.

Following his resignation, Talleyrand was entrusted by the Revolutionary government with a mission to England in 1792. He was to try to persuade England not to join in the imminent war against France. It was a congenial mission for him, because as he wrote at the time, "Two neighboring nations, one of which founds its prosperity principally upon commerce and the other upon agriculture, are called upon by the eternal nature of things to have good understanding and mutually to enrich one another." He was one of the few Frenchmen before or since his day to advocate a close and special British-French relationship as the best guarantee of mutual prosperity and peace in Europe. He was a man of peace, entirely opposed to the old French ambition to make France the Great Nation of Europe.

"We have learnt," he wrote in a report to his government in 1792, "a little late no doubt, that for States as for individuals real wealth consists not in acquiring or invading the domains of others, but in developing one's own. We have learnt that all extensions of territory, all usurpations, by force or by fraud, which have long been connected by prejudice with the idea of 'rank,' of 'hegemony,' of 'political stability,' of 'superiority' in the order of the Powers, are only the cruel jests of political lunacy, false estimates of power, and that their real effect is to increase the difficulty of administration and to diminish the happiness and security of the governed for the passing interest or for the vanity of those who govern. . . . France ought, therefore, to remain within her own boundaries, she owes it to her glory, to her sense of justice and of reason, to her own interest and to that of the other nations who will become free."

. He never changed these points of view. They were his central policy as foreign minister. His belief in them constitutes the entire reason why, as history says, he sold the fruits of victory at the conference table, and ultimately betrayed Napoleon when that adventurer became emperor of the French. But since these were his beliefs, a question arises as to why Talleyrand ever conspired in the *coup d'état* that brought Napoleon to power, particularly when the young victor of Italy had told Talleyrand, in writing, what a cold, pertinacious man would do. The answer seems to be that Talleyrand was always consistent. He recognized political lunacy when he saw it, whether it be in the grandiose schemes of an adventurer of genius or in the sentimental claptrap of a politician lying to his electorate. Talleyrand was sardonic and venal. But he consistently acted in what he thought was in the best interest of his country, and he always believed he could be more effective inside the government, no matter what the form of that government, than he could be outside it. At one point during the Terror, Talleyrand's name was put upon the proscribed list: he fled to the United States. While in America, he supported himself by speculating in the sales of western wilderness lands, and, according to one report, by cynically selling the state secrets of France. It is easier to believe the one thing than it is to believe the other, but the point is that he did not, like Genet, remain in American exile. As the Terror devoured its own leaders, he managed to have his name removed from the list of the proscribed, and made his way back to France, and into the government again. He served the Bourbons, he served the Directory, he served Napoleon, and he served the restored Bourbon monarchy—which is to say, he served France. In the process, he also served himself. In this twofold purpose, he was not always successful, as the following events suggest:

After the Treaty of Campo Formio in the fall of 1797, France no longer had a foe upon the Continent. But she remained at war with Great Britain and involved in an undeclared war at sea with the United States. Turning to the major problem, the Directory asked the luminous young Napoleon to undertake the invasion of England. Napoleon inspected the state of the French navy, stared across the Channel, and said no. France could more easily injure Great Britain, he said, by doing what she could do, rather than attempting that which she could not do. He suggested France first take Malta, then invade Egypt. Since Egypt was a Turkish possession, this would mean war with the Ottoman empire, but he considered Turkish enmity piffling. He would strike through Egypt to the east, destroy the Turkish empire *en passant*, with India as the ultimate objective. Thus France would shut the British out of the Mediterranean, and, coming on India by the back door, ruin Britain's trade with the East and gain that trade for France. The combination of Napoleon's overpowering presence, and the Directory's fear of it, allowed him to have his way.

Off he went to the Near East in 1798, studying the Koran, proclaiming himself the Sword of Islam, come to free the people of Egypt from the tyranny of the Turk. And while he sailed off to his astounding victories, with Nelson in pursuit, there remained the problem of the United States. The Directory chose to ignore it.

The Americans did not. While there was a large reservoir of good feeling for the French among the American Republicans, it was being diminished by the French capture of American ships and seamen. President Adams asked his Cabinet what to do. Hamilton was for war, but the decision was to send a mission to try to negotiate with the Directory which refused to accept an American ambassador. Three men, John Marshall, Charles C. Pinckney, and Elbridge Gerry, comprised the mission. On arriving in Paris, they were shortly told that the Directory would have nothing to do with them; the Directory would not see them, much less talk with them. But while they were digesting this bleak news, they learned that Talleyrand wished to have a word. From Talleyrand they learned that all things are always possible, although many of them must be approached with a certain circumspection. Shortly thereafter, the Americans made the acquaintance of three Frenchmen, known to them and to history as Messieurs X, Y, and Z. These mysterious gentlemen suggested that the United States should buy thirty-two thousand florins' worth of Dutch bonds from them. France had acquired these bonds in the course of its conquest of Holland, and since that country could not redeem them, and since France certainly did not intend to redeem them, the bonds were actually worthless. By purchasing the worthless bonds, therefore, America would actually be giving France—or X, Y, and Z—thirty-two thousand florins, although there would be nothing in writing to show this was the case. The transaction could be made to appear that the Americans had simply bought Dutch bonds. If the Americans did this, and if in addition they made a present of $250,000 to M.

Talleyrand, then, said X, Y, and Z, it was virtually certain that the Directory would change its mind, and that negotiations could begin.

Talleyrand was perhaps trying to be helpful. The Americans took a quite different view, which Pinckney expressed in immortal bombast: "Millions for defense, but not one cent for tribute!" The three Americans returned to the United States in anger, and when reports of the XYZ Affair were published in the Federalist press, the Federalists were as furious as Marshall, Gerry, and Pinckney had been, and the Republican friends of France simply could not believe it. They asked to see the correspondence, and when President Adams obligingly published it, there was nothing the Republicans could say. It would seem the Federalists had been right and the Republicans wrong, in their evaluation of French friendship. Bills were promptly passed in Congress to put the United States in readiness for war. All treaties with France were abrogated. The United States army was enlarged, and the creation of a United States navy was authorized. George Washington came creaking out of retirement, offering to serve again as commander in chief of the army, with Hamilton as his second-in-command. Hamilton urged that an army invade Louisiana, the Floridas, and Mexico, together with that would-be liberator of New Spain, Francisco Miranda. Hamilton's excuse was that the United States could strike now against Spain because Spain had made an alliance with France. An alliance with Great Britain and cooperation with the British navy in operations against French and Spanish possessions in the Americas seemed very probable. In the event, no such alliance was formed, but the threat of it was always there. Nor was war ever declared, although what has been called "John Adams' War" was now begun at sea. American fighting ships were built, and their captains were ordered to destroy or capture French warships. The first of the United States undeclared wars, fought under Presidential rather than under Congressional authorization, took place in the earliest years of the nation; in it, the new navy acquired success and prestige against the French, and allowed patriots to continue to imagine their new nation was invincible.

The situation was distressing to both Jefferson and Talleyrand, although for different reasons. Jefferson thought it obscene that the two republics were fighting one another, and Talleyrand, although no proponent of the notion that France should become the Great Nation of Europe, was no enemy to the idea that France should have a colonial empire. Moreover, he shared the Girondists' earlier view that the old French possessions on the Mississippi should be regained from Spain. He feared that in the course of the undeclared war, the United States might take New Orleans and Louisiana away from Spain before France could get them back. Talleyrand's door was therefore open when one Victor Du Pont arrived in Paris. Du Pont, a manufacturer of gunpowder whose French family had established itself in the state of Delaware, was a private emissary sent by Vice President Jefferson to the French foreign minister. Jefferson, it seems, was indulging himself in personal diplomacy that, properly speaking, was none of his business. His message for Talleyrand, via Du Pont, was that France would certainly drive the United States into the arms of Great Britain if this sea war persisted, and that this would be dangerous to the remaining French possessions in the Caribbean. He wanted Talleyrand to persuade the Directory to end the war and reopen normal diplomatic relationships with the United States. Talleyrand saw the point clearly enough; it had already occurred to him. But he saw no point in dealing through the Directory; he was then assisting in arrangements for its downfall, for great events were at hand.

The result of Napoleon's conquest of Egypt was that Great Britain, Austria, and Russia immediately formed a Second Coalition. The Treaty of Campo Formio went the way of all treaties, and an allied army surged into Italy, dismantling Napoleon's ephemeral Cisalpine Republic. When Napoleon heard this news, there followed the high drama of his desertion of the Army of the Nile, his lucky crossing of the Mediterranean in a small ship practically under the bowsprits of the British navy, his sudden appearance in Paris, and the touch-and-go series of events culminating in the replacement of the Directory by a dictator.

Something called the Consulate was established in 1799, with Napoleon Bonaparte as First Consul. Ever wishing to give his usurpation the color of legality, Napoleon sought popular confirmation of his power by holding a plebiscite: he proclaimed a new constitution for what he continued to call the republic, asking the electorate to accept it in its entirety—but offering no alternative. The people could vote yes or no; all or nothing. His majority was roughly three million to one thousand in a nation sick of chaotic leadership and ready to be ruled by someone who at least seemed to offer them law, order, and a program. And none, to the French, seemed more able and more certain of what he was doing than the undefeated young general from Corsica. With the assurance of popular support, Napoleon then began to rule by decree. He presented himself as the savior of the Revolution, as the man who had arrived to put an end to ten years of drift and terror, and who would now put the principles of the Revolution into effect. He would be the simple, and unique, leader and servant of the French.

In all this, Talleyrand was at his side. Talleyrand's role in the *coup d'état* derived from his conviction that facts take precedence over principles. It was Napoleon's hour; Talleyrand had seen it coming, therefore Talleyrand helped prepare the way. He could not serve France if he did not serve her master. Only if he, too, were sitting on the wagon box could he make suggestions as to the direction the journey should take.

One of his suggestions was that the First Consul should put an end to the irritating, wasteful, undeclared war at sea with the Americans. The Americans seemed on the point of an open declaration of war, with operations in Louisiana and the Caribbean in consequent view. Talleyrand also suggested the advisability of reacquiring New Orleans and Louisiana from Spain, and Napoleon immediately saw the advantages of that. A French position on the Mississippi would put an end to the dreams of the Americans and give France a base from which simultaneously to threaten Britain in Canada and support the French islands in the Caribbean. Finally, the sea war with the Americans was something France could not afford. The British navy, which had annihilated the French fleet that had carried Napoleon's army to Egypt, was much more than the French navy could handle— quite apart from any assistance the British navy might receive from the new, small, but remarkably effective United States navy. What France needed to do was build a navy that could compete with the British one; meanwhile, the fewer foes she had at sea, the better.

So the First Consul offered peace. He repealed the Directory's decrees under which French warships harried American merchantmen, and he let the Americans know that if they wished to send a delegation to discuss matters of mutual interest, he would be glad to receive them. He also opened conversations with Spain with respect to New Orleans and Louisiana and ordered a wholesale increase of the French naval establishment. He needed command of the sea, or at least parity with the British navy, if he were to defeat Great Britain in both the Old World and the New. There was meanwhile France to govern—and to defend. A Russian army had reached Switzerland, and the Austrians were once again in possession of northern Italy.

The First Consul led the Grand Army of France across the Alps, this time through the high snowfields and dangerous passes, falling on the Austrians in Italy and defeating them in a pitched battle at Marengo in the early summer of 1800. He forced the Austrians to reconfirm the Treaty of Campo Formio. He appeared in Europe in that year as an ever-victorious young god of war; in fact, he thought of himself as such; and he appeared as the liberator of oppressed peoples, bringing them the blessings of the new freedom. To the French, he appeared as their wise lawgiver, a benevolent despot by their sufferance who gave them order and prosperity at home, victory beyond the borders. He ruled by a combination of popular support, the power of the army, his own amazing energy and imagination, and the sinister suggestions of his secret police. He assured the dazzled French that they were the new Romans of a latter-day Roman republic. The implication was that he and they should impose a Pax Romana upon the world. There was conscious symbolism in his use of terms: consul, senate, tribunate, prefects, eagles for his legions; in the names he gave to the conquered lands. They were client states: the Cisalpine Republic, the Helvetic Republic, the Ligurian Republic, the Illyrian states. He called Great Britain "Carthage"—a nation of sea traders. Here the implication was one of Punic War. And there was always the implication that the First Consul was Caesar. Like Caesar, he could read, write, and dictate at the same time; he could govern captured territories and France by decrees dictated from his carriage or from horseback while he rode to his victories and disposed of kingdoms. He was only thirty years old, born two thousand years too late.

On September 30, 1800, a three-man American delegation to Paris had the great satisfaction of concluding a peace with the First Consul. It reestablished formal relationships between the two republics, and brought an end to their strife at sea. The Americans sailed for home in happy ignorance of a great and ominous secret. They did not know that the discussions begun in 1795 between France and Spain had culminated in agreement.

The pact, which the French knew as the Treaty of Montefontaine, and which the Spanish called the Treaty of San Ildefonso, had been signed the day after agreement was reached with the Americans. Its terms were hidden from the world. It stated that His Catholic Majesty of Spain "promises and engages on his part to retrocede to the French Republic . . . the colony or province of Louisiana with the same extent it now has in the hands of Spain, and that it had when France possessed it, and such as it should be after the treaty subsequently entered into between Spain and other States."

In brief, France now held title to the Mississippi River and all the land west of it to Mexico and the Rocky Mountains, from the Gulf of Mexico to Canada. She had at last torn up the Treaty of Paris and regained the bulk of her former possessions, and there was no thought on Talleyrand's part, much less on Napoleon's, of creating any of Citoyen Genet's sister republics in this region. They wanted a continental base from which to mount a sea power to protect the French Caribbean islands and from which to apply pressure against United States diplomacy. The Americans would think twice about alliances with Great Britain if exposed to attack from the Mississippi. While French thought bore on military considerations, it also envisioned the exploration and exploitation of this tremendous area once Napoleon had Europe in his fist and a profitable peace had been wrung from a defeated Great Britain.

France urged the treaty on Spain on the grounds that French control of Louisiana would be a guarantee that neither Great Britain nor the United States would attack Mexico or any other Spanish possessions in New Spain. The Spanish could hardly have believed this would be much of a protection: certainly not a protection from France. The appalling reason why the Spanish signed away the very heart of North America is that they thought the Grand Duchy of Tuscany was a much more important piece of property.

In all the centuries they had been in North America, and in all the decades they had the specific governance of New Orleans and the Mississippi River valley, the Spanish had failed utterly to realize the possibilities that lay open to them. And because they had failed to put something into it, they had got nothing out of it. New Orleans was a lackadaisical, ramshackle wet mess of a town;

it and the hinterland were expensive to govern and, the Spanish thought, too difficult to defend. They did not give up Louisiana to Napoleon at gunpoint, although they might have had to do so. They gave it up, rather, because of a failure of imagination and will. They were willing to trade a potential empire for a duchy. Feudal Spain still thought in terms of dynastic advantage, entirely missing the point of what was taking place in Europe.

Talleyrand and Napoleon must have smiled when they learned that Spain would give them territories vaster than all Europe if Napoleon would give Tuscany to the son-in-law of the king of Spain, the duke of Parma. It seemed that Parma wanted to be called a king. If Tuscany were added to his other possessions, he could call himself one, could he not? Of course he could, Napoleon assured the Spanish—France would be glad to call Parma a king if Spain would give France all the territory west of the Mississippi. France would call him the king of Etruria. There was no such kingdom, but it was a wonderful title, and Parma could have Tuscany and 1,200,000 Italian subjects. France would also give Spain six ships of the line, and a mutual alliance against any nation that might try to object to their treaty—and here the French and Spanish had the United States in mind. Moreover, Napoleon promised Spain he would never sell Louisiana to anyone else; if the French tired of it, title would revert to Spain.

It was altogether a curious bargain. As everyone knows, Tuscany is a beautiful, fruitful garden full of handsome and hardworking gardeners. In 1800, it might well have seemed more desirable to a Spanish grandee than several million square miles of nothing in particular, full of Indians. And so the Spanish traded Louisiana away before they received anything but a tinsel title to a nonexistent kingdom, on Napoleon's promise to make the title good. The bargain is otherwise curious for the light it throws upon Napoleon. That heroic young liberator of the people of Europe, the champion and savior of revolution, would blandly hand over 1,200,000 of his fellow Italians to a Spaniard who wanted to

[handwritten marginalia: 3 WEEKS LATER HE SOLD IT TO THE U.S.— THE LYING S.O.B.]

play at being a king. If he gave this a moment's thought, Napoleon probably reasoned he could take Tuscany away from Parma, together with anything else Spain or Parma owned, whenever he wished to bother. In any case, Napoleon now had title to Louisiana, and as soon as he could create a sufficiently potent navy, he intended to take possession of it. The Spanish would remain in actual possession until French warships would arrive, and all this was to be kept a secret from the world.

17

The River
Was the Key

THREE centuries had elapsed since the discovery of America, but to the civilized world in 1801, lands west of the Mississippi River were almost as unknown as the surface of the moon. A few white men had penetrated these regions, bringing back reports. In addition to Welsh-speaking Indians, who might prove to be the descendants of a Welsh prince, there was a curious people whose ears were so large as to serve them as umbrellas against sun and rain. Another strange people had only to smell food to be nourished by it. There was somewhere out there an even more exotic people who had one central leg rather than two legs. They bounded faster than deer in prodigious hops across limitless plains. Griffons had been seen there; the country was positively infested by them. There was after all a Missouri River, and it led to China. This was the Northwest Passage to the Orient.

Apart from griffons, unipeds, and distant Chinese, the few and random reports reaching civilization told of stupefying distances, fiery deserts, mountains that made the Alps seem simple hills, great pasturelands populated by game animals in herds numbering tens of thousands. Huge wolves, bears, and lions preyed on these herds, as did swarms of warlike Indian nomads who, it seemed, also preyed on one another. It was not altogether certain whether the North American continent was an island or a peninsular appendage of continental size joined at its northwest corner to Asia; reports differed. But the civilized world was aware that North America's west coast slipped into the Pacific Ocean. Presumably a man could walk west from the Atlantic to the Pacific, but no one knew how long it would take him to do this, nor what he would find in the way of wonders and perils once he crossed the Mississippi River and trudged away northwest. Those who pondered this matter on the basis of prior experience of eastern North America tended to disbelieve the more imaginative reports of griffons, although giving credence to those of Welsh Indians. They more prosaically thought in terms of plains that had never known a plow; of forests that had never known an ax; of animals and birds that had never been hunted; of mountains as yet unmined. In short, they thought of western North America as being a very great deal more of eastern North America, and they thought of moving into it. Still, no one could be sure of what to expect.

Since politics, like nature, abhors a vacuum, the presence of this vast *terra incognita* invited political speculation. So far as the Americans knew, the Spanish apparently held title to the unexplored heart of the continent, but whether they could make good their grip on that title or be persuaded to let go of it, was another matter. United States policy was to trade with all nations while avoiding military alliances with any one of them, meanwhile moving west to the Mississippi River and creating new states out of the western territories assigned to it by the treaties of 1783. But there were many Americans, including Thomas Jefferson, who thought it would also be politic for the United States to keep moving west, past the Mississippi and on across the continent to the Pacific Ocean. If this should be at the expense of Spain, so be it: to paraphrase Clausewitz, war is the continuation of politics by other means.

In 1801, Jefferson was President of the United States. His election followed one of those dramatic shifts of public opinion that have customarily characterized the behavior of the American electorate. In taking advantage of the discomfiture of the Republican party that derived first from Genet's activity and then from the XYZ Affair and war with France, the Federalists had overreached themselves. They had passed the Alien and Sedition Laws—measures allegedly designed to prevent radical Republicans from conspiring with the Directory in Paris to overthrow the government of the United States with the assistance of French armies and to replace the Constitution with a Reign of Terror. But hardly had these laws been passed when the public on second thought found them as repellent as they had first seemed attractive. In the ensuing convulsion, the Republicans came to power.

Jefferson did not believe the time was ripe to dispossess Spain of her holdings in North America, but he was sure that time would presently arrive. He saw the power of Spain as steadily declining. He also saw the advisability of filing a claim, by right of discovery, to that unknown western expanse before it occurred to the British to do so. There might or might not be a Northwest Passage to Cathay, but if there should be one, Jefferson thought Americans should find it. If there should not, an American route overland to the Pacific would at least provide a shorter way to China, and a quicker means of bringing Mr. Astor's furs from the Pacific Coast to eastern markets, than the long and perilous sea route around Cape Horn.

Eight years earlier, Jefferson's young friend and Virginia neighbor, Meriwether Lewis, had wanted to explore northwest to the Pacific. Jefferson now commissioned Lewis and another army officer, William Clark, to gather an expedition. They were to cross the Mississippi, proceed northwest, mapping the country, noting its flora, fauna, and geology—and to report on the military strength of the people they might meet: Spanish, British, Indians, or whoever else might be out there. The members of the expedition would be United States soldiers. Not to put too fine a point on it, Jefferson was going to send a column of troops on an armed reconnaissance of the territory of a chosen enemy. He told the Spanish, however, that the expedition would be a purely scientific one, and he requested their permission to send it into Spanish lands. Sullenly, the Spanish consented.

Perhaps Jefferson should have wondered why the Spaniards should have given passage to what they must have known would be more than a botanizing field trip. But then, before the expedition could be mounted, rumors suggested a frightening explanation. The proposed journey of Lewis and Clark was immediately postponed.

The rumors, circulating in Europe, spoke of a secret pact between France and Spain. They said Spain had given New Orleans, the two Floridas, and the entire huge hinterland of Louisiana to France. If the rumors were true, as the British thought they were, then the problem of the United States would no longer be one of choosing the moment to chase a few futile Spaniards off the Mississippi. It would be one of trying to defend United States territory against invasion by the victor of Marengo —for it was inconceivable to Jefferson, or to anyone else, that Napoleon would not know what to do once he got his hands on New Orleans. He would certainly use the Mississippi River valley as the base of a new French empire in America.

American agents and diplomats in Europe were told to try to track down the rumor and ascertain what truth there might be in it. Jefferson and Madison, who was now Jefferson's secretary of state, meanwhile tried an oblique approach. Ambassador Robert R. Livingston was told to ask France to sell West Florida to the United States. Presumably, the answer would at least indicate whether the rumor was true. If France disclaimed possession of the Floridas, then Livingston was to ask the French to assist the United States in purchasing West Florida from Spain. In either case, the ostensible interest of the United States in West Florida was to acquire this land and its rivers leading to the Gulf of Mexico as a route to the sea for the goods and produce of American settlers in Kentucky as an alternative to the route down the Mississippi and New Orleans. At the same time, the American ambassador to Spain, Charles Pinckney, was told to try to buy West Florida from Spain. Here again, a reason for this negotiation was to discover whether Spain had the land to sell—or whether she had, as rumor said, given it to France. This stratagem got Jefferson nowhere. The French said they did not own West Florida, and the Spanish refused to discuss it.

The following year, 1802, opened with the Americans still ignorant of the truth and with Napoleon's ascendant star soaring ever higher above Europe. Napoleon forced the Peace of Amiens upon his defeated enemies. Under the terms of this treaty, France acquired Belgium and lands west of the Rhine; she surrounded herself with client republics of Napoleon's creation. Holland became the Batavian Republic; Switzerland, the Helvetic Republic. There was a Ligurian Republic with Genoa as its capital; the Cisalpine Republic was re-created in the Po Valley. Britain had to return to France those Caribbean islands she had seized during the war, and to agree to withdraw from Malta, Minorca, Trinidad, and Elba. No one expected this peace to last. Napoleon was not through with the British, nor they with him. The British would never leave Malta unless they were willing to concede control of the Mediterranean to the French. But for the time being, the British had said they would leave Malta, and everyone pretended to believe this, and so for the time, there was peace in Europe. Whereupon, Napoleon began to plan operations elsewhere.

During the first two years of his consulship, Napoleon had done more than electrify Europe by his victories. His brilliant and lucid governance of France had brought unity, internal peace, and good order out of the ten earlier years of revolutionary confusion. Napoleon mobilized the energies of this most populous and technically advanced nation of Europe, bringing it prosperity as well as victory and giving it for the first time a uniform legal code. He also gave France every political goal of the Revolution except that of political liberty. But the populace was more than glad to have him reign as a benevolent despot: he gave them equality of opportunity. No longer were offices bought and sold. Talent, and talent alone, was the key to any career. Napoleon did not simply reform France, he transformed it. Under his rule, France became more than the Great Nation of Europe. She became the Great Nation of the world, and as if this was not more than enough of a good thing, she also had the world's largest military establishment commanded by the world's first warrior. Almost as important to Napoleon's power as armed force was Europe's good opinion of him at this time. It was not shared by the princes he had dispossessed, nor by the British, but it was by nearly everyone else, including Beethoven and Goethe. To European populations, Napoleon seemed to be what he proclaimed himself to be: the servant and champion of the republican cause and the enemy of tyrants.

But Napoleon knew no limits. There is no evidence he ever sat down and cold-bloodedly planned to become master of the world, but there is every evidence that he simply went from one thing to the next, and that, as he once said, "Peace is opposed to my interests." During his consulship, he had greatly expanded the French naval establishment, and in 1802, with Europe momentarily pacified and Great Britain badgered into a suspension of hostility, Napoleon turned his attention to America.

The New France that Napoleon (and Talleyrand) envisioned was to be built by stages. First, the position of the Caribbean islands would be made secure. At that time, the islands were a profitable source of sugar, an important commodity in itself, apart from its commercial trading value. But for their protection, the sugar islands needed a continental hinterland to serve at once as a source of military and naval supply, and as a trading partner. France was too far away, with too many British warships on the ocean between. America, however, was close at hand, and the first purpose of acquiring New Orleans and Louisiana from Spain was to provide the Caribbean islands with the convenient hinterland necessary to them. The next step would be to convert the Gulf of Mexico into a French pond, and the Mississippi into a French stream. If this could be done, then the British and the Americans could be shut off from trade in the Gulf and in the Caribbean—and from incursions into the interior of North America. The Americans would be confined, as Talleyrand put it, to the space nature seemed to have intended for them, and Canada could be attacked from the south and returned to France. At a later time, Napoleon could give his attention to Mexico. Then, of course, there was Asia . . . but first things first: the first thing to do was to regain Santo Domingo for France. That island was the richest of them all. Its slaves had revolted and established a republic of their own: Napoleon would attend to that.

He sent a fleet, and an army of fifty thousand veterans under the command of his brother-in-law, General Leclerc, to brush the black republic out of existence. That having been rapidly accomplished, the warships and the troop transports would then proceed to New Orleans, dismiss the Spanish, and take possession of the city and its immediate Louisiana hinterland.

Since espionage has always been one of the world's largest light industries, particularly in multinational Europe, and since the departure of an army and a battle fleet can seldom be entirely concealed from the curious and the garrulous, fast packet boats, bearing news of this expedition, arrived in American waters before the topsails of Napoleon's warships rose out of the sea off Santo Domingo. The British fleet on the Jamaica Station prepared for action: recent history indicated to them that peace was an anomalous interval between wars, and the presence of a French battle line, and a Napoleonic army in Caribbean waters, warranted certain basic precautions.

There was also apprehension in the muddy new capital city of Washington. Jefferson, Madison, and Monroe, like Ambassador Livingston in Paris and many another Republican, were all of them Francophiles as well as believers in the essential brotherhood of all republics. Jefferson suspected that Napoleon might prove to be more of an opportunistic, counterrevolutionary dictator than a paladin of human rights, but he and the men around him still clung to the rather romantic notion that there was a French Republic, and that there should always be friendship between the United States and France. Their faith had been tortured by recent experience, but it had been somewhat revived by Napoleon's putting an end to the war at sea. Reports of the French fleet's intentions were, however, a cause for alarm and despondency. The imminent arrival of a French army in New Orleans was the very thing that Jefferson and the United States had most to fear. For one thing, it indicated that the rumors of a secret pact between France and Spain were true. Livingston had at last asked Talleyrand, point-blank, if there was such a pact, and Talleyrand had blandly denied it. But unless France was going to go to war with Spain, which was quite improbable, no French force could occupy New Orleans unless a treaty did exist between the two nations. Therefore, there was a secret treaty, and from this, all other fears followed. Friendship with France could not stand such close acquaintance.

The threat to the United States was far more serious than the enmity of Great Britain had been during the Revolutionary War. Then, Britain had been alone against the world, whereas the American colonies had had the direct and indirect support of several European nations. But with general peace in Europe, France could bring all of her enormous power to bear upon a friendless United States, whose military establishment was not strong enough to deal with the French force already en route to New Orleans. Much less could the United States hope to cope with the French forces that would surely follow. War with France was simply unthinkable. But equally unthinkable was the prospect of Napoleon on the Mississippi.

But what could be done? Jefferson's one, best hope was that France and Britain would soon go to war again. He said he hoped "to endure" until that happy day. His next-best hope was that he could form an alliance with Britain when the French arrived in New Orleans. To seek a British alliance was, in a way, running home to mother when a bully appeared in the neighborhood. The future risk was that after mother thrashed the bully, she would retie the frightened child to her apron strings. That risk had to be accepted. There was nothing else to do.

"The day that France takes possession of New Orleans fixes the sentence which is to restrain her forever within her low-water mark," Jefferson hopefully and militantly wrote to Livingston in Paris. "It seals the union of two nations who in conjunction can maintain exclusive possession of the ocean. From that moment we must marry ourselves to the British fleet and nation. . . . This is not a state we seek or desire. It is one which this measure, if adopted by France, forces on us as necessarily as any other cause, by the laws of nature, brings on its necessary effect."

Ah, those laws of nature. They could be invoked to prove anything. Once upon a time it had been a violation of natural law to be united with Britain; now it would be unnatural to be separated from Britain. Union with Britain, marriage with Britain, was now the most natural thing in the world.

Before sealing his letter to Livingston, Jefferson gave it to a friend to read. The friend was another Delaware Du Pont, Pierre S. Du Pont de Nemours. Like Victor Du Pont, Pierre was to act as Jefferson's private messenger to France. He was to disclose the contents of Jefferson's letter to Livingston to Talleyrand and, if possible, to Napoleon himself. Jefferson also gave Du Pont a letter, written ostensibly as a note from one friend to another, but also intended for public consumption. This letter, too, predicted that if France ever took possession of Louisiana, the result would be an Anglo-American attack that would annihilate the French navy and destroy French commercial shipping. Du Pont was to show this letter to his French friends.

Perusing these letters, Du Pont embroidered upon the theme. He suggested that he should try to bargain with Talleyrand. He would tell him that the United States was willing to buy New Orleans and the Floridas, and in addition to paying money for these properties, the United States would guarantee forever French possession of the west bank of the Mississippi River—and help France take Canada in the course of her next war with Britain. Doing a bit of arithmetic in his head, the powder-maker of Delaware told Jefferson it would be cheaper for the United States to buy New Orleans than it would be to buy enough powder, shot, and ammunition to fight a war which the United States would probably lose, anyway. He said he would tell Talleyrand, who certainly understood the language of money, that Jefferson and his administration had nothing but admiration and friendship for France, whereas a subsequent American administration might not. The implication was that France would be able to get more money for New Orleans out of a friendly and generous Jeffersonian administration than out of a suspicious one.

While Du Pont set off on his private mission, Livingston persisted in his official one. He, too, embroidered upon the theme. He asked Talleyrand and Napoleon to cede not only New Orleans to the United States but also all of Louisiana above the Arkansas River. This, he told them as smoothly as they had said precisely the same thing to the Spaniards, would rid them of the expense of an unprofitable colony and place a buffer between British Canada and French Louisiana, thereby protecting French possessions from British attack.

It was all quite hopeless. The arguments of the ambassador

were as unavailing as those of the private messenger. Talleyrand and Napoleon meant to build an empire, not to sell one. New Orleans was the key to the Mississippi, and the river was the key to the empire.

The French fleet arrived in Santo Domingo. Put ashore, the French army defeated the black republic and for a time imposed martial law in sectors of the island. But in the course of this military exercise, French sailors and soldiers perished in hecatombs. General Leclerc was among the victims. They were not killed by their black enemies; they died of yellow fever. The epidemic left too few survivors among the French for them to succeed in pacifying the entire island, much less to press on with the expedition's much more important assignment, the occupation of New Orleans. Disease thus served the Americans where diplomacy failed, but the relief was a temporary one. Napoleon ordered another fleet and another army to be made ready. This time the warships would sail directly to New Orleans.

In Washington, Jefferson breathed a bit easier on hearing news of the French disaster; he was spared for a while from having to think of the dubious virtues of a British alliance. The dubious aspects included the price the British would ask for such an alliance, and the personal political price that Jefferson would have to pay for it. Jefferson's entire political life had hitherto been predicated on his fear and suspicion of his mother country. To throw the United States into Britain's arms would cost him credibility and, very likely, the Presidency. He continued to hope that war would erupt between France and Britain to delay further Napoleon's arrival in Louisiana. He said he despaired of making any sort of bargain with Napoleon "till a war took place between France and England" and that he "believed the event was not very distant." His policy would be to keep the United States well out of that war, to have the country look to its own defenses, and to grow relatively more powerful while the two European powers weakened one another.

At this point, late in 1802, the Spanish threw matters into complete confusion when the Spanish intendant at New Orleans canceled American trading privileges in the city and on the river. He said briefly that they no longer existed. There was fear in Washington that Napoleon had put the Spanish up to this, for if the French intended to take over the governance of Louisiana, it would be to their advantage to take over a governance to which no strings were attached. The Spanish intendant, however, may have acted entirely on his own authority. He, too, had heard rumors of a secret treaty between his government and France, and he refused to believe them. His unilateral abrogation of American trading rights could have been his way of testing the truth of the rumors. If the rumors should be true, then his action would represent his protest: he would thus show the Americans, the French, and his own government in Madrid that he was in command of the river.

The Spanish intendant's action did not close the Mississippi to the American ships, rafts, and keelboats. They could sail or float on it as they pleased—provided that they paid duties and port fees at New Orleans like any other foreigners. Perhaps the intendant had paid insufficient attention to the proximate causes of the American Revolution, or did not understand that the now-flourishing American settlements in the Mississippi valley were filled with veterans of that war and survivors of Indian wars—a population quick on the trigger to whom tax was a fighting word, a population then in the throes of a Protestant religious revival, and one who in any case did not admire the Spanish, their religion, or anything else about them. Perhaps the intendant did not care.

But the western Americans cared. Their shrieks of outrage carried clearly to Washington and were plainly audible in Massachusetts and Georgia as well. The westerners took the view that being asked to pay port duties was the same thing as being denied the use of the Mississippi. They formed militias. They sent angry statements to Congress. "The Mississippi is ours by the law of nature," one such statement said. "If Congress refuses us effectual protection, if it forsakes us, we will adopt the measures which our safety requires, even if they endanger the peace of the Union, and our connection with the other States. No protection, no allegiance."

In other words, Mother Nature just naturally demanded that they go down to New Orleans and clean those thieving, idolatrous Spaniards out of there, even if this meant getting the Union into a war, or even if it meant the westerners would have to split off from the Union to start a nation of their own. They were going to do what they wanted to do whether Congress or the President or anyone else liked it or not. Out in Kentucky, Andrew Jackson put himself at the head of a militia force and said if the Federal government failed to talk the Spanish out of New Orleans, he would take care of things himself and, after that, sweep "through the damned greasers to Mexico City." The westerners' point was that they were not afraid of anybody. They, too, had heard those rumors about the secret treaty between France and Spain, but if their chasing the Spaniards out of Louisiana meant war with the French, that was all right with them. They didn't give a damn for the Frogeaters, either. Americans had beaten Frenchmen before, in the French and Indian wars, and they would beat them again.

These artless opinions were passionately shared throughout the older states. Petitions were sent to Congress demanding that war be declared if Jefferson could not negotiate with Spain. From Paris, Livingston, exasperated by his inability to pin Talleyrand to a simple yes or no answer as to whether France owned Louisiana, urged Jefferson to send an army to take New Orleans. Once we have taken the city, he said, then we can negotiate with whoever turns out to be the owner. The Federalists were all for war. Since the westerners had largely supported the Republicans in the election that brought Jefferson the Presidency, the Federalists now loudly championed the westerners' warlike protests, hoping to wean the west away from the Republican party. The Federalists argued that the United States was in imminent peril of war, and that Jefferson's vacillations were dangerous to the nation. This presumption was quite true—truer than the Federalists might have actually known. But it was also true, as the Federalists and Jefferson knew, that war would mean the ruin of the Republican party. It would mean a British alliance in a war with France, and thus represent a complete vindication of Federalist policy, which would then be seen as having been consistently correct while the Republican policy would be seen as having been consistently wrong. Jefferson's option was whether to save his country or to save his party, and he sought to save both by refusing to make a choice, meanwhile hoping that his popularity among the westerners would lead them to trust in his judgment: to give him time until France and Britain went to war.

Time, however, was rapidly slipping away. As the year entered its last weeks, a French force was assembling at the Dutch port of Helvoët Sluys. Napoleon was spending two million francs to equip this fleet which, with its troop transports, would sail for New Orleans.

In London, the British government considered the advisability of sending a British fleet there first—unless the Americans should come to their senses, take the city as the Federalists were stridently suggesting, and so come to grips with facts. For the British clearly saw a threat to their own possessions in a Napoleonic presence in America.

In America, Jefferson sought for the words that would show the American people that he understood the situation and would at the same time, inform the French. He decided to accept the rumors of a secret treaty as being true. On December 15, 1802, Jefferson told the Congress that "The cession of the Spanish province of Louisiana to France, which took place in the course of the late war, will, if carried into effect, make a change in the aspect of our foreign relations."

These diplomatic words did him little good in a country anxious to hear harsher ones.

He tried again, a week later. He told Congress that "he was aware of the obligation to maintain in all cases the rights of the nation, and to employ for that purpose those just and honorable means which must belong to the character of the United States." The spectacle of a President of the United States pleading with Congress, begging them to believe that he knew what his duties were, illustrates Congressional disbelief in Jefferson's judgment. Worse, the House of Representatives sent Jefferson a reminder of what his duties were. The House members said they must "express their unalterable determination to maintain the boundaries and the rights of navigation and commerce through the river Mississippi as established by existing treaties."

At this point, Jefferson received a note from the Spanish government in Madrid, asserting that the intendant at New Orleans had acted without their knowledge or consent. Jefferson showed this communication to Congress, and tempers there and in the western territories were somewhat assuaged, but the Spanish were no longer the real problem. It was the French, not the Spanish, who were preparing for military operations on the Mississippi. Squeezed by this overt military threat on one side and by mounting political pressure at home on the other—a pressure applied not only by Federalists and hotheaded westerners like Andrew Jackson, but also by men in his own party, including his own Vice President, Aaron Burr—Jefferson saw nothing for it but to seek the odious British alliance. He instructed the American Embassy in London to discuss with the British government the possibility of a military alliance in the event of a war between the United States and France.

In this bleak winter, as the old year died and the new one

began, Jefferson received a wholly unlooked-for letter from Pierre Du Pont in Paris. Du Pont said he had been led to believe that France might possibly sell New Orleans and both Floridas to the United States for six million dollars. Du Pont did not say why he thought France might enter into such a bargain, and there was no evidence to suggest she would. Instead there was every reason to believe she would not, and the best evidence to support such logic was the French fleet taking supplies aboard in Holland. But Jefferson acted on the faint hope Du Pont's letter gave him. He privately asked Congress for money and was promised two million dollars in return. He then wrote to his old friend, James Monroe:

"I have but a moment to inform you that the fever into which the western mind is thrown by the affair at N. Orleans, stimulated by the mercantile, and generally federal interest, threatens to overbear our peace. . . . I shall tomorrow nominate you to the Senate for an extraordinary mission to France."

When he found another moment, he wrote again to Monroe:

"The agitation of the public mind on occasion of the late suspension of our rights of deposit at New Orleans is extreme. . . . Remonstrances, memorials, etc., are now circulating through the whole of the country . . . The measures which we have been pursuing, being invisible, do not satisfy their minds; something sensible, therefore, has become necessary, and, indeed, our object of purchasing New Orleans and the Floridas is a measure likely to assume so many shapes that no instructions could be squared to fit them."

Monroe was therefore to feel around in the dark in Europe and return with something or other that the American public could see. The first large problem was that no one really knew who actually owned Louisiana, or for that matter, the Floridas— for neither France nor Spain would admit that any secret treaty existed. But Monroe was to join Livingston in Paris to "procure

. . . a cession to the United States of New Orleans and of West and East Florida, or as much thereof as the actual proprietor can be prevailed on to part with." Failing this, they were to try to obtain an agreement that navigation of the Mississippi River, from source to ocean, "shall be equally free and common to citizens of the United States and of the French Republic." If France or Spain or whoever owned New Orleans would not sell the entire city to the United States, then Monroe and Livingston were to bargain for just a part of it, or for some little site on the riverbank where the United States could maintain a dock and warehouses, or at least a right of deposit on New Orleans docks, or some sort of claim to some real estate at the mouths of those Florida rivers whose sources were in United States territory. What Jefferson wanted was something, anything, to show the electorate for the time being. He was in no doubt that whatever his envoys could obtain would be too little. But anything would be a palliative, he said. He said, he wrote, he knew that possession of the Mississippi River was something the United States "must have." The trouble was, the United States could not then have it without going to war with the most powerful nation in the world, and no matter what the end of such a war, the Republican party would certainly be one of the corpses. Anything his envoys could gain would be more than welcome, even if all they might gain would be time.

To appoint Monroe as an envoy might seem to be taking a very long last chance. Monroe's previous mission to France had ended with his expulsion from that country. But the failure of Monroe's mission had not entirely been his fault—and then, there had been a different French government. Perhaps Jefferson hoped that Monroe's radical republicanism and ardent Francophilia would be accepted at face value by the French this time. But Monroe's appointment was also a palliative. His mission to Paris was intended to have more effect on the minds of the westerners than on Napoleon's. As a member of Congress, Monroe had championed the rights of western Americans to use the Mississippi River. For Jefferson to send Monroe to Paris was to reassure the westerners that their point of view would be taken directly to France by a man in whom they believed. Presumably the westerners would refrain from provoking a war while their man in Paris talked with Napoleon. Then, when and if the mission failed, the westerners would not place all the blame for it at the Republicans' door: they would realize that the Republican administration had tried.

Monroe sailed for France on March 8, 1803. Neither he nor Jefferson thought that Napoleon would sell or concede anything. There was no assurance that the young master of Europe would even grant Monroe an audience. The only good news for Jefferson in all that wretched winter was that the French fleet at Helvoët Sluys had not got out of harbor in time. It had been on the point of sailing in February, but that winter in Europe was exceptionally cold. There were early frosts, and ice formed sooner than normal, and just as the ships were to sail, ice sealed them in the harbor, and there they still were, creaking and groaning in the ice. Saved from one Napoleonic invasion by pestilence, America had been saved from another by the weather. But warmer winds were blowing, and soon the ice would melt.

18

The Noblest
Work
of Their Lives

Both Napoleon and Talleyrand envisioned the greatness of France. To Napoleon, who cared nothing for the French or any other people, the greatness of France was a means to an end. The end he sought was immortal glory, the foremost place in history. France provided him with arms and men. It was the base from which he would create and then govern a greater-than-Roman empire. He had an intelligent distrust of Talleyrand, but he would gladly make use of Talleyrand's talents whenever it seemed that they could serve his purposes.

To Talleyrand, the greatness of France was the desired end. France was his country, not Napoleon's. He wished his country to be preeminent in Europe in order that the French people could safely pursue their own destinies. He had an intelligent distrust of Napoleon, but he would gladly make use of Napoleon's talents whenever it seemed they could serve his purposes.

In the spring of 1803, Napoleon looked upon the world with all the confidence of a fortunate gambler who feels his luck running strong. Thinking in Roman terms, envisioning Great Britain as Carthage, Napoleon contemplated the invasion of England. Once ashore, he would rapidly defeat the British army which was much less powerful than his own. The difficulty lay in getting there. Every time he saw a puddle, he said, there was a British warship on it. But Carthage had been a sea power, too, and Carthage had been destroyed.

Talleyrand's view was that of a gambler who feels the cards are about to turn and knows it is time to leave the table. The Treaty of Amiens had been a wonderful treaty for France, and a very bad one for Britain. Now, he said, was the time for diplomacy. It would be better to conciliate the British than to fight them—and meanwhile consolidate one's gains. Talleyrand saw the wars between Britain and France in the last two centuries as having been mercantile wars between powers seeking to create colonial empires. The British had an extensive one, despite the recent loss of their American colonies, and the French had just reacquired Louisiana. Difficult as such a thing might be to achieve, Talleyrand wanted a commercial alliance with Britain. This, he said, would be the best and simplest way to guarantee the security of France and peace in Europe. The interests of the two nations would eventually collide in North America, but when they did, it would be better to discuss matters from a position of strength. Peace would provide the time to build that strength. Although he was convinced that wars were lunacy, Talleyrand was no pacifist. The unnecessary war was the one he found objectionable: it was worse than lunacy; it was a mistake.

Since these were Talleyrand's beliefs and since he knew that Napoleon was preparing to make war on Great Britain and that there were no limits to Napoleon's ambition, it might seem that honor would have required Talleyrand to resign his office as foreign minister. But Talleyrand's sense of honor was entirely his own. He remained close at Napoleon's side while the distance grew between them. Neither was afraid of the other. The two gamblers respected and faintly despised each other. Each knew the relationship could not possibly last, but each was confident that he would be the sole survivor.

On the morning of April 11, 1803, Napoleon summoned Talleyrand and François Barbé-Marbois to his office. Like Talleyrand, Marbois was a member of the ancient aristocracy who had once served the Bourbon king and who had managed to survive in the wild seas of revolution, serving the successive governments in the French foreign ministry. He was now the minister of the public treasury.

The First Consul had something to tell his ministers that morning. He began by reviewing the general situation. He had recently put himself at the head of the client republics he had created, against Talleyrand's advice, and the British were arguing that this was a distortion of the Treaty of Amiens. The British were using this as an excuse for their failure to evacuate Malta and otherwise comply with their responsibilities under the treaty. So there would be war with Britain very soon, Napoleon said. In fact, next month.

That being the case, there was the matter of the British navy to consider. Facts must be faced: France was a sea power, but second to the British. The French navy had been weakened by the loss of so many experienced officers and men in the yellow fever epidemic in Santo Domingo. This loss would be made good in time, but it had not yet been made good, and meanwhile the British had increased their naval force in the Caribbean. Perhaps it was just as well that the French fleet in Holland had been icebound that winter, for at least the ships were still in European waters. The power of Britain could be broken only in Britain, which required the invasion of Britain, and for this purpose the French would need to put every ship they owned into the Channel in order to obtain local superiority at sea for a long enough time to put the Grand Army ashore in England. In other words, the French navy was not strong enough to protect French possessions in America while at the same time gaining control of the Channel.

Meanwhile war was imminent; the Americans in London were reportedly conferring with the British as to the possibility of a military alliance, and the addition of the American navy to the British forces in American waters would render defense of French possessions there impossible. This raised the question of Louisiana. Napoleon assumed the British would attack down the Mississippi River basin from Canada, and north from New Orleans, seize Louisiana for themselves, join it to Canada, thus boxing the Americans in along the line of the Mississippi—and await future opportunities. But—

"They shall not have the Mississippi, which they covet," Napoleon assured his ministers. "The conquest of Louisiana would be easy if they only took the trouble to make a descent there. I have not a moment to lose in putting it out of their reach. . . . I think of ceding it to the United States."

Marbois listened to the angry argument that followed; his own role in the conference had not yet been made clear. Talleyrand argued for peace, not war; Napoleon said it was the British who were about to break the peace, not himself. Then the British should be given some concessions, Talleyrand suggested. Ever since the ancient regime it had been French policy to try to recover Canada and Louisiana for France—there was the site of empire; there was the opportunity; having at last regained possession of Louisiana, it would be ridiculous to throw away a potentially fruitful portion of the earth's surface that was several times larger than Europe.

There was no question of throwing anything away, Napoleon replied; there was only the question of facing facts and putting first things first. The last thing he needed was war in America, either with the British or the Americans or both, when Europe was the decisive theater. The first thing was to defeat

Great Britain and create a united Europe under French command. Thereafter, France could turn her attention back to America. As both he and Talleyrand well knew from the reports of the French ambassador to the United States, feeling against France was rising there. Since the Americans were so anxious with respect to the Mississippi, why not give them what they wanted at this time, and so make friends of them and prevent their alliance with Britain—an alliance that would make the French task in Europe more difficult than it already was?

"They only ask of me' one town in Louisiana," Napoleon said of the Americans, "but I already consider the colony as entirely lost; and it appears to me that in the hands of this growing power it will be more useful to the policy, and even to the commerce of France, than if I should attempt to keep it. It is not only New Orleans that I will cede, it is the whole colony without any reservations. . . . To attempt to retain it would be folly."

Talleyrand thought it was the war with Britain that would be folly, that Napoleon had his priorities exactly backward. On the other hand, the enmity of the British might very well be implacable. Their historic policy was to oppose the creation of any preponderating power in Europe, and Napoleon's victories, and his seizure of control of the Swiss, Dutch, and Italian republics, had created just such a power. Napoleon's victories were dangerous to France. Yet, if this Corsican genius should defeat the British, then Canada would be returned to France, and many things would then be possible.

Napoleon discussed the alternative. If the war with England should not go as well as one might wish, France could console herself. For, by giving the Americans an empire, he said, he would be placing a southern limit to British Canada, and giving Britain a real rival—one that would eventually forge ahead of Great Britain as a world power. In which case it would be to the advantage of France to have such a power as a friend.

But there was meanwhile no question of throwing anything

away: Napoleon intended to sell that which he already considered as entirely lost. This is where Marbois came in. He had been secretary to the French legation in the United States in 1779; he had married a Philadelphia woman; the Americans would regard him as a friend. Ordinarily negotiations with the Americans should be handled by the foreign minister, but in view of Talleyrand's opposition to the cession of Louisiana, it was possible that Talleyrand would sabotage the sale instead of consummating it. Moreover, Talleyrand should not discuss money with the Americans. The last time he had done so, the result had been an undeclared war. Napoleon could understand a man's asking for a bribe, but unfortunately the Americans could not. For the purposes of this transaction, it was necessary to use Marbois. Lacking imagination, the fellow was honest, and would do what he was told.

Marbois wondered what the price would be.

"Well," Napoleon mused, "you have charge of the treasury. Let them give you one hundred million francs . . . and take the whole country."

When Marbois was able to speak, he said such a thing was impossible. One hundred million francs would be more than seventeen million dollars, and there was not that much money in the United States.

"I will be moderate in consideration of the necessity in which I am making a sale," Napoleon said.

He thought for a moment, and said he would accept fifty million francs.

"But keep this to yourself," he said.

When Marbois protested that this, too, might be more than the Americans could afford, Napoleon was irritated.

"Beh!" he said. "Let them borrow it."

When Marbois wondered where the Americans could borrow that much money, Napoleon must have wondered what sort of fool he had made a treasurer. Who did he think had all the money? As evenly as he could, Napoleon suggested that the Americans should borrow it from British banks.

It was a rather Florentine touch. Wars were expensive. Let the British pay for their own defeat. After the British were defeated, the Americans would be making payments to banks now under French control, and thus France would in effect hold the mortgage to Louisiana. All sorts of advantages might flow from that arrangement, including foreclosure by military means. In any event, Napoleon could look forward to the receipt of several million dollars for nothing. Since he did not have possession of Louisiana and could not possibly hold it if he did, anything he got for it would be clear gain. The fact that the British would give him the money was an irony to be cherished. To be sure, the Spanish would be furious. He had given them his word that he would never alienate Louisiana to any third party. But Napoleon cared neither for the friendship nor the enmity of Spain. If the Spanish tried to hold Louisiana against the Americans, the result could only be a war that would delay American exploitation of the empire he was giving them—and so weaken the United States at a time when it might be to the advantage of France for the United States to remain a relatively weak nation. Napoleon could see nothing but good things ahead.

Talleyrand saw matters in a very different light. His pride had suffered no particular harm when Napoleon had brought in Marbois to deal with the Americans. His pride, like his honor, was his own. He was, however, disgusted and therefore coldly amused. What a wonderful thing it was to be a dictator. To be able to dispose of a continent as if it were a lame horse. To be able to glance toward heaven and say "one hundred million francs," and the next moment, to say, "Very well: fifty million." Never in all history had a continent depreciated so rapidly. And the purpose of it all was to raise money for an unnecessary war. War was necessary only to Napoleon. The future dead might entertain other opinions. It was true the British were preparing for war. It was also true that the British were supplying the French army with its boots and overcoats. The British would lend money to the Americans who would give it to the French who would give it to the British for boots and overcoats that the French could wear in England to enhance the glory of a Corsican. It seemed that two hundred years of French effort in America was to be bartered for haberdashery.

In such a world, anything was possible, including the possibility that the British might prefer peace to war; that the Americans might be mollified by a few docks and warehouses on a riverbank; that, given peace, France might fulfill the dreams of Champlain, Frontenac, and La Salle and create a great New France in America. The ancient regime had been unable to do this, but republican France could. The Revolution had opened many avenues to the French people: Talleyrand viewed his task as trying to make sure that Napoleon did not close them. He had just seen the dictator close one of the larger doors, and he had been unable to prevent this. There would, however, be other occasions.

It was in this mixed mood that Talleyrand saw the American ambassador that evening. And it was in this mood that Talleyrand had interrupted Robert Livingston's talk of rights of deposit and free navigation to shout in the deaf man's ear, "What will you give for the whole?"

It was none of his business now; that was in the hands of Marbois, but Talleyrand amused himself at the spectacle of Livingston's incredulity. He was so plainly half-believing what was so impossible to believe, so obviously wondering whether he had heard what he thought Talleyrand had said, and so anxious to believe that he had.

Talleyrand smiled and smoothly evaded the thrusts of Livingston's anxiety; he said he could not say more; he could not say less; his question had been purely hypothetical. He suspected Livingston's questions had to do with Livingston's pride. The new

envoy extraordinary, James Monroe, was to arrive next day, and
Livingston, as the United States ambassador, could not help feeling that Monroe's appearance in Paris was a rebuke to his own
abilities. Naturally, therefore, it would be to Livingston's advantage to be the one who found the key to the treasure chest before
his unwelcome colleague could start to look for it. But Talleyrand
would give Livingston no more than a hint that evening.

Next morning, Livingston presented himself at the Foreign
Ministry and handed Talleyrand an aide-mémoire of their discussion the night before. Talleyrand read it, and told Livingston that
last night he had only been speaking for himself, out of curiosity
—that after all, Louisiana was not his to sell. Livingston was left
to wonder what that meant. Were they back to square one? Despite all the rumors and expeditions was there in fact no secret
treaty? Or did the secret treaty not include Louisiana, or was
Talleyrand trying to tell Livingston something else?

Livingston inclined to the latter belief. He immediately
wrote to James Madison, the secretary of state, that Talleyrand
"told me he would answer my note, but that he must do it eva-
sively, because Louisiana was not theirs." In other words, if Louisiana was not French, then there was no reason for Talleyrand to
be evasive. Since he was evasive, Louisiana was French, and since
Talleyrand was a diplomat of genius, and since diplomats never
speak to one another without a purpose, Talleyrand's question
had been far from hypothetical. Talleyrand in effect had told him
that the French would be willing to sell the Americans something, and the problem now was to find out what it was and how
much the French would want for it. Pierre Du Pont's belief that
this was so had been verified by Talleyrand's evasions.

When Monroe arrived at the American embassy that day,
Livingston told him of his suspicions, but when Monroe told him
that the embassy was authorized to offer the French two million
dollars for the Floridas and New Orleans, Livingston thought

they would never accept it. Together they went over the instructions Monroe had brought to Paris:

1. The envoys were permitted to bid as high as ten million dollars for New Orleans, East and West Florida, and a guarantee of free navigation of the Mississippi River for citizens of France and the United States.

2. They were also to offer France free trading rights for French ships, and a port of deposit.

3. If necessary, the United States would guarantee forever French possession of all that part of Louisiana west of the Mississippi River.

4. If the French offered property other than New Orleans for sale, then the Floridas were to be considered as worth only a quarter of the value of New Orleans, with East Florida considered as worth only half the value of West Florida.

5. If the French would not sell New Orleans property to the United States for use as a port of deposit, then the envoys were to try to buy real estate in some other Mississippi River town for use as a port of deposit.

6. If France would not sell either of the Floridas, then the envoys should try to obtain a port of deposit on one of the rivers of West Florida.

7. If the French refused to negotiate and instead meditated hostilities against the United States, or if they closed the Mississippi River to American shipping, then Monroe and Livingston were to leave Paris for London and at once seek a military alliance with Great Britain—one that would prohibit either the United States or Great Britain from making a separate peace with France.

8. Should France refuse the Americans a port of deposit, but agree to permit American ships to navigate the Mississippi, then Livingston and Monroe should return to the United States and let Congress decide on war or peace with France.

More than dubious, Livingston told Monroe, "Only force can give us New Orleans. We must employ force. Let us first get possession of the country and negotiate afterwards."

The French were playing for time, he said. The thing to do was move in now, before the French could get to the river: that French fleet in Holland was no longer icebound. Monroe could assure Livingston there were many Americans who agreed with him—but there were political problems. Livingston could imagine what they were: they would include probable defeat for Jefferson and the Republicans. Livingston had Presidential ambitions of his own. A successful negotiation for New Orleans would enhance them; war with France would diminish them.

That evening, however, Marbois presented himself at the American embassy to meet Monroe, who had not yet been formally presented to the French as envoy extraordinary, and to tell Livingston and Monroe that Napoleon might be willing to sell all of Louisiana to the United States. He said that Napoleon had asked him, as the treasurer of France, to investigate this possibility. As Marbois later wrote, "Instead of the cession of a town and its inconsiderable territory, a vast portion of America was in some sort offered to the United States. They only asked for the mere right of navigating the Mississippi, and their sovereignty was about to be extended over one of the largest rivers of the world."

The Americans knew Marbois from Philadelphia days and regarded him as a decent man grown gray in the honorable service of his country, and were compelled to believe he was serious, however incredible his suggestion. Talleyrand's question of the day before had not been hypothetical, that much was now clear, but it was not at all clear to the Americans why Napoleon should make such an offer, or why Marbois had been chosen as the man to make it. The one thing that was very clear, was that Livingston and Monroe were not authorized to accept it. To negotiate for the entire central region of North America would ridiculously exceed their instructions, particularly in view of the fact that Napoleon's price (if he were serious) would as ridiculously exceed the United States ability to pay it.

Where Monroe was anxious to hear more from Marbois, Livingston backed and filled and talked around and away from the subject, just as the evening before, Talleyrand had evaded him. He felt there must be something wrong, and one of the things that was apparently wrong was that none of the three men knew precisely what they were all talking about. The dimensions of Louisiana were as mysterious as its contents. Marbois left the Americans without having received any answer more definite than the assurance of their immediate interest and the certainty of an early reply. He could well imagine their deepening shock as they began to consider the enormity of the opportunity so unexpectedly thrust beneath their noses.

By morning, Livingston felt he had the answer to at least one of his questions.

"I now plainly saw the whole business," he wrote in a dispatch to James Madison, "first, the Consul was disposed to sell; next, he distrusted Talleyrand, on account of the business of the supposed intention to bribe, and meant to put the negotiation of Marbois, whose character for integrity is established."

While it might have been plain enough why the Americans should talk about money with Marbois rather than with Talleyrand, there remained the problem of where to find the enormous sum that would certainly be required. The answer was obligingly sent to Monroe the following day by a man he called "a confidential friend."

The mysterious stranger who called at the American embassy told Monroe that he was an agent of the British banking firms of Hope and Baring. He said the London bankers knew all about Monroe's mission, and felt that he might need money to accomplish it. He said the bankers had authorized him to say that they would loan Monroe whatever he needed. When Monroe asked how far the bankers meant to go, and on what terms, the confidential friend promised up to ten million dollars, at six percent per year.

Monroe and Livingston were left to speculate that their dubious visitor was remarkably well-informed. Ten million dollars was exactly what they had been authorized to offer for New Orleans and the two Floridas. If their mission was common knowledge to London bankers, they felt it must be known to the British government—which, as a matter of fact, it was: one of the American embassy's secretaries was a British spy. Livingston and Monroe did not know that, but they could conclude that the British government wanted their mission to succeed, even though the British must surely know that Napoleon would use the money to make war on them.

It was indeed a risk the British were willing to accept. First, they were not afraid of Napoleon, and next, there was six percent in it. But more important, the British did not want to see Napoleonic France established in the center of the North American continent, with all the means this would give France of augmenting her naval force, and of threatening Canada and British possessions in the Caribbean. Moreover, with Napoleon obviously threatening Britain with invasion, it was no time for the British to have to divide their naval forces between the Channel and American waters. It was much more to their liking to have the Americans as their friends at this time—and to have a relatively weak United States as Canada's neighbor, rather than a virulently potent France.

The man who visited the American embassy may have been an agent for the London bankers, but it also seems it was the French who sent him to call on Monroe. Livingston and Monroe were being led at a smart trot to the negotiating table by the French, and once there, they learned from Marbois that he would not discuss the sale of New Orleans or the Floridas. He told the Americans that if they wanted anything, they would have to take all of Louisiana or nothing. Take it or leave it. He said the asking price was one hundred million francs, but the First Consul might be willing to accept a little less if the Americans acted right away.

For all that Monroe was Livingston's junior by some twenty years and a radical Republican whereas Livingston was a conservative one, it was he who drew back while Livingston wanted to push ahead. Monroe objected that to treat for Louisiana would exceed their instructions and that he and Livingston should tell Madison and Jefferson of Napoleon's offer and wait for a reply. The older man felt that this was such a fantastic offer, such an incredible opportunity to more than double the area of the United States without firing a shot, that they would be criminally responsible if they did not sign a contract—and that the sooner they signed it, the better. He was certain that Jefferson, the Congress, and the nation in general would agree. The price, however, might be trimmed. The United States had filed claims against France for damage done American shipping. These claims could be laid against the price; there was at least no harm in asking.

Sixteen days later, on April 30, a bargain had been struck. The United States agreed to pay France sixty million francs for Louisiana and to pay another twenty million to American shipowners in satisfaction of their claims against France.

It is perhaps niggling to remark that the Americans promised to pay ten million more francs for Louisiana than Napoleon would have taken, and in addition gave France a free gift of another twenty million francs by agreeing to pay American citizens' claims against France. For Marbois to have got this extra thirty million francs out of the Americans may well attest to his diplomatic skills, if not to theirs. A more serious point is that Livingston and Monroe committed the United States to pay eighty million francs, or fifteen million dollars, to be hired at six percent. And fifteen million dollars was not only more money than the United States Treasury possessed, it was more money than existed in the entire nation.

But the truly serious defect in the agreement had nothing to do with money. Difficult as it may be to believe, Monroe and Livingston pledged their country to buy, sight unseen, a parcel of land that had not been described to them, with no certainty that the seller actually owned it, but with every reason to believe that the seller did not, and that war with Spain was implicit in the contract. They had no clear idea what they were buying, nor did Marbois know what he was selling. At one point, Marbois went trotting off to Napoleon to ask what the western boundaries of Louisiana were, telling the First Consul that he regretted the fact that they seemed to be rather obscure.

Napoleon favored him with a charming smile.

"If an obscurity did not already exist, it would, perhaps, be a good policy to put one there," the Corsican suggested.

It was even more important to the French to keep the eastern boundaries obscure, for it was New Orleans and West Florida that the Americans particularly wanted to buy, in order to obtain control of rivers emptying into the Gulf of Mexico. Obscurity was therefore built into the controlling sentence of the agreement. The sentence said the Americans were buying "Louisiana with the Same extent that it now has in the hands of Spain, and that it had when France possessed it; and Such as it Should be after the Treaties subsequently entered into between Spain and other States." During the negotiations, Marbois led the Americans to believe that West Florida had been part of the recent cession of Louisiana to France, although this was not the case. West and East Florida were separate properties that belonged to Spain.

Only after the bargain had been agreed upon and the document signed were the boundaries of Louisiana discussed in any detail—and now that the haggling was over, Talleyrand reentered the scene.

"What are the eastern boundaries of Louisiana?" Livingston asked him.

"You must take it as we received it," Talleyrand replied,

meaning that the Americans must take what, it was now tacitly admitted, the French had in fact received from Spain.

"But what did you mean to take [from Spain]?" Livingston wanted to know.

Talleyrand shrugged. "I do not know," the foreign minister said.

"You mean," Livingston said, beginning to understand all the implications of that lie, "that we shall construe it in our own way?"

"I can give you no direction," Talleyrand said. "You have made a noble bargain for yourselves, and I suppose you will make the most of it."

Livingston and Monroe were lawyers, and at this point one might think that all the defects of the agreement would now come flooding into their minds. But the point escaped Monroe. He presumed the French had been deliberately obscure merely in order to increase the putative extent of the property, and therefore the price. Livingston had a shrewd appreciation of the truth, particularly after what Talleyrand had just said, but as he later wrote to Madison, "I was willing to take it in any form."

"We can afford to overlook any defects in the treaty details," the American historian Binger Herman lightly said in retrospect, "and forever hold in gratitude the illustrious men who, by their diplomatic skill, their earnestness of purpose, well-directed efforts, achieved one of the greatest triumphs in the world's history. . . . It well justified the boast of Livingston as he placed his name to the treaty of cession, and rising and shaking hands with Monroe and Marbois, said, 'We have lived long, but this is the noblest work of our lives.' "

It is also possible to think of these illustrious men, who bowed and smiled and shook one another's hands upon completion of their skillful labors, as three revolutionaries meeting in a back room to concoct among themselves one of the shadiest real-estate transactions in the long and sordid history of land-jobbery. The fact that it was the largest real-estate transaction in history might seem to lend it glory, but only in the sense that a million-pound swindle might seem more glorious than a two-shilling one.

No sooner had the Americans signed the agreement than Napoleon and Talleyrand asked for an immediate down payment, before the treaty had been ratified by either government, much less the land delivered by France to the United States. If the American envoys did not agree, Marbois explained, the deal was off. Moreover, the Americans must act at once, he said, because either the British or the Spanish might seize Louisiana if they learned the Americans were thinking of buying it from France.

Monroe, that envoy extraordinary, actually believed this nonsense. He seemed to forget that Spain did not have to seize Louisiana—she already possessed it—and that if France could not deliver the goods, there was no reason for the Americans to pay France a cent. And, since British banks were going to underwrite the purchase, it ought to have occurred to Monroe that the British government knew all about the negotiation and approved of it. Perhaps Monroe was frightened out of his wits by the mere suggestion the deal could fall flat. At any rate, to Livingston's endless surprise and disgust, Monroe blurted out that he was em-powered to put two million dollars down right away. He said he hoped his colleague, Ambassador Livingston, would agree.

Fortunately for the Americans, Napoleon did not simply pick up two million dollars for nothing at all. It seemed the French were merely testing the probability that the Americans could meet the price and knew where to get the money. They said Monroe's generous offer was enough: they withdrew their demand for the actual money. Livingston sighed. He told Monroe afterward that he was glad Monroe had made the offer, "as he likewise was that it had been refused."

Still jittery, Monroe was all for galloping off to Spain to dis-cuss metes and bounds and other matters that would certainly be of mutual interest, but Talleyrand told him this would be inadvisable and premature. Monroe could not see why it should be, but then he did not know that Napoleon had promised Spain he would never sell Louisiana to any third power. Nor did Talleyrand enlighten him. Napoleon explained that it would be best if the French first took over from Spain in Louisiana, and then handed the province to the Americans. It was all a matter of procedure, he said.

Monroe accepted this, but on subsequent reflection, his suspicions darted up again. He felt he saw it all, now: the French had not only cleverly inflated the price, but no part of the Floridas was included in the transaction, and the French were trying to keep him away from Madrid long enough to get there first themselves, so that they could tell the Spanish to sell the Floridas to the United States for as much money as the United States had agreed to pay for Louisiana. In other words, he felt the French intended to sell the same property twice—that the French and Spanish were acting together.

These suspicions were very wide of the mark. As Talleyrand had all but said, the French expected the United States to take the Floridas from Spain by force. As far as Napoleon was concerned, he wanted the agreement ratified at once (for he wanted those sixty million francs for the coming war), and he had no doubt that the American Congress would jump to it.

As to the latter point, Livingston and Monroe were by no means as confident as Napoleon was. Once the excitement of negotiation began to chill, there was every question in their minds. Congress might very well repudiate the transaction. So, for that matter, might Jefferson. The problem was not entirely one of money, although Congress might balk at that. The overwhelming question in their minds, now that they had time to think about it, was whether the Constitution permitted the Federal government to buy foreign lands.

Livingston and Monroe might not have acted much like lawyers in their scurry to buy an undescribed property with a clouded title, but they read the Constitution very narrowly. So did Jefferson, Madison, and all other Republican leaders. Jefferson's career, and that of the Republican party, was based on their allegiance to strict construction of the Constitution. Jefferson had once been burned when he fell in with Hamilton's schemes to have the United States assume the debts of the former colonies: Patrick Henry had acidly called to his attention the fact that this was to give the Federal government powers not specifically granted it in the Constitution—and that all other powers remained with the states. The Republicans had recently come to power on that very issue. They had charged the Alien and Sedition Acts were unconstitutional because they gave the Federal government powers to which it was not entitled.

Livingston and Monroe had been instructed to negotiate with France for ports of deposit and navigation rights. True, they had been empowered to buy property, but it had been riparian property, and its purchase might conceivably have been excused on grounds that natural law ordained the right of men who live on a river to go down to the sea which all mankind had a natural and common right to use. But they had not bargained for riparian rights. They had bargained for an empire, and not one word in the Constitution said they could. The two envoys were quite sure the Federalists would gleefully point this out, and that a great many Republican Congressmen might, however sadly, concede the point. So might Jefferson, when it was plainly put to him that he could not possibly agree to the purchase of Louisiana unless he was willing to repudiate a cardinal principle of his political life.

No doubt the American envoys had forgotten their law and their political principles once Napoleon had offered them all the property west of the Mississippi. No doubt they had seen in this offer the solution of many problems: no more Spaniards on the river; peace rather than war with France; unlimited opportunity for Americans to walk west into their continent and make money out of it; no need for the United States to become entangled in the sticky embraces of Great Britain; and in addition to all this, personal glory for themselves for having brought all these good things about. Their dazzlement had persisted even after they learned that they had bought someone else's pig in a poke, and that the instrument of sale would have horrified a first-year law student. But in the heady moments of dealing with Napoleon for an empire, they had been borne away and aloft far above the law and principles and into the realms of nations and princes.

They now returned to the law, and their principles, with a thud. Some way around both would have to be found if the document they had signed was to be worth more than the sand scattered over their signatures. The view from Paris was a little unclear. It was possible that their mission to Paris had not ended in triumph, but in a fiasco ruinous to their party and their nation.

19

The Mountain
of Salt

O N July 15, 1803, President Thomas Jefferson read the dispatches from Paris, and wrote at once to Meriwether Lewis. "We received the treaty from Paris, ceding Louisiana according to the bounds to which France had a right."

The expedition, which had been postponed for fear of a possible French reaction, could now proceed.

General James Wilkinson, in his capacity as Secret Agent No. 13, also sat down to his writing desk. He wrote to the Spanish intendant at New Orleans, warning him of Lewis and Clark's forthcoming reconnaissance, suggesting that the Spaniards arrest the Americans if they wandered into Spanish territories in the west.

The Spanish ambassador called on the secretary of state to say that he "had orders to warn the Federal Government to suspend the ratification and execution of the treaties of cession to Louisiana, as the French Government in securing the province had contracted an engagement with Spain not to retrocede it to any other power."

He said that "France not having executed that engagement, the treaty cession was void."

He wanted the United States to understand that the two Floridas were in no way a part of the cession in any case, and not to imagine that Texas was, either.

The Spanish point of view was prickly with threats of war, and one rumor going around Washington said that the British were behind all this, that they had warned the Spanish of the Franco-American treaty, told them to object to it, and had promised to help them if it came to war.

War with the Spanish was the least of Jefferson's problems, however. Spain's objections could be safely ignored, no matter that they were solidly based on every legal and moral right. Spain was being robbed by the Americans and the French, with Napoleon holding the pistol. Therefore, Jefferson could discount the threat of Spanish war, and if the Spaniards in Louisiana tried to defend their property, there were two hundred thousand Americans in the Mississippi River valley, and only sixty-four thousand French and Spanish Creoles.

Jefferson's real concern was for American law, not international morality. He said he feared he had "gone beyond the Constitution" in agreeing to purchase Louisiana. Much as he believed the United States "must have the Mississippi"; much as he wanted there to be one nation on the continent, and an overland route to the Pacific coast, he was at least as much concerned for human liberty. With respect to foreign affairs, he believed that only a strong Federal government could conduct them. But with respect to internal affairs, he believed the Federal powers were very narrowly defined, and that all other powers, including the right to secede, belonged to the states. He utterly rejected the Federalists' theory that the Constitution "implied" that the government could assume any powers not specifically spelled out in that document. If that were so, he felt, a future Federal government could justify almost anything on grounds that the laws it passed were helping to promote the public welfare, even if their effect was to convert the republic into a monarchy.

The only protection the people had, he felt, lay in their control of their state governments. If the several states did not retain all powers not granted the Federal government, they might as well give up any pretense to having rights of their own. The issue of states' rights versus Federal rights was a basic problem to the framers of the Constitution, as the vague language of the Constitution suggests; it was a basic problem to Jefferson; it became a bloody one during the Civil War, and it still to great extent plagues the United States tóday. In 1803, Jefferson was acutely aware that the Constitution did not give the Federal government specific authority to buy foreign real estate. On the other hand, he meant to have Louisiana.

His first reaction was to draft an amendment to the Constitution—and give it to his Cabinet to consider. Since an amendment must be ratified by state governments, this in effect would put the purchase of Louisiana up to the states. It seemed, however, that the states might very well refuse to adopt any such amendment, for Congress was in an uproar over the proposed treaty, which the Senate would have to ratify. Instead of regarding an opportunity to buy Louisiana as a heaven-sent gift to the nation, not a few Congressmen from Virginia to Massachusetts saw nothing ahead but unmitigated disaster.

Representative Cyrus Griffin of Virginia spoke for Southerners who felt that a tremendous addition to the nation would drive down land values and increase the price of labor. He also objected that the climate in the west would kill off immigrants like flies.

"We have already without Louisiana more uncultivated lands than we can sell," Senator William Plumer of New Hampshire said, "and I am confident that the ratification of this treaty & the possession of the immense territory will hasten the dissolution of our present government. We must form different empires and

The Mountain of Salt

the form of our governments will then result more from the circumstances of the times in which the change is effected, than the will of the people or the fitness and propriety of the measure."

Senator Plumer expressed the fears in small Eastern states when he added, "Admit this western world into the Union, and you destroy at once the weight and importance of the Eastern States and compel them to establish a separate, independent Empire." The same point was put by Senator James White of Delaware, who said:

"But as to Louisiana—this new, immense, unbounded world—if it should ever be incorporated into the Union, of which I have no idea [and if it] can only be done by amending the Constitution, I believe it will be the greatest curse that could, at present befall us. It may be productive of innumerable evils, and especially of one that I fear ever to look upon. . . . Thus our citizens will be removed to the immense distance of two or three thousand miles from the capital of the Union, where they will scarcely ever feel the rays of the General Government—their affections will become alienated; they will gradually begin to view us as strangers—they will form other commercial connections, and our interests will become distinct. . . . And I do say that under existing circumstances, even supposing that this extent of territory was a desirable acquisition, fifteen millions of dollars was a most enormous sum to give."

The last point was made clear to the man in the street: newspapers amused themselves by trying to estimate how many wagons, stretched for how many miles, would be required to move fifteen million dollars' worth of silver, assuming there was that much silver in the world. Money was never a serious argument in the debate, however. Nevertheless, Jefferson thought it was important enough to meet, and sought to assure the Senate that Louisiana was, economically speaking, a bargain. Neither Napoleon, Talleyrand, Marbois, Livingston, Monroe, Madison, nor Jefferson had ever seen Louisiana or ever would, and none of

[343]

them knew how large the property was or what it contained, but these facts did not prevent Jefferson from describing the wonders of that unknown land his envoys had bought. He assured the Senate that there was a tribe of giants who lived out there. There were antique towers standing on one riverbank, he said. There were meadows of tremendous extent, whose land was far too rich to allow the growth of trees. And, there was a mountain of pure salt that was 180 miles long and 45 miles wide. All a man had to do to get the salt was drive a wagon up to the mountain, take out a shovel, fill the wagon, and drive home again to market. He did not know just exactly where this mountain was, but he knew it was there, he said—a whole mountain of pure salt.

What Mr. Jefferson ought also to have mentioned, the New York *Evening Post* reported, was that "some leagues to the westward . . . there was an immense lake of molasses, and that between this lake and the mountain of salt, there was an extensive vale of hasty pudding, stretching as far as the eye could reach, and kept in a state of comfortable eatibility by the sun's rays, into which the natives, being all Patagonians, waded knee deep, whenever they were hungry, and helped themselves with salt on one hand to season their pudding, and molasses with the other, to give it relish."

The comment was deserved: Jefferson thereafter confined his speculation to the law as, during that summer of 1803, the Congress and the nation debated the wisdom of buying Louisiana, the size of which, only dimly perceived, was nonetheless perceived as being of fantastic extent.

"It is not consistent with the spirit of a republican government that its territory should be exceedingly large; for, as you extend your limits you increase the difficulties arising from a want of that similarity of customs, habits, and manners so essential for its support," Representative Roger Griswold of Connecticut very rightly and wisely said. "It will not be found, either in the report of the secret committee which has recently been published, or in any document or debate, that any individual entertained the least wish to obtain the province of Louisiana, our views were then confined to New Orleans and the Floridas. . . . The vast and unmanageable extent which the accession of Louisiana will give the United States; the consequent dispersion of our population, and the destruction of that balance which it is so important to maintain between the Eastern and Western States, threatens, at no very distant day, the subversion of our Union."

The threat in fact was a clear and present danger, as Representative Griswold had personal reason to know, for he and Senator Timothy Pickering of Massachusetts, together with other New England politicians, were at that moment seriously discussing secession from the Union if Louisiana was purchased. They hoped that Vice President Aaron Burr could lead New York into their Northern confederacy; they were Federalists, and he, a Republican, but it was not only the Federalists who feared that to purchase Louisiana would be dangerous to the Union, as well as being illegal. Griswold's point, that republics are a function of size, was well-taken—as everyone who lives in any large city today can now well understand. During the debate over the acquisition of Louisiana, it was seriously proposed that the United States ought to be divided into at least three republics—a Northern one, a Southern one, and one in the West. Jefferson rather agreed.

"Whether we remain in one confederacy, or form into Atlantic and Mississippi confederacies, I believe not very important to the happiness of either part," he wrote. "Those of the Western confederacy will be as much our children and descendants as those of the Eastern, and I feel myself as much identified with that country in future as with this."

If these remarks seem strange in a man who believed there should be one republic throughout North and South America, and that the conduct of foreign affairs required strong central powers to accomplish this purpose, the explanation is that Jefferson passionately believed in states' rights—and that he wanted Americans to take possession of their continent even if this meant they had to form separate republics for administrative purposes. That he could entertain mutually exclusive points of view is an illustration of his ability to see value in each of them—and the immense difficulty of trying to resolve them.

War between Britain and France had erupted just two weeks after Livingston, Monroe, and Marbois had signed the treaty of purchase, but so far as the American politicians were concerned that summer, the war might as well have been taking place on the dark side of the moon. The one issue in the United States was whether to take what people were now calling an empire, and the issue came down to the Constitutional question.

"It is declared in the third article [of the proposed treaty] that 'the inhabitants of the ceded territory shall be incorporated in the Union of the United States,' " Senator Pickering pointed out. "But neither the President and Senate, nor the President and Congress, are competent to such an act of incorporation." He added that he believed the assent of each state was necessary for the admission of a foreign country as an associate in the Union.

"We can hold territory, but to admit the inhabitants into the Union, to make citizens of them, and States, by treaty, we cannot constitutionally do," Senator Tracy of Connecticut agreed, "and no subsequent act of legalization, or even ordinary amendment to our Constitution, can legalize such measures. If done at all, they must be done by universal consent of all the States or partners to our political association."

Thomas Jefferson could hardly have put it better. But the irony was, these men were Federalists. In the course of debate, the Federalists, who from their earliest days had been the advocates of the government's use of its "implied" powers, now appeared as the champions of states' rights and of a strict construction of the Constitution. They were not just playing politics, using Jefferson's stick to hit him over the head with it. Some were concerned for fear they would lose money if the acquisition of immense lands in Louisiana cheapened the value of their properties; others for fear that the political center of gravity would wander over the mountains. But it is reasonable to assume that most Federalists were just as concerned as Jefferson was for the good of their nation and the rights of its people, and that they looked beyond Louisiana to see something much more important: precedent and principle. Like Jefferson, they too could see value and danger in each concept. Even if their reasons were selfish, they opposed the purchase on principles that had considerable validity.

To complete the irony, Jefferson, that champion of strict construction and states' rights, now invoked the government's right to use powers not specified but implicit in the Constitution. It was perfectly clear to him now that the United States could legally buy land and absorb alien populations, because the Constitution granted the government power to make war. Now, he argued, in the course of a war, the government could certainly find itself in the position of acquiring foreign lands and ruling alien populations. Therefore, since the Constitution did envision war, it also envisioned the acquisition of property, and therefore if the Constitution permitted the acquisition of property by military means, it certainly ought to admit the acquisition of property by peaceful ones. The power to do so was clearly implied in the Constitutional requirement that the government should provide for the common defense—and of course possession of the Mississippi River was essential to the military security of the United States. The staunchest Federalist could hardly have put it better.

There is no point in saying, as the Federalists did, that Jefferson's blowing hot and cold demonstrated his utter lack of principle. True, he meant to have Louisiana by any means he could find, but he was not picking up the Federalists' stick to hit them over the heads with it. Like them, he thrashed the matter out on grounds of principle and selected one that had considerable validity: some powers of government must be assumed at need in cases where the Constitution's silence could be construed as consent.

What is particularly interesting in this case is the fact that the men who drafted the Constitution were, most of them, alive and well and taking part in the discussion—changing sides, looking at matters differently from the way they had only a few years earlier, still uncertain in their minds as to the proper relationship between the Federal government and the several states. Nor did the subsequent vote resolve the issue. During the summer, the Senate agreed to ratify the treaty of purchase, and Congress voted to hire the money, but not because the theory of implied powers was seen to be superior to that of states' rights. It was rather because a majority in Congress wanted that land, as did the large majority of the national electorate. The vote to take it plainly showed that men had changed their political skins in saying yea or nay, and since an excellent case could be made for either side of the Constitutional question, it all came at last to using the argument that would excuse the action. Practically to a man, the westerners were states' rights Republicans, but practically to a man they wanted the Louisiana territory. The nation had been creeping steadily west since Colonial infancy, walking steadily west since the Revolution. It now saw opportunity to leap into the west—and took it. The Senate vote was 24-7.

Jefferson and the Republicans did not come out of this affair with their principles in shreds and their party in disarray; in the public eye, at least, they emerged with glory. Never had the Republican tide run so full.

If it seems a wonder that a westward-moving nation took so long a time and spent such argument before deciding to do what it plainly intended to do, the reason is that the Americans felt, and still feel, a need to give their actions some color of legality. The nation, after all, was founded on treason: the Declaration of Independence, written by Jefferson, was an elaborate and eloquent excuse for it. The declaration is, in another sense, an admission of treason and an exercise in rationalization. It was important in 1776, and in 1803, and again to Americans today, to appear to be always in the right; to claim that whatever they do is legally correct, morally sound, and in the interest of all mankind. Of course if they had ever really concerned themselves with the legal and moral aspects of the Louisiana Purchase, it would have occurred to them that the Spanish were quite correct to say that France had no legal right to convey the property, and therefore that the United States could not buy it from France. But no one gave this matter more than a passing thought. Everyone's attention was instead riveted on the property itself, and the nation was willing, as Livingston said in Paris, to take it in any form. To a nation with a guilt complex born of matricide, form was important.

While America debated ratification of the purchase treaty, Napoleon bullied the Spaniards. As a result of both actions, a French commissioner set off from Paris in the fall of the year, and his ship having evaded capture by the British, arrived on November 23 in New Orleans. He brought with him a letter from the king of Spain, dated a year earlier. The letter ordered the Spanish governor of Louisiana to hand the province over to France. He also produced a letter to himself, written by Napoleon, ordering him to take possession of Louisiana in the name of France. The Spanish gave him the keys to the city, and to the intense joy of the French Creole population, the French flag flew again over New Orleans.

Twenty days later, a column of American troops appeared. The French flag came down and that of the United States was raised, while the Spanish and French Creoles of New Orleans looked on with profound misgivings. After 311 years of hardship, war, glory, mismanagement, and opportunity, the Latin adventure in North America was at an end. The present and future belonged to the confident, grinning Anglo-Saxons.

Republican democracy had thus displaced monarchical tyranny, and so the fortunate populace of New Orleans was immediately placed under martial law. Two joint rulers were given them. One was a William Claiborne. The other was a familiar figure, that of the affable, bibulous swindler known to the Spaniards as Secret Agent No. 13—and to the United States as Brigadier General James Wilkinson, U.S.A.

20

A Possibility
of Paradise
An Epilogue

Talleyrand spoke of a noble bargain, and in simple terms of money and power, he was certainly right. The Louisiana territory turned out to embrace some nine hundred thousand square miles of North America. For something under four cents an acre, the least of nations acquired an inland empire that contained virtually every sort of climate, topography, soil, and ore. Every sort of crop and domestic animal could be produced in it, pools of petroleum and natural gas awaited discovery and invention to serve the uses of a future industrial society. The timber in Minnesota alone was worth more than the purchase price of the entire region, and so, for that matter, were the pelts of the animals found in those northern forests. Briefly, the natural resources of Louisiana were such as to enable whatever nation held the territory to become the richest nation on earth. A conventional view of the Louisiana Purchase is that it enabled the United States to so exploit these resources as to become a major power in the world. That, of course, is what happened.

It is also possible to look at the purchase from several other points of view. For example, there was nothing inevitable about the United States coming into possession of its current geographic boundaries. Had Napoleon invaded and defeated Great Britain in 1803, the political map of North America would appear quite different today. Had the British not been otherwise occupied in 1812, the United States could have been dismantled. Had Europe not been caught up in social revolution in the 1860s, any of several nations might have allied themselves with the Confederacy and defeated the Union in the Civil War, with the result that several flags could be flying in America today. In this context, it is possible to regard the Louisiana Purchase as a stupendous and fortunate accident that befell the United States and to say that a further series of accidents, including one at Waterloo, enabled the United States to enjoy possession of a region so strangely, if not illegally acquired.

Another view of the Louisiana Purchase is that it marked the beginning of the end of several dreams.

The original dream was to do God's work on earth. Columbus with eighty men and boys set off to convert the Great Khan of Cathay and all his myrmidons and to defeat the forces of Satan in whatever islands and continents they might be found. This, as he said, was the alpha and omega of the enterprise. The medieval Spanish warriors might have been as full of vices as Cortés said they were, but they nonetheless felt themselves embarked upon a great crusade. When they grew hugely rich from their conquests, they used their wealth to continue the crusade in Europe—and to search for new treasure troves in the realms of the Devil. For reasons they were never able to understand, their faith, their wealth, and their medieval political system led the Spaniards to the ruin of all their hopes three centuries later. Just as they feared it would, the acquisition of Louisiana by Anglo-Saxon republican heretics led directly to the dissolution of New Spain.

The Renaissance French were next to attempt the seas that were believed to be full of monsters, to enter a mysterious part of the world they, too, believed to be the Devil's realms, filled with evil spirits, imps, and creatures drawn from medieval bestiaries. They also sought the high road to Cathay, but once arrived in America, their responses to its opportunities were different from those of the Spaniards. The more visionary of the French leaders saw the possibility of a great New France, but for reasons having to do with religious wars, emergent political systems in Europe, and a want of popular will, the French never did what they might have done. Like the Spaniards, the French never sent to America sufficient numbers of the kind of men and women capable of creating a civilization. When at last the French became the Great Nation of Europe under Louis XIV, that autocrat's attention was given to Europe; when the French once again dominated Europe under Napoleon, that autocrat's attention was also riveted upon Europe. By then it was all too late. When Napoleon sold Louisiana, he also sold the dream of New France.

In contradistinction to the Latin nations, the English voyagers in Tudor times immediately envisioned a New England. They, too, were in the grip of God in those days, but rather than viewing America as the land of Satan, they saw it as the Promised Land. To be sure they gave a thought to locating the Northwest Passage to Cathay, but once they had glimpsed the North American continent, their primary purpose was not to find wealth but to create it. Here, as a Tudor sailor said, was work for a prince, for only a prince possessed the money necessary to send out colonists to labor for years to convert the wilderness into a garden. Fortunately for the English, they had monarchs who agreed that this could and should be done. As soon as their circumstances at home and in Europe allowed them to, the English began to sail for America in such numbers as to suggest a resumption of the ancient migrations of their Teutonic ancestors. A popular will was there, and for reasons having to do with the course of European events, English traditions, political structure, and traits of character, they succeeded where the Latin nations failed or defaulted. In the years immediately following the American Revolution, there was reason to believe that the former colonies might rejoin the British empire, but the purchase of Louisiana was the beginning of the end of the dream of a New England in the Promised Land. Thanks to the accidents of European history, the United States was given sufficient time to grow away and apart from Europe. As it turned out, the acquisition of Louisiana was the last necessary act of the Revolution.

It also delayed, for more than a hundred years, the appearance of a distinctive civilization in America. Up to the time of the Louisiana Purchase, North American history was the story of Europeans adventuring in a world theirs for the taking. But neither the Spanish nor the French nor the English created facsimiles of the civilizations of their mother countries in North America. For one thing, the Europeans who went out to America were not representative of their national populations. The larger number of the Latins were dropouts and rejects who had little reason to replicate the civilizations they had left, and just as little ability to do so in any case. The English likewise transported their share of misfits to America, but they did not administer their colonies by martial law, and in the course of reacting to pioneer necessity, the English colonists became self-reliant egalitarians who were quite different from their kinsmen in England in outlook and attitude. Their Revolution was a parting of the ways with respect to many of the social forms that undergird English civilization. In brief, the English became Americans while living in America, and they developed a distinctive American culture. But they did not develop a distinctive civilization.

The difference has to do with senses of time and purpose. A tribe of Stone Age nomads who have legends, weave baskets, make weapons, and wear feathers may be said to have a culture. But they live always in the present in a state of constant motion that has as its entire purpose a simple acquisition; they have no clear knowledge of the past and no image of a future. Another tribe may also use stone implements, but if it devises a calendar and a literature, keeps records, charts the stars, builds enormous and beautiful cities, creates a coherent theology and an intricate political system, it may be said to have a civilization. As Kenneth Clark points out, a civilization is essentially distinguished by its quality of permanence. It is the creation of a people who have a decent respect for the past and for the future, and who create works that are meant to endure—works that represent the abiding genius of their nation, that they believe to be beautiful, and that enlarge for them the quality of human experience. Unlike a nomadic culture, a civilization is not exclusively concerned with acquisition. Its attention is turned inward upon itself, not outward into limitless space.

The distinctive American culture that the English settlers developed had something in common with that of a nomadic tribe. Faced with the lack of almost every necessity, they lived very much in the here and now. Their efforts chiefly centered upon acquisition, and particularly upon the acquisition of land. Their parents were sleeping in parish churchyards half a world away; most of them never expected to see England again. England and the past were behind them, and unknown and apparently limitless space lay ahead of them to the west. They were in a state of motion; they had to be if they were to survive. Their attention was necessarily turned outward to see what use could be made of the products of their new and savage environment. The process of invention and encroachment in the present tended to confirm them in a frontier culture whose attitudes had much to do with egalitarian push, grab, and get—and with enterprise free to a point of license. They were not in the least concerned with permanence: they were immediately concerned with change. They needed at once to go from something dangerous and bad to something safer and better. It was a need that determined their responses, and led to an opinion that something new is probably better than something old, that more is better than less, that most of the newest is best of all. A frontier culture put a premium on size: in a savage world, a big strong man was safer than a little spindly one, and a large landhold offered greater security than a small one. It was furthermore seen that more money offered a means to greater safety and comfort than less money did. Apart from that, in a frontier society lacking many of the hierarchies and social classes of a civilized one, the possession of money became a determinant of social position in America to an extent it never did in Europe. At the time of the purchase of Louisiana, the Americans had by no means filled the lands granted them as a result of the Revolution, nor had they yet achieved security for themselves in a world filled with predatory nations abroad and on their borders. They were still essentially dedicated to immediate acquisition, never mind by what means. When Napoleon suddenly gave them another nine hundred thousand square miles, more than doubling the nation's area, this locked the Americans into frontier attitudes, and into a frontier culture, for the next hundred years.

For all that time, with the exception of the years of civil war, the principal business of Americans was the exploration, settlement, and exploitation of their new empire. In all that time, there was no respite to think in terms of permanence; to think in terms of an American past and future and to create those works that would endure and express the genius of the nation and enlarge the quality of the American experience. There was no time to build the city of man nor any desire to do so. There was only time to expand, exploit, and acquire: to build the city of power.

To make the point is not to say that the purchase of Louisiana was a cultural disaster: it is simply to suggest that if anyone is puzzled as to why the Americans never created or conserved much that speaks to the human spirit, the answer largely is that the Americans were too busy doing something else instead. To the world's astonishment, the Americans practically exploded across their continent, and barely a century later, they stood grinning down on little Europe. The Americans regarded their unprecedented success as a complete justification of their frontier attitudes, and as the twentieth century began, they carried those attitudes into it.

Today, the frontier mentality is changing as the American space constricts; as it becomes ever more apparent that there is simply no more space to take; as the suspicion grows that the biggest and newest is not always the best, that money is not the measure of all things, and that there might be limits to growth and acquisition. Now that the frontier is closed, American attention is turning inward, and a distinctive American civilization may well begin to emerge. It will take time. Less than two hundred years ago, President George Washington was riding a horse on a muddy Virginia road. Today a President can fly northwest to Cathay at the speed of sound. That sort of progress is both remarkable and measurable. But two hundred years are required to make a decent lawn, and often something more to build a decent cathedral. That sort of progress is also remarkable, a bit more difficult to measure, but at least as necessary.

Just here, another view of Louisiana emerges. It is that of Paradise Lost. The image of Eden was never far from the minds of the sixteenth-century explorers: Ponce de León perished looking for it. Nor was the vision of Eden ever lost in subsequent centuries. Eden always existed west over the next rise. The trouble was, it disappeared the moment people entered the virginal garden. They came in with their surveying chains, staking out their claims, shooting the fur and feathers off of all that hopped, ran, or flew; they whacked down the trees, ruined the fields, dammed and poisoned the streams, raised Cain and slew Abel, and then wandered over the next rise to enter another Eden and repeat the process. It is altogether wrong to blame them, for they had no idea what they were doing. They believed that natural law, if not God, gave them dominance over nature. It was also impossible for riflemen emerging on the Great Plains to look upon hundreds and hundreds of thousands of bison, and to think in terms of conservation. It was just as impossible for them to imagine that the savage tribes who moved about, following the herds, had any shadow of right or claim to these lands, or anything to offer mankind than their enmity. In the course of proceeding from horse to spacecraft in less than two hundred years, the Americans very thoroughly and systematically destroyed the garden and its indigenes. Yet in all this time, the American soul quickened to the beauty of the wilderness. To this day, Americans prefer a tangled stand of virgin brush and forest to the tidy European forests they regard as artificial parks. Wilderness was the American experience, and the Americans were drawn to it, and loved it. When they ruined it, they were not obeying Wilde's dictum that each man kills the thing he loves; they naïvely thought there would always be more because, for more than a century, there always *was* more. It was just over the next rise. Now that the hours-long rolling thunder of the passage of a bison herd will never be felt again, the concussion of it stirring the grasses and the leather fringes of hunters' jackets; now that the forests will never reappear, nor many kinds of birds and animals; now that Paradise has been lost and the Americans realize that they once had it and destroyed it—now they have grown nostalgic and sad. No small reason for the sudden loss of American self-confidence in recent decades has been a growing feeling that the ruin they wrought can never be made good and that their progress was, after all, away from Eden—and to a parking lot.

As the American attention turns inward, there is an emergent wish among them that they had preserved more of their past than they did; that most of the Colonial buildings had not been pulled down to make way for progress, and the lakes and rivers poisoned, and the blacksmiths sent to factories. Unlike their now-distant European kinsmen, the Americans lack a sense of home. They have never had a home in the three and a half centuries since the first English colonists arrived. Their home was England,

and they left it. Almost ever since then, the Americans have been in motion, putting up temporary structures and committed to constant change. The temporary quality of American life may be best, if rather ludicrously, expressed in their time capsules. These are metal tubes filled with writings, photographs, and artifacts, buried in the ground in the hope that someone will one day happen upon them, want to dig them up, and see who the Americans of the twentieth century were. Instead of building a new Florence as a testimony, and for the purposes of enlargement of the quality of life for the present and the future, the Americans put a few mementos of their often trivial and certainly transitory present life in holes in the ground.

The time capsule mentality is giving way, now that the American wandering is over, and as the realization dawns that they will have to build a home out of what they have left. It is interesting to note that the huge heartland of the continent is being progressively deserted. The Americans are leaving those broad lands of the Louisiana territory that they had hitherto rushed upon, turning away from what had once been Eden to disappear into America's great city complexes. The region was and still remains a primarily agricultural one, but machines have replaced men, women, and children in the fields, and other machines have replaced the artisans in the villages. The great republic of intelligent agrarians that Jefferson envisioned is, to all intents and purposes, nonexistent. The cities, those panders to every vice, are everywhere triumphant.

For what it may be worth, there is a contrary emigration from the city to the country and to what scraps of wilderness yet remain. The émigrés are very nearly as incompetent to look after themselves as the first Europeans who arrived in the American wilderness. But they are possessed of the old dream of Eden, and those who would regain Paradise are, again like the majority of those who first came from Europe, largely those who have dropped out or have been driven out of contemporary American

[359]

society. They are mostly young, and rather like Jefferson they believe that human liberty and happiness are to be realized only in close contact with the earth. They wish to live freely in obedience to what they imagine to be natural laws; to eat foods grown without artificial aids; to exist at one with nature. They entertain a somewhat romantic view of the American Indian, believing him to have been a worthy example. It would seem that some of the notions of Locke and Rousseau are still echoing around the nation. The attitude of the disaffected young is chiefly interesting as a peculiarly American cry of grief, homelessness, and nostalgia. To the extent that it is a frontier attitude, it is not helpful. Almost by definition, civilization arises in cities. It now remains for the Americans to build cities fit for human habitation, to create at last a home for themselves in what never was their native land.

Bibliography

It is customary when writing an outline of history to justify or excuse one's statements by shifting the blame to someone else.[1] I have not followed the custom here because, as a reader, I find footnotes distracting.[2] But again as a reader, I often find myself wanting to know more about the subject or wondering what books the author could possibly have read that led him to say the things he did. Since you may share my aversion to footnotes, but also share the same sense of curiosity, I have arranged a compromise. I will cite below, in Section A, the books that were particularly important to the construction of each section of this book. Following that, in Section B, I will list books that I found generally useful and/or interesting. This is by no means a definitive list, for there are thousands of titles relative to the subjects my book discusses, but the list is at least my own, and I am sure that if you read the titles, they will flesh out for you the large contours of the story I have set forth. You will find, for example, no less than three titles concerning that strange and wonderful man Aaron Burr, whom I have barely mentioned; a description of

---

[1] Via footnotes that pinpoint the scholar's plagiarisms.

[2] See what I mean?

Creole life in New Orleans (which I have totally ignored), and works on frontier life that evoke all its color and nastiness. All these books found their way into mine, even if between the lines, as I sought to pursue my central argument that America was a mere function of European activities up to the time when Napoleon suddenly presented America with an opportunity to gain an empire of her own.

SECTION A

The nature of American Indian society: I have primarily followed (or borrowed from) *Works* by Francis Parkman, published by Little, Brown & Co., Boston, 1896. I have followed Parkman rather than Samuel Eliot Morison with reference to the effect of Champlain's making war upon the Iroquois. It may have been a foolhardy judgment on my part, for I have immense respect for Morison, but Parkman's explanation made sense to me. For *Aztec society,* the leading source was *Conquistadors in North American History* by Paul Horgan (New York: Farrar, Straus & Co., 1963).

The nature of the Spanish and the voyages of Columbus: Here the primary sources were Horgan, and the *Admiral of the Ocean Sea* by Samuel Eliot Morison (Boston: Houghton Mifflin Co., 1942). My view of the Spaniards was also colored by Parkman and by *The Armada* by Garrett Mattingly (Boston: Houghton Mifflin Co., 1950).

Early voyages of discovery: The primary source was Haklyut's *Voyages.*

Warfare among the early Spanish, French, and English in the New World: I have followed Parkman here and Haklyut. (My remarks on the British royal navy and its ships are largely my own, deriv-

[362]

Bibliography

ing from considerable outside reading and visits to the museum at the Royal Naval College in Greenwich.)

The French and Indian Wars: The primary source was again Parkman.

The development of European societies and nations from medieval to modern times: I have followed *A History of the Modern World*, revised edition, by R. R. Palmer and J. Colton (New York: Alfred A. Knopf, 1963).

The emergent American society, the frontier, the Revolution and formation of a new nation: I have followed Daniel J. Boorstin's *The Colonial Experience*, Vol. 1 of his *The Americans* (New York: Random House, Vintage Books, 1958); Palmer and Colton; John Bach McMaster's *History of the People of the United States* (New York: D. Appleton & Co., 1885); and F. L. Paxson's *History of the American Frontier, 1763–1893* (Boston: Houghton Mifflin Co., 1924). My remarks on the nature of guerrilla warfare and my evaluation of the military aspects of the Revolution stem from my own investigation of guerrilla operations, published by J. B. Lippincott of Philadelphia in 1961 in my book, *They Fought Alone*.

Louis XIV: The more important book was *Louix XIV* by Vincent Cronin (Boston: Houghton Mifflin Co., 1965); the more delightful was *The Sun King* by Nancy Mitford (New York: Harper & Row, 1966).

Napoleon and Talleyrand: The leading biographies, which I followed, are *Napoleon* by Emil Ludwig (New York: Liveright, 1926), and *Talleyrand* by Duff Cooper (London: Jonathan Cape, 1932). Each of these works is enormously informed, and I was dumbfounded to discover that neither book contains the word "Louisiana." Quite apparently each author felt that the sale of Louisiana to the United States was of such small moment to his protagonist as to be entirely insignificant in the story of his life. How interesting it is to reflect that this might have well been true. Yet it also seems true that the sale of Louisiana had its effect upon the relationship between Napoleon and Talleyrand; my feeling is that this may have been the point at which Talleyrand determined to betray his master.

The Founding Fathers: For the relationships among Jefferson, Monroe, Madison, Hamilton, Burr and Livingston, I am indebted to *Ordeal of Ambition*, by Jonathan Daniels (New York: Doubleday & Co., 1970).

The course of American diplomacy: The leading source was *A Diplomatic History of the United States* by Samuel Flagg Bemis (New York: Henry Holt & Co., 1936).

The Purchase of Louisiana: The leading sources were government documents, listed in Section B, and *History of Louisiana* by François de Barbé-Marbois (Philadelphia: Carey & Lea, 1830). Marbois' book was also published in the original French by Carey & Lea as *Histoire de la Louisiane, et de la cession de la colonie par la France aux États-Unis.* Both French and English versions may be found in the Reading Room of the British Museum, if not in United States libraries. The *Encyclopædia Britannica* authors warn against your believing Marbois' statements with respect to his having Napoleon and Livingston looking into the future, on the ground that Marbois was writing in retrospect in 1829. My feeling is that since Marbois was one of the actual negotiators, he knew what he was talking about. (You are also supposed not to read *History of the Louisiana Purchase* by J. K. Hosmer [New York: D. Appleton & Co., 1902] but I read it anyway.)

Arguments over the purchase of Louisiana: Some are found in Daniels; others in *History of the People of the United States* by John Bach McMaster (New York: D. Appleton & Co., 1885).

Bibliography

SECTION B

Here follows in alphabetical order the author's suggested reading list; the works by Cable are fictions. Most of the histories are important. Some of the other books are merely latter-day entertainments.

Adams, Henry. *History of the United States*, Vols. 1–2.

Barbé-Marbois, François de. *History of Louisiana*. Philadelphia: Carey & Lea, 1830.

Bemis, Samuel Flagg. *A Diplomatic History of the United States*. New York: Henry Holt & Co., 1936.

Boorstin, Daniel J. *The Colonial Experience*, Vol. 1 of *The Americans*. New York: Random House, Vintage Books, 1958.

Cable, G. W. *The Grandissimes*. New York: Charles Scribner's Sons, 1880.

———. *Old Creole Days*. New York: Charles Scribner's Sons, 1879.

Coates, Robert M. *The Outlaw Years*. New York: Macaulay Company, 1930.

Cooper, Duff. *Talleyrand*. London: Jonathan Cape, 1932.

Cronin, Vincent. *Louis XIV*. Boston: Houghton Mifflin Co., 1965.

Daniels, Jonathan. *Ordeal of Ambition*. New York: Doubleday & Co., 1970.

De Voto, Bernard. *The Course of Empire*. Boston: Houghton Mifflin Co., 1952.

Documents, Government. American State Papers, Foreign Relations, Vol. 2; Public Lands, Vol. 2; House Document 431,

Bibliography

57th Congress, 2nd Session, 1903; Historical Sketch of "Louisiana" and the Louisiana Purchase, U.S. General Land Office, Washington, D.C.: U.S. Government Printing Office, 1912.

Dos Passos, John. *Prospects of a Golden Age.* New York: Prentice-Hall, 1959.

Early, Eleanor. *New Orleans Holiday.* New York: Rinehart & Co., 1947.

Encyclopædia Britannica. 11th edition.

French, Benjamin Franklin. *Historical Collections of Louisiana and Florida.* New York: J. Sabin & Sons, 1869.

Haklyut, Richard. *Voyages.* Any edition will do, providing it carries the full text.

Horgan, Paul. *Conquistadors in North American History.* New York: Farrar, Straus & Co., 1963.

Hosmer, J. K. *History of the Louisiana Purchase.* New York: D. Appleton & Co., 1902.

Kane, Harnett T. *The Bayous of Louisiana.* New York: William Morrow & Co., 1944.

———. *Queen New Orleans.* New York: William Morrow & Co., 1949.

Ludwig, Emil. *Napoleon.* New York: Liveright, 1926.

McMaster, John Bach. *History of the People of the United States.* New York: D. Appleton & Co., 1885.

Mattingly, Garrett. *The Armada.* Boston: Houghton Mifflin Co., 1950.

Mitford, Nancy. *The Sun King.* New York: Harper & Row, 1966.

Bibliography

Morison, Samuel Eliot. *Admiral of the Ocean Sea.* Boston: Houghton Mifflin Co., 1942.

Morse, John T., Jr. *James Monroe.* Boston: Houghton Mifflin Co., 1895.

———. *Thomas Jefferson.* Boston: Houghton Mifflin Co., 1895.

Palmer, R., and Colton, J. *A History of the Modern World.* Rev. ed. New York: Alfred A. Knopf, 1956.

Parkman, Francis. *Works.* Boston: Little, Brown·& Co., 1896. The titles in this series include *Pioneers of France in the New World*; *La Salle and the Discovery of the Great West*; and *A Half-Century of Conflict*, Vols. 1 and 2.

Parton, James. *Life & Times of Aaron Burr.* 5th ed., 1858. New York: Johnson Reprint Corporation.

Paxson, F. L. *History of the American Frontier, 1763–1893.* Boston: Houghton Mifflin Co., 1924.

Stoddard, Major Amos. *Sketches, Historical and Descriptive of Louisiana.* Philadelphia: Mathew Carey, 1812.

Thwaites, R. G. *Jesuit Revelations.* Cleveland, 1896.

Winsor, Justin. *Narrative and Critical History of America.* Vol. 7. Boston: Houghton Mifflin Co., 1888.

Wise, William. *Aaron Burr.* New York: G. P. Putnam's Sons, 1968.

Index

A

Index

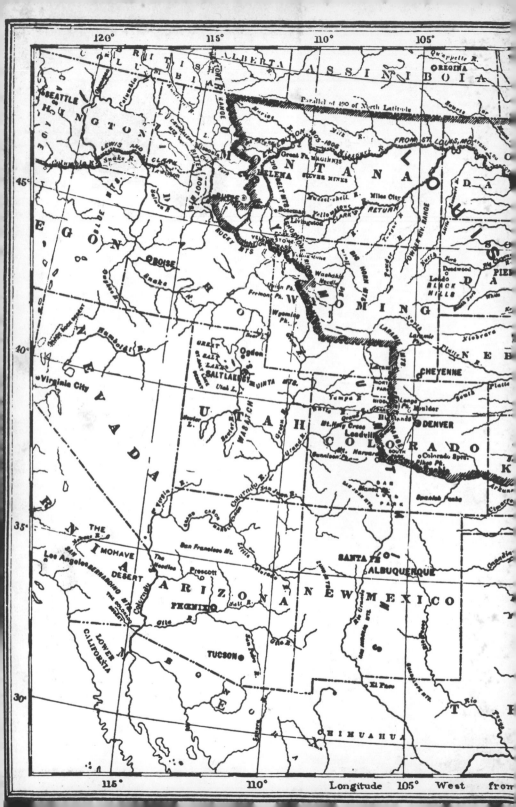